NATIVE NORTH AMERICAN VOICES

NATIVE NORTH AMERICAN VOICES

Deborah Gillan Straub, *Editor*

U·X·L®
AN IMPRINT OF GALE

DETROIT • NEW YORK • TORONTO • LONDON

NATIVE NORTH AMERICAN VOICES

Deborah Gillan Straub, *Editor*

Staff

Sonia Benson, *U·X·L Developmental Editor*
Carol DeKane Nagel, *U·X·L Managing Editor*
Thomas L. Romig, *U·X·L Publisher*

Susan Salas, *Permissions Associate*

Shanna Heilveil, *Production Associate*
Evi Seoud, *Assistant Production Manager*
Mary Beth Trimper, *Production Director*

Michelle DiMercurio, *Art Director*
Cynthia Baldwin, *Product Design Manager*

 This book is printed on acid-free paper that meets the minimum requirements of American National Standard for Information Sciences—Permanence Paper for Printed Library Materials, ANSI Z39.48 1984.

Library of Congress Cataloging-in-Publication Data
Native North American Voices/Deborah Gillan Straub.
     p. cm.
    Includes bibliographical references and indexes.
     ISBN 0-8103-9819-2 (alk. paper)
      1. Speeches, addresses, etc., Indian–North America. 2. Indians of North America–History. I. Title.
E98.O7S77 1996
973'.0497—dc20

                                                         96-34164
                                                         CIP

Printed in the United States of America
10 9 8 7 6 5 4 3 2 1

Contents

Black Hawk

Speech Topics
at a Glance

For a more detailed listing of information covered in this volume, consult subject index.

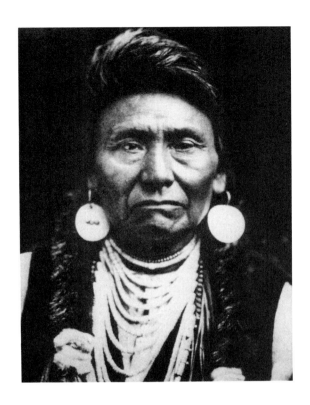

Joseph

Civil rights

Confederacies and coalitions among tribes

Cultural values

Discrimination—racial

Education

Employment; economics

Reader's Guide

Gertrude Simmons Bonnin

Over the past two hundred years the orations of American Indian speakers have powerfully shaped the national consciousness, changed government policy, raised pride and determination among the many groups of native peoples, and countered stereotypes and complacency in the American public. *Native North American Voices* collects in a single source a wide range of these speeches, complete and excerpted, as they were delivered by Native American tribal leaders, activists, political figures, religious leaders, and other prominent men and women from the late eighteenth century to the present.

Voices selections include well-known historical moments, such as Chief Joseph's words upon surrender ("From where the sun now stands I will fight no more forever") and the legendary ecological warning credited to Chief Seattle. From more recent times, the militant protest of the Red Power Movement in the early 1970s prompted the powerful addresses of activists such as Russell Means and Vernon Belle-court included in this volume. Also featured are the spoken words of contemporary Indian leaders like Ada Deer, head of the Bureau of Indian Affairs, and Wilma Mankiller, former principal chief of the Cherokee Nation. Cultural and religious ideas are expressed in the poetry of Suzan Shown Harjo, a spiritual message delivered by Smohalla, and an inspirational address by Ben Nighthorse Campbell.

It is not possible in this first edition of *Native North American Voices* to include all of the many prominent Native American speakers who have contributed to American culture and history. Due to the unavailability of certain materials for publication, some important speeches of the last two centuries were regretfully omitted from the volume. *Voices* does, however, provide a compelling array of diverse Native American viewpoints. The book's twenty entries were selected: a) to encompass a wide range of perspectives and backgrounds; b) to be engaging and accessible to students; and c) to provide firsthand—and often quite dramatic—insight into the key issues, events, and movements of Native North American history.

The entries in *Native North American Voices* are arranged alphabetically by speaker. Each begins with introductory material, providing a brief biography of the speaker and the historical context of the speech that follows. Informative sidebars expand on topics mentioned within the entries. A "Sources" section, directing the student to further readings on the speechmaker and his or her speeches, concludes each entry.

Native North American Voices also contains approximately 60 black-and-white photographs, a subject index, a listing of speeches by major topics, and a timeline. Words and phrases are defined in the lower margin of the page on which they appear.

Related Reference Sources

Native North American Voices features a comprehensive range of historical and current information on the life and culture of the Native peoples of the United States and Canada. Organized into 24 subject chapters, including major culture areas, activism, and religion, the volumes contain more than two hundred black-and-white photographs and maps and a subject index.

Native North American Biography profiles 112 Native North Americans from the United States and Canada, both living and deceased, who are notable in fields ranging from civil rights to sports, politics and tribal leadership to literature, entertainment to religion, science to military. A black-and-white portrait and a list of sources for further research accompanies most entries. The alphabetically arranged volumes feature cross references and an index listing all individuals by field of endeavor.

Native North American Chronology explores significant social, political, economic, cultural, and educational milestones in the history of the Native peoples of the United States and Canada. The chronologically arranged volume spans from prehistory to modern times and contains more than 70 illustrations and maps, extensive cross references, and a subject index.

Acknowledgments

The editor wishes to thank the following people who served as advisers on this project: Wil A. Linkugel, Professor of Communication Studies, University of Kansas, Lawrence, Kansas; and Hilda K. Weisburg, Media Specialist, Sayreville War Memorial High School, Parlin, New Jersey.

Your Suggestions Are Welcome

The editor welcomes your comments and suggestions for future editions of *Native North American Voices*. Please write: The Editor, *Native North American Voices*, U•X•L, 835 Penobscot Building, Detroit, Michigan 48226-4094; call toll-free: 1-800-877-4253; or fax: (313) 961-6347.

Introduction

Speaking in/of Native America

Reaching reliable generalizations when speaking of oratorical tradition in Native America is exceedingly difficult for two very important reasons. First, much of what comes down to us as Native American oratory was preserved by people who had, at best, a modest understanding of the speaker's language. Christopher Columbus's journals are filled with what various Native Americans supposedly said, for instance, even though no one in Columbus's group had a working knowledge of the languages they encountered. Then, too, among many of the translators we find either or both of two major biases: a desire to make Native American speakers "sound" more like someone of European extraction or a need to make Native American speakers "sound" like savages who didn't deserve an audience among "civilized" people.

Second, there is no such thing as "Native American culture." Films, television shows, books, advertisements, school mascots, and humor of all sorts consistently have created the

Ben Nighthorse Campbell

impression that Native Americans belong to a single, monolithic culture in which all "Indians" look, act, and speak pretty much the same. Yet it makes no more sense to think of Native Americans as belonging to a single culture than it does to speak of Europeans as belonging to a single culture. In fact, in some ways it makes considerably *less* sense. Europeans were hugely influenced by the spread of Christianity, by the promulgation of Latin, and by a widespread reverence for Greece and Rome. Among Native Americans, contrary to popular belief, there is no single religion, no single reference-language, and no single literary tradition.

One consequence of all this is that people who speak of *the* Native American culture, *the* Native American religion, *the* Native American worldview, or *the* Native American anything else do considerably more damage than good. It is worth bearing in mind, then, that the Native American speeches that follow are not representative—not because *Native North American Voices* is flawed or its editor incompetent, but because no single volume can possibly represent all of the oratorical traditions of Native America.

With these points in mind, we nevertheless can make some useful observations that hold fairly well for many of the hundreds of Native American cultures, particularly prior to the twentieth century and particularly among contemporary traditionalists in Native America. We may begin with two communicative precepts: first, that breath is sacred, and second, that the communicative well-being of the tribe must take priority over all other communicative commitments.

Because breath is sacred, Native Americans generally have maintained an oral rather than a literary tradition. Until the resurgence of Native American organizations in the 1950s, Native American languages were falling rapidly into disuse. Since the 1950s, however, Native Americans have been working hard and long to revitalize their languages, which has led to a new vitality for Native American speaking.

Structurally, Native American cultures generally are horizontal (where people are considered equals) rather than vertical (where people are considered either dominant or subordinate). Therefore, anyone is entitled to speak insofar as they actually have something important to say. Older speakers—if they are also wiser speakers—typically were and are given greater respect than younger, less experienced speakers. This was and is true of women as well, for contrary to popular belief, women in most Native American cultures are not second-class citizens and have therefore always been the equals of men in all areas, including speechmaking.

Regardless of who is speaking, however, shorter speeches—speeches that get to the point—typically are preferable to long-winded, flowery speeches. Notice that this runs contrary to typical media portrayals, where "Indians" seem to go on and on about "cherry blossoms" and "long rifles" and "the autumn moon" and such.

From these generalizations about Native American oratory spring a number of guiding principles. Some of the more obvious ones include:

- never lie;
- always communicate *with;*
- always and only communicate through the sacred principles of life;
- always and only permit one person to speak at a time, provide a period of silence following the speaker's speech to permit the speaker's revisions and/or amendments, and permit no shouting or interruptions;
- always and only speak to educate or persuade and never to confront;
- always preserve the principle that sharing is a requirement of life;
- always remember that gratitude can be shown only in deeds and never in words;
- always preserve the horizontal, egalitarian social environment, and never think someone less worthy than yourself;
- learn by doing rather than saying;
- always acknowledge leadership that is fostered by responsibility and never leadership that wields power;
- always speak when you have something to say and never otherwise;

- always demonstrate respect for the other—both human and nonhuman, both living and dead—and for the relationship that communication establishes;

- always protect the communicative rights of all tribal members;

- always remember that one's duty to the children of others is no less than one's duty to one's self; and

- always remember that conflict requires understanding, which is growth, rather than resolution, which is death.

As you read through the speeches that follow, please bear the above points in mind as much as possible. Or, if all this is too much to take in at once, please try to remember that we are not all the same and that we have the same kinds of thoughts and hopes and fears and concerns and dreams as you do.

Dr. Richard Morris
Professor of Communication Studies
Northern Illinois University
DeKalb, Illinois

Suggested Readings

Crow Dog, Leonard, and Richard Erdoes, *Crow Dog: Four Generations of Sioux Medicine Men,* HarperCollins, 1995.

Deloria, Vine, *Custer Died for Your Sins: An Indian Manifesto,* Avon, 1970.

Deloria, Vine, and Clifford Lytle, *The Nations Within: The Past and Future of American Indian Sovereignty,* Pantheon, 1984.

Gilbert, Bil, *God Gave Us This Country: Tekamthi and the First American Civil War,* Doubleday, 1989.

Josephy, Alvin M., *The Indian Heritage of America,* Houghton, 1991.

Mankiller, Wilma, and Michael Wallis, *Mankiller: A Chief and Her People,* St. Martin's, 1993.

Riley, Patricia, editor, *Growing Up Native American: An Anthology,* Morrow, 1993.

Weatherford, Jack, *Native Roots: How the Indians Enriched America,* Crown, 1991.

Credits

Ada Deer

Grateful acknowledgment is made to the following sources whose works appear in this volume. Every effort has been made to trace copyright, but if omissions have been made, please contact the publisher.

Bellecourt, Clyde. From "The Longest Walk," in *Native American Reader: Stories, Speeches and Poems*. Edited by Jerry D. Blanche. The Denali Press, 1990. Reprinted by permission of the publisher.

Bellecourt, Vernon. From "American Indian Movement," in *Contemporary Native American Address*. Edited by John R. Maestas. Brigham Young University, 1976. © 1976 by Brigham Young University. All rights reserved. Reprinted by permission of the publisher.

Black Hawk. From "Black Hawk's Farewell," in *Literature of the American Indian* by Thomas E. Sanders and Walter W. Peek. Macmillan College Publishing, 1973. Copyright © 1973 by Macmillan College Publishing Company, Inc. Reprinted with permission of Macmillan College Publishing, a division of Simon & Schuster, Inc.

Bonnin, Gertrude Simmons. From a speech delivered on December 14–15, 1928, addressed before the Indian Rights Association on "Problem of Indian Administration" in Atlantic City, New Jersey. Reprinted by permission of the Brigham Young University Archives.

Seattle. From "Chief Seattle's Speech, Version 2—Revised by William Arrowsmith," in *Recovering the Word: Essays on Native American Literature*. Edited by Brian Swann and Arnold Krupat. University of California Press, 1987. Copyright © 1987 by The Regents of the University of California. Reprinted by permission of the publisher.

Harjo, Suzan Shown. From a keynote address delivered on September 18, 1992, at the Fourth Annual "Seeds of Change" conference in Santa Fe, New Mexico. Reprinted by permission of the author.

Mankiller, Wilma. From "Inaugural Address," in *Native American Reader: Stories, Speeches and Poems*. Edited by Jerry D. Blanche. The Denali Press, 1990. Copyright © 1990 by Jerry D. Blanche. Reprinted by permission of the publisher.

Means, Russell. From "The State of Native America," in *Native American Reader: Stories, Speeches and Poems*. Edited by Jerry D. Blanche. The Denali Press, 1990. Copyright © 1990 by Jerry D. Blanche. Reprinted by permission of the publisher.

Sitting Bull. *Great Plains Observer,* January 1969. Reprinted by permission of the publisher.

Smohalla. From "Smohalla Speaks," in *Literature of the American Indian* by Thomas E. Sanders and Walter W. Peek. Macmillan College Publishing, 1973. Copyright © 1973 by Macmillan College Publishing Company, Inc. Reprinted with permission of Macmillan College Publishing, a division of Simon & Schuster, Inc.

Swimmer, Ross. In a speech "An Indian Crossroad." Reprinted by permission of the author.

Trudell, John. From "Commitment," in *Contemporary Native American Address*. Edited by John R. Maestas. Brigham Young University, 1976. © 1976 by Brigham Young Universi-

The photographs and illustrations appearing in *Native North American Voices* were received from the following sources:

Cover: AP/Wide World Photos: Russell Means.

Timeline: Archive Photos: Tecumseh; **The Granger Collection, New York:** "Trail of Tears" and Geronimo; **National Archives and Records Administration:** Treaty signing between Sioux and U.S.; **The Bettman Archive/Newsphotos, Inc.:** Native Americans stand guard at Wounded Knee, The Longest Walk protest, and Museum of the American Indian, New York; **AP/Wide World Photos:** Wilma Mankiller and Rally for Leonard Peltier on steps of Federal Court Building.

The **Bettmann Archive/Newsphotos, Inc.:** pp. v, xiii, xxi, 4, 6, 25, 27, 31, 36, 45, 50, 65, 143, 159, 166, 188, 201; **Archive Photos:** pp. vii, 107, 110, 192, 209, 211, 215; **AP/Wide World Photos:** pp. xvii, 1, 8, 20, 54, 59, 90, 124, 133, 136, 146, 219, 227; **National Archives and Records Administration:** p. 42; **The Granger Collection, New York:** pp. 77, 82, 119, 156, 172, 185, 196; **Stephen Lehmer/Art Dept. UCLA:** p. 223.

Timeline of Important Native North American Events

1750–1996

Boldface indicates speakers featured

1754 The Iroquois Confederacy receives several visits from Pennsylvania statesman Benjamin Franklin, who views the alliance among Iroquois nations as a model for unifying the American colonies.

1763 Ottawa war chief Pontiac leads a confederacy of Indian tribes in a war against the British.

1777 The American Revolution permanently disrupts the nations of the Iroquois Confederacy, who have held different alliances. **Joseph Brant** and his followers move to Canada.

1787 The Continental Congress declares that no land is to be taken from Indians without their consent.

1790 The first U.S. Naturalization Act allows only "free white persons" to become American citizens.

1803 The U.S. negotiates the Louisiana Purchase with France, acquiring the territory west of the Mississippi River to the Rocky Mountains and south from Canada to the Gulf of Mexico. President Thomas Jefferson proposes that Indian nations living east of the Mississippi River should be removed west to open eastern land to settlers.

1810–13 Shawnee chief **Tecumseh** tries to forge an alliance of several Indian tribes to resist white expansion westward into the Great Lakes region.

Tecumseh

1754–63 French and Indian Wars	**1775–76** American Revolutionary War	**1787** U.S. Constitution approved	**1812–15** War of 1812

•• **1745** •• **1760** •• **1775** •• **1790** •• **1805** •• **1820** ••

Trail of Tears

1824 The Bureau of Indian Affairs is established under the jurisdiction of the U.S. War Department.

1827 **Red Jacket** is ousted as chief of the Seneca nation for his outspoken opposition to the white man's religion and customs.

1830 Congress passes the Indian Removal Act. Many Indian groups living east of the Mississippi River are forced to give up their land and relocate west of the river to present-day Oklahoma. Thousands die of disease, exposure, and starvation during the long journey to Indian Territory, prompting the Cherokee to name the route the "Trail of Tears."

1832 Sauk Chief **Black Hawk** leads bands of Sauk and Fox in an attempt to regain their land. U.S. troops quickly and brutally crush the uprising, known as the Black Hawk War.

1835–42 The Second Seminole War erupts when Seminole Indians of Florida led by Chief Osceola resist efforts to remove them to a reservation in the west. U.S. forces struggle to overcome the resistance for nearly seven years and many Seminoles remain in Florida permanently, despite U.S. policy.

1840–60 The U.S. government proceeds in its plans to remove all Indians to Indian Territory, then present-day Oklahoma and Kansas. Once there, Indians are told they will be able to form their own state and elect officials to represent Indian interests in Congress.

1847 The Oregon Trail opens, encouraging an increasing number of white settlers to head westward.

1849 The Bureau of Indian Affairs is transferred from the War Department to the new Department of the Interior.

1850–80 Non-Indians in California kill and terrorize Indians for three decades. The Indian population in California falls from 100,000 in 1850 to 16,000 in 1880.

1828
Democratic Party forms, elects Andrew Jackson as president

1833
First national abolitionist association formed

1846–48
Mexican-American War

1848–49
California Gold Rush

• • **1820** • • **1830** • • **1840** • • **1850** • • **1860** • •

1861–65	Colonel "Kit" Carson defeats Navajo and Apache in New Mexico and places about 10,0000 Navajo on a reservation.

Sioux leaders and U.S. delegates negotiate Second Fort Laramie Treaty, 1868

1864	Several hundred peaceful Cheyenne men, women, and children are massacred by U.S. troops at Sand Creek, Colorado.
1867	Medicine Lodge Creek in Kansas Territory is the site of the largest gathering of Indians and whites in the history of the United States. Kiowa chief **Satanta** is among the Native Americans who attend.
	The U.S. Surgeon General orders the collection of Indian skulls from graves and battlefields for the Army Medical Museum.
1868	Sioux Leaders sign the Second Fort Laramie Treaty, establishing the Great Sioux Reservation in present-day North and South Dakota. Chief **Sitting Bull** refuses to sign.
1871	After nearly a century of negotiating with Indians by treaties, a Congressional act ends all treaty-making with Indians. According to the act, Indians are no longer recognized as independent nations.
1874	The discovery of gold in the Dakotas attracts hordes of miners to the area, most of whom ignore treaties protecting Indian lands.
1876	In the Battle of the Little Bighorn, a contingent of Sioux and Cheyenne warriors led by Crazy Horse and **Sitting Bull** defeat General George Armstrong Custer and his troops.
1877	With U.S. troops in pursuit, **Chief Joseph** of the Nez Percé leads his people in an escape to Canada. He is forced to surrender just a few miles from the Canadian border.
1879	Accompanied by Chief Standing Bear of the Poncas, **Susette LaFlesche** tours the eastern United States as an advocate for Native American rights.

1861–65
American Civil War

1867
United States
buys Alaska

1870
15th Amendment grants all
male American citizens the
right to vote

1880
Buffalo on Plains
threatened with
extinction

•• **1860** •• **1865** •• **1870** •• **1875** •• **1880** ••

Miniconjoux Sioux perform Ghost Dance, 1890

Geronimo in 1905

1881 **Sitting Bull** and his followers surrender to U.S. troops.

1886 Apache chief **Geronimo** surrenders to U.S. troops.

1887 Congress passes the General Allotment Act (also known as the Dawes Act), which breaks up lands owned by Indian tribes and parcels it out to individuals. Dishonest public officials then sell the remaining reservation land to whites, sometimes at very low prices.

The earliest known version of **Chief Seattle**'s famous speech is published in a Seattle newspaper.

1889 Indian Territory (present-day Oklahoma) is opened to white settlers.

1890 The Ghost Dance religion sweeps across the Plains, leading to fears among whites of a violent new Indian uprising.

Sioux chief **Sitting Bull** is killed in an uprising while being arrested.

U.S. troops massacre some 300 Sioux women, children, and elders at Wounded Knee in present-day South Dakota.

1924 Congress grants citizenship to all Native Americans in gratitude for their service during World War I.

1926 **Gertrude Simmons Bonnin** forms the National Council of American Indians and becomes its first president.

1928 The Institute for Government Research publishes the Meriam Report, a landmark study describing the deplorable living conditions among Native Americans.

1934 The Indian Reorganization Act (also known as the Wheeler-Howard Act) is signed into law, reversing the policies of the General Allotment Act and once again permitting tribal ownership of land.

1898–99
Spanish-American
War

1907
Oklahoma is admitted
as forty-sixth state of
the Union

1914–18
World War I

1929
Stock market crashes;
Great Depressions
begins

• • **1880** • • **1890** • • **1900** • • **1910** • • **1920** • • **1930** • •

1941-45 More than twenty-five thousand Indian men and women join U.S. military services in World War II.

1952–57 The Bureau of Indian Affairs launches a "relocation program" designed to foster Indian assimilation into mainstream society by moving Indians into major U.S. cities.

1953 Congress approves the Termination Resolution. This leads to efforts during the 1950s to dismantle the reservation system, end most federal obligations to Indians as specified in earlier treaties or by congressional actions, and terminate the legal status of Indians tribes as nationalities and independent cultural communities.

Indian airmen in World War II

1968 The American Indian Movement (AIM) is founded by **Clyde Bellecourt**, Dennis Banks, and other activists.

Congress passes the Indian Civil Rights Act, which guarantees reservation Indians many of the same civil rights and freedoms in relation to tribal authorities that the Constitution guarantees to all persons in relation to federal and state authorities.

1969–71 Indians from many different tribes occupy Alcatraz Island to lay claim to the land and protest federal government policy toward Native Americans. Short-term occupations continue to take place at Fort Lawton and Fort Lewis, Washington, Ellis Island, New York, and elsewhere.

1972 **Russell Means** leads 1,300 Indians to Gordon, Nebraska, to protest a local court's leniency toward two white brothers who brutally murdered Raymond Yellow Thunder, an Indian.

Armed participants in Wounded Knee takeover, 1973

A group of about 500 Indians arrive in Washington, D.C., at the end of the Trail of Broken Treaties protest march. Some demonstrators—including a number of AIM activists—occupy the headquarters of the Bureau of Indian Affairs.

1939–45
World War II

1950–53
Korean War

1965–73
United States troops fight in Vietnam War

1968
Student protest demonstrations hit 221 U.S. campuses

• • 1940 • • 1947 • • 1954 • • 1960 • • 1967 • • 1973 • •

Wilma Mankiller

1973 AIM protestors clash with police in Custer, South Dakota, while protesting the local court's treatment of a case in which a white man murdered an Indian.

Some 200 Indians under AIM leadership occupy the hamlet of Wounded Knee on the Pine Ridge Reservation in South Dakota, resisting heavy federal forces for seventy-one days. Two thousand Indians join the occupation.

1975 A shoot-out on the Pine Ridge Indian Reservation leaves two FBI agents and one Indian dead. AIM activist Leonard Peltier is subsequently tried and convicted for the crime and sentenced to life in prison. Decades after his conviction he is viewed by many as a political prisoner.

1978 The Longest Walk, a protest march calling attention to the federal government's poor treatment of Indian people throughout history, begins at Alcatraz Island off the California coast and ends in Washington, D.C., with some 30,000 participants.

Congress passes the American Indian Religious Freedom Act to protect the rights of Native Americans to believe, express, and exercise their traditional religions.

Congress passes the Indian Child Welfare Act to promote the stability and security of Indian tribes and families by giving tribal courts rather than outside welfare officials jurisdiction over foster care and adoption practices.

1979 Two thousand Indians demonstrate against the development of uranium mines in the Black Hills of South Dakota.

1987 **Wilma Mankiller** becomes the first woman elected principal chief of the Cherokee Nation.

1988 Congress repeals the Termination Resolution of 1953.

The Longest Walk protest march, 1978

1974
President Richard Nixon resigns after Watergate investigation

1976
United States celebrates bicentennial

1979–81
Fifty-two hostages are held at U.S. Embassy in Iran

1989
German reunification; Berlin Wall falls

•• **1973** •• **1977** •• **1981** •• **1985** •• **1989** ••

| 1989 | President George Bush signs into law the National American Indian Museum Act, establishing the National Museum of the American Indian as part of the Smithsonian Institution and ordering the return of Native American human remains in the Institution's collection to tribes that request them. |

Museum of the American Indian, New York

| 1990 | President George Bush signs into law the Native American Graves Protection and Repatriation Act, which requires federal agencies and private museums receiving federal funds to return Native American human remains and sacred objects in their collections to tribes that request them. |

The U.S. Supreme Court rules that the state of Oregon can enforce its drug laws against a Native American who had used peyote during a religious ceremony.

| 1991 | The name of the Custer Battlefield National Monument is officially changed to Little Bighorn Battlefield National Monument. |

| 1992 | **Ben Nighthorse Campbell** becomes the first Native American elected to the U.S. Senate since 1929. |

| 1993 | **Ada Deer** becomes the first woman to head the Bureau of Indian Affairs (BIA). |

President Bill Clinton signs the Religious Freedom Restoration Act, a law that compels legislators to prove that either health or safety are threatened before outlawing any religious act.

Rallies for Leonard Peltier continue into the 1990s

| 1994 | President Clinton meets with hundreds of tribal leaders at the White House to discuss self-government and other issues of concern to Native American groups. |

| 1995 | The U.S. Congress proposes deep cuts in funding for Native American programs that drastically reduce the BIA budget and direct payments to tribes. |

1990–91
Persian Gulf War

1991
Dissolution of the
Soviet Union; Cold
War ends

1995
Million Man March,
Washington, D.C.

• • **1990** • • **1991** • • **1992** • • **1993** • • **1994** • • **1995** • •

Native North American Voices

Clyde and Vernon Bellecourt

Activists of the Ojibwa tribe

During the 1960s and 1970s, the American Indian Movement (AIM) was at the forefront of the struggle for Native American rights. Brothers Clyde and Vernon Bellecourt both played important roles in the founding of the group, which was the most militant of the Indian protest organizations. While AIM no longer makes headlines as it once did, it lives on through the activism of the Bellecourts and others who continue to demand justice for Native Americans.

Early Lives

The Bellecourts were born on the White Earth Reservation in Minnesota. They grew up there with ten brothers and sisters, struggling against overwhelming poverty and the racist attitudes of neighboring communities that branded them as "dirty Indians." Both left the reservation for Minneapolis while they were still in their teens in search of what they hoped would be a better life. But their experi-

"THE AMERICAN INDIAN MOVEMENT IS A SPIRITUAL MOVEMENT FIRST AND A POLITICAL ORGANIZATION SECONDLY.
—*Vernon Bellecourt*

"THIS IS ALL WE HAVE LEFT HERE. OUR WAY OF LIFE. AND IT WAS TOLD TO US THAT IF OUR DRUM WAS EVER STILLED, YOU TOO WOULD BE THROUGH AS A NATION.
—*Clyde Bellecourt*

ences as members of the city's so-called "Red Ghetto"—the term used to describe the local Indian population—only added to their feelings of despair and frustration. Unable to find work, it was not long before the Bellecourts turned to crime. A string of burglaries and armed robberies eventually landed them lengthy prison sentences.

By the early 1960s, Vernon was out on parole and working as a barber, a trade he had learned while in jail. (He eventually owned a beauty salon and later an import business specializing in gift items.) Clyde, however, was still doing time in Minnesota's Stillwater State Prison. Facing the possibility of having to spend many more years behind bars, he went on a hunger strike, intending to stay on it until he died. One of his fellow inmates, another Ojibwa named Eddie Benton, did not want to see that happen. Benton began talking to him about their shared heritage and about the "Red Power" civil rights movement that was starting to attract attention on the West Coast. At first, Clyde resisted Benton's efforts to make him see how important it was for him to go on living. By 1962, however, he had given up his hunger strike and was working actively with his friend to promote Indian awareness within the prison.

After being released on parole in 1964, Clyde returned to Minneapolis. He was convinced by then that the federal government's supervision of the Indian people was slowly but surely destroying them. He felt the only way they could survive was to take charge of their own future. He tried to establish a fairly traditional civil-rights association that worked within the existing system to secure for Native Americans their full rights as citizens of the United States. But the church groups and government agencies he approached over the next few years showed little interest in supporting his goals. A frustrated Clyde finally came to the realization that "the system" didn't care much about Indian citizenship or independence.

Clyde Bellecourt Joins with Other Activists to Form AIM

Faced with this lack of interest, Clyde, his prison friend Eddie Benton, and another ex-convict named Dennis Banks banded together in mid-1968 to start a new group they called "Concerned Indian Americans." As they soon realized, however, the acronym resulting from this choice—CIA—was not at all acceptable. They then changed the group's name to the American Indian Movement (AIM).

At first, AIM leaders focused their efforts on reaching out to Native Americans in the nation's urban areas. Most of them had been relocated there from reservations during the 1950s as part of official U.S. government policy. The idea behind the forced moves was to encourage Indians to give up their culture and their language so that they could assimilate (blend) into white society. But experiencing such a drastic change in their lives had left many of these Indians confused and **demoralized**. The racism and discrimination they faced at almost every turn only made their situation worse, as did their ongoing struggles with poverty and alcoholism.

Clyde Bellecourt, 1973

AIM members helped these urban Indians deal with police harassment and obtain education, job training, housing, and health care. With the support of Minnesota's judicial system, they also set up a program that offered young Indians who had broken the law an alternative to prison. In addition, they worked with people who had already served time to keep them from ending up in prison again. They taught children to take pride in their history and to observe their traditions. And because they felt alcohol abuse was a major source of misery in the Indian community, AIM leaders spoke out forcefully against drinking. In fact, anyone who wanted to become involved in the movement had to promise to remain sober.

Meanwhile, Vernon—who had done very well for himself in business—was enjoying a comfortable life in suburban Minneapolis. But when he saw the difference AIM was beginning to make in the Indian community (especially in the lives of young men and women), he joined up, too.

demoralized: discouraged, unenthusiastic.

Vernon Bellecourt, 1977

AIM Adopts a More Militant Image

As AIM grew and changed over the next few years, it took on a much more militant look. Members allowed their hair to grow long so they could wear it in braids. They dressed in Indian-style clothing to show their pride in their heritage. They also carried weapons, which they claimed were for self-defense. In addition, direct confrontation replaced nonviolent protest as their preferred method of dealing with the outside world.

The image they created of themselves and their movement was very dramatic and, to some, threatening. It often left AIM members at odds with reservation Indians, who faced a different set of problems than urban Indians. But AIM attracted national attention to the struggle for Native American civil rights and captured the imaginations of young Indians in a way no other activist group had ever been able to do.

During the early 1970s, the Bellecourts were involved in most of the major AIM demonstrations. Just before the November elections in 1972, for example, about five hundred Native Americans from all over the country arrived in Washington, D.C., to protest government Indian policy. Known as the Trail of Broken Treaties march, it was led primarily by AIM members. Clyde Bellecourt had even helped draw up a list of twenty proposals for improving U.S.-Indian relations, including demands for a separate government for Indians, the restoration of Indian lands, and the renegotiation of all treaties. The plan was to present the list to White House officials.

Once they arrived in Washington, however, events took an unexpected turn. President Richard Nixon went back on his promise to meet with the marchers. There were also problems obtaining decent food and housing. Angry and frustrated, some of the activists went to the offices of the Bureau of Indian Affairs (BIA). There they encountered riot police who tried to turn them away. Instead, the activists took over the building. Their standoff with federal authorities lasted five days and resulted in damage to the building as well as to furniture and files inside. The government blamed the Indians for the vandalism, and the Indians accused federal agents of causing most of the destruction.

In any case, the incident generated lots of publicity—mostly negative—for AIM. It also led the FBI to classify the group as an "extremist" organization like the Black Panthers. Two months later, the Nixon administration officially rejected AIM's twenty proposals. Later, criminal charges were filed against Clyde Bellecourt for his part in the march; they were later dismissed.

AIM Spearheads the Wounded Knee Occupation

In 1973 Clyde Bellecourt was among the leaders of the famous Wounded Knee takeover. It began on South Dakota's Pine Ridge Indian Reservation on February 27, after several hundred AIM members and sympathizers decided to take a stand against the mistreatment of Indians. Their anger was focused in particular on the reservation's head **administrator**, Dick Wilson, who was elected president of the tribal council in 1972, and was considered by many to be a puppet—someone who is controlled by an outside influence— of the U.S. government.

Most of Wilson's support at Pine Ridge came from Indians who believed that they should try to give up their native customs and assimilate into white culture. This caused conflict because many of the tribal elders and the young people at Pine Ridge wanted to preserve or restore the old traditions. There was more at issue. Accusations were widespread against Wilson of corruption and relying on violence and **intimidation** when dealing with people who disagreed with him. In fact, one of his many questionable practices as tribal leader was keeping a large private police force known on the reservation for drunkenness and brutality. Wilson faced impeachment by his own tribal council several times because of the criminal corruption of his administration, yet the FBI and the BIA supported him strongly. Wilson hated AIM and asked for government arms

administrator: a person appointed to manage and carry out the policies of others.

intimidation: actions intended to frighten or threaten.

Armed participants of the Wounded Knee occupation, 1973

and support against the group. Soon Pine Ridge was overwhelmed with guns and federal marshals.

When the Sioux elders asked AIM for help against Wilson and his puppet government, the group agreed to take action. Aside from the desire to get rid of the heavy government control on the reservation, AIM members chose to occupy the village of Wounded Knee in part to draw public attention to the site of the 1890 massacre where more than two hundred Sioux men, women, and children had been killed by U.S. Army troops under orders to crush a spiritual movement known as the Ghost Dance.

After AIM took over Wounded Knee, three hundred federal marshals and FBI agents immediately moved in to reestablish government control. The resulting armed stand-

Clyde and Vernon Bellecourt

off lasted seventy-one days. The occupation peaked when the two sides began firing on each other and two Native American men were shot and killed. It finally ended when federal negotiators promised to set up a meeting between Sioux elders and White House representatives. The meeting never took place, however, and once again AIM leaders—including Clyde Bellecourt—found themselves facing a variety of criminal charges. The evidence against Clyde was so flimsy, however, that he never actually went to trial.

Following the Wounded Knee takeover, AIM established a defense fund to help pay the legal fees of those who had been arrested. The organization's leaders took on much of the responsibility for raising money, often by giving speeches and asking for donations. On one such occasion, Vernon Bellecourt gave the following talk in which he described AIM's beginnings and discussed its tactics and goals. The date of this speech is around mid-1975, shortly after two FBI agents were shot and killed on the Pine Ridge Reservation in a confrontation with AIM members and supporters. (See box on page 18 for more information.) It is reprinted from Contemporary Native American Address, *edited by John R. Maestas, Brigham Young University, 1976.*

[The American Indian Movement] was formed in mid-1968 in the ghetto community of Minneapolis, Minnesota. It had to go back to the policy of the United States government which for many years ... was called *relocation*. It was an effort to train people in some area of trade or education to bring them into the mainstream. Generally, the program was ill-devised and ill-planned. In fact, it was never really successful because the program was designed to fail. [The federal agents in charge of the relocation program] would never provide enough assistance. They would just provide enough to get [the Native American people who were being relocated] in the city and drop them off—only **compounding** the problem for Indian people.

Because of the inadequacy of those services provided under the law by the government, [the relocated people]

compounding: increasing.

Vernon Bellecourt at AIM's first international conference, White Oak, Oklahoma, 1973: "We stand together as red people first and then we stand together as tribes."

were completely severed from Indian people when they went into urban areas trying to make that transition from a reservation environment into a city environment. For a lot of our people this has created some social problems. So the organization then started in Minneapolis, and when they looked around and saw that in spite of all the work that the various churches were doing in their missions, in spite of all the programs that were designed by the federal government, in spite of all the efforts of liberal do-gooders to do something for Indian people, they never at one time said, "Let's do it with you." They were always trying to do it for us and failed. The American Indian Movement recognized that we had to form to draw attention to these conditions....

[AIM] has been able to break down tribalism, and we have representation from every tribe in our organization. We stand together as red people first and then we stand together as tribes and fuse together a strong **coalition** from the young people today who are once again identifying with their traditional religion. AIM is first of all the religious rebirth, a spiritual movement, and then, of course, comes the new Indian pride, new Indian dignity. And it has been described as an organization where the people have gone back to an old religion of their tribes, away from the confusion of the society that has made them slaves of unguided lives.

We strongly believe that the movement has been able to unite our young people. It has been able to unite them together with our traditionalness, our elders, our more respected leaders and with a conservative element in between the **bureaucrats** and the people who for some strange reason see us as a threat to their existence. Although we have never attacked Indian people we have always found out that they were not our enemy. We have defined the system. We know what the problems are. We are quite capable of dealing with them as we are dealing with them today.

We recognize in Wounded Knee, as with the case of the Bureau of Indian Affairs occupation during election week, that the primary purpose of the AIM has been as a **catalytic** organization that was going to focus not only national attention but international attention on what has become a national disgrace in this country—the conditions in which Indian people are forced to live.... Now, we recognize that in addition to the confrontation that is taking place between the **sovereign** people at Wounded Knee and the government that AIM and other tribes represented there are not only confronting the bureaucratical impression of the United States government, the Department of Interior's Bureau of Indian Affairs, but most important we see that we are confronting the conscience of America and the conscience of the world.

Indian people, particularly the young people today who have taken a very active role in the AIM, have recognized that for close to 482 years the American Indians have tried to oppose western expansion of the European culture in our land which we recognize could survive and could go on by itself. But what they have tried to do is brainwash us into

coalition: an alliance of different people or groups who come together to take action.

bureaucrats: government officials, especially ones who follow a narrow and rigid set of rules.

catalytic: causing change.

sovereign: free from control by others.

bringing our people into that mainstream and, in doing so, our people have become poor. We recognize that the efforts toward entering the so-called "mainstream" concept has not only failed our people but has also failed a lot of people in the country. We have exhausted our diplomatic efforts. We have negotiated. We have pleaded. Our people have been going to Washington for years and nothing changes, the conditions only get worse. So, what has happened in Wounded Knee is that a declaration of **sovereignty** was made. It is a start of a revolution among the Indian people today, not only a revolution that is taking place in our own existing tribal form of government on the reservations, but we recognize that we have to take a position of sovereignty in relationship to the treaties.

Sovereign treaties or congressionally ratified treaties were made with Indian nations as sovereign people, and it is really immoral, at this time, to suggest that in negotiating those treaties that we should play it by their ground rules within their judicial system and within their courts.... The government in Pine Ridge has totally failed their people while the bureaucracy gets stronger and they buy more guns and police cars and build bigger buildings on the Bureau of Indian Affairs Agency.

Meanwhile, the reservation people are suffering with a forty-two-year life expectancy and still suffering from three times the national average in infant mortality rates and five times the national average suicide rate. Chronic ill-health and diseases that first appeared in the white world yet **prevail** in reservations. When we can see these kinds of conditions, we recognize that the system has totally failed us, and now we should have the right to pool our **self-determination**, our interpretation of which is total self-government. This is a whole new attitude being created at Wounded Knee, and it will continue to become a reality.

The term "revolution" which has become stereotyped now leads the people to believe that it is a violent revolution or that it is some type of thing where we are going to assassinate a lot of people. That is not what we are talking about. We are basically talking about a philosophical revolution which is really going to free our people. We see among the new generation, people who are willing to put meaning into those

sovereignty: freedom from control by others.

prevail: continue to occur frequently.

self-determination: freedom to choose one's own political future.

Clyde and Vernon Bellecourt

words of support instead of words of sympathy. We talk about revolution and we talk about a philosophical revolution brought about by political confrontation.... We recognize that, unfortunately, we live within a system and society in our country here where a society exists that can only respond to some kind of strong confrontation. We can see the success that we have already had in that area....

There are a lot of responsible tribal leaders in this country. And I am not trying to throw them all into the same category, but we see in spite of the reservations that some of the people are being abused. They are poor; the conditions of poverty are getting worse, and we realize that we have to have some type of revolution to bring about these changes so that we can exist and survive as a society.

There have been two attempts by responsible Indian people in the Pine Ridge Reservation to remove their existing tribal chairman [Dick Wilson]. They recognize that he has become a puppet of Washington and, in fact, never really an advocate of Indian people.... They have indicated to us very strongly that they no longer want that kind of puppet government, and they want to cast it off. In doing so, the people and the AIM met with the traditional chief on the Pine Ridge Reservation.

It has always been our feeling that the American Indian Movement has been a traditional organization, going back to our traditional way of life, our traditional ties, values, standards, etc. The tribal form of government, as the government exists today, was set up by Washington some years back. The whole impression of their policy is being threatened, and, of course, this is why they are opposing any type of stand by the people up there. And so we are having meetings with the traditional chiefs. And the wishes of the overall people are to restore the government back to the chiefs who are in fact serving as advocates of their people.

This is what is happening so far as the issue on the Pine Ridge Reservation is concerned. We have recognized that in several of these non-Indian communities that the whole economy depends on the monies that Indian people spend in those communities. It is ironic that those same communities are the ones that are practicing racism against Indian people. Indian people are assaulted, arrested, charged with drunkenness when they aren't drunk so that they can post fines on them and get their money. They view the Indian people as a parasite living off the economy, and they abuse them. We can see what a complete double standard of justice we have in this country affecting the Indian people....

We have always recognized our credibility as a sovereignty. We have always recognized that several nations [tribes] have never given up the feeling of sovereignty. The United States government has never given up the feeling that we are sovereign people and have been subjected to tyranny and actually a conquered people. Because of this strong feeling of sovereignty, we always recognize that Indian people perhaps have had to fight to bring about social change in this country. If you really evaluate and look at the conditions we have to live in today, we can bring clear-cut **indictment** against the government and system along with an unconcerned society for allowing these conditions to exist and continue. We always recognize that we have a valid cause to also stand up the very same way that this country stood up in 1776 and wrote a document called a Declaration of Independence....

It is defined in the Declaration of Independence very clearly that when, for long periods of time, a government becomes a tyranny to the people, when it becomes abusive to people, committing **indignities** and continually **suppressing** them, you have not only a legal responsibility but a moral responsibility to change that form of government or attempt to destroy it. All we have said at Wounded Knee today is that we are trying to change that form of government. We are trying to bring about change, social change....

We recognize the whole civil rights movement across this country has recognized that the American Indian people are going to take the lead as far as bringing about social change. We have had several national organizations who have indicated to us clearly that they could see in our efforts that we have rekindled the flame again in this land of bringing about justice for a change, to bring about truth where there hasn't been any.

We believe that we are going to be a primary force in the history of this country. Our prophecies told us that one day a

indictment: formal charge of a crime.

indignities: insults, humiliations.

suppressing: put down by authority or force.

Clyde and Vernon Bellecourt

man would come from the North, and his skin would be the color of death, and he would be here for a short while, and he would leave, and then again he would return and be here for a long time, and our people would suffer. But in the fifth generation after the second coming of the white man, small fires would crop up about our nations, and confrontations at Fort Lewis, Alcatraz—these are those small flames. The conditions are the same as they were when the white man came the second time to our land. People are fighting and children are fighting with their parents. Our prophecies tell us when trees would start dying from the top, a black cloud would settle, and there would be rioting, and the small fires would become one gigantic flame, and, at that time, the red people would stand once again in power. We can see the answer to our prophecy is coming true now.

This is the time we have to stand as a sovereign people. We have to stand and give direction to the society and our country which has been lost for the most part. We know that we can take that role and provide the truth, spirituality, freedom not only for the redman but for all people in this land and that is the role that the AIM is going to play.... We have been able to sit down with our Sioux brothers and so-called tribes of Indians who supposedly were enemies with one another. We have been able to completely overrule that problem by joining together spiritually.

The American Indian Movement is a spiritual movement first and a political organization secondly. It has been very good for us to see the outcome of this new awareness, the new pride that has been introduced to our young people. Every day young people are getting off alcohol and narcotics because of this new awareness.... As far as Indian people are concerned, going back to our ways is the way we want to do it.

I am sure the government also recognizes the fact that we have this fuse in our hand right now, and they want to extinguish it.

The movement itself is going to continue in an effort to confront the conscience of American people. We are going to continue confronting the establishment. We are going to continue working within the system....

We're going to work on and be involved in controversial issues, and in spite of all the criticism we are getting today, our movement is getting stronger because it is a movement of people wanting change. We recognize that Wounded Knee has become a memorial for freedom not only for Indian people but for all people for a better way of life. If that can be crushed, and this society allows it to be crushed, they are perhaps crushing an opportunity to really have peace in the world. We have recognized our spiritual leaders. And our old people tell us that the reason this government has never been able to find peace in the world is because they have never made peace with the sovereign people here. Until they make peace with the redman in our part of the universe, they will never find peace.

For thousands of years, ever since the time of creation, it has been our position that we were **imbued** by the Creator, the Great Spirit, with certain rights that could not be **alienated** by any foreign power, and certainly in this case, we can only see the United States government as a foreign power. The traditional people, the people on the reservations, have maintained their culture, language, spiritual ways, their way of life as much as they can within a contemporary society, of course. And their society has been really disrupted.

In 1934, the United States government, in order to impose a so-called process of government, patterned a government, after the United States government, on the reservations to impose leadership on people who went through their Bureau of Indian Affairs schools and other **indoctrination** so the mining interests could gain the resources of our land. They had to impose this kind of leadership. I think it only fair to say that within this alien form of government that has been imposed upon the people since 1934, passed by Congress without ratification by the tribe, forced upon them, that many tribal leaders have tried to function within that system. We have been honest, very sincere people, very much handicapped by government-Washington bureaucracy.

We have always maintained and respected the traditional **hereditary chiefs.** In their place the government has put puppets, people who have sold their own people out to the mining corporations who are now strip-mining vast lands that no one wanted at one time. We were forced at the point

imbued: endowed.

alienated: transferred or withdrawn, usually by means other than the law.

indoctrination: the act of teaching someone while also trying to influence them to believe a certain way.

hereditary chiefs: chiefs who became leaders of their tribes by reason of birth—that is, they were heirs to leadership because of their family lines.

Clyde and Vernon Bellecourt

Indian Reorganization Act (IRA) 1934

After many years of trying to **assimilate** American Indians into mainstream U.S. life and to divide Indian reservations into individually owned plots of land through its allotment program, the U.S. government was forced to change its policy. At the end of the 1920s Native Americans' right to sovereignty was becoming acknowledged. Public opinion shifted toward valuing Indian cultures and trying to preserve them. The Meriam Report, an investigation commissioned by John D. Rockefeller in 1928, described terrible conditions on American reservations and in Indian boarding schools. In the early 1930s John Collier, President Franklin D. Roosevelt's commissioner of Indian affairs, began a program known as the "Indian New Deal," which set out to strengthen and protect Indian cultures. In 1934 Congress passed the Indian Reorganization Act, or the IRA, which ended allotment, returned some land to Indian groups, granted Native Americans the right to live in their traditional manner, and encouraged a prescribed (though not traditional) form of partial self-government on reservations.

The IRA tribal governments on reservations had constitutions and elected tribal councils. But the measure was not as effective in providing self-government as it may have been intended. The Bureau of Indian Affairs still held control of the federal funds on which most reservations relied and could therefore override tribal council decisions. Moreover, the processes of democracy in traditional Indian decision-making often conflicted with the voting system prescribed by this act. Only 77 of the 258 tribal communities eligible for the IRA accepted the measure.

---

of a rifle. So, the traditional view is that we are a civilization, we are a sovereign people, we have our own form of government with imposed leadership....

We [of AIM] have provided an alternative voice, an alternative voice of action for Indian people. We have almost total support of the traditional people. Also the young people today can see what is happening. They have the vision as to what is happening to our nations and civilization. They see they are destroyed through practices of the Christian church, the anti-Indian concepts of education, and the federal bureaucracy. These are the three major enemies of the Indian people. We have identified them, and we know that in order to survive as a people we must go back to our lands. We must rebuild our tribal form of government, we must take control of our destiny and our future. We must control the Dick Wilsons across this country who are controlled by the

assimilate: cause to become more like the dominant culture.

Interior Department, the agency of government who has the trust, the protective status over our resources. This is the same agency of government that gives our leases to the mining companies, the strip-mining corporations, the power plants.... This is the enemy we have identified—the federal bureaucracy.

And so the traditional people cannot **compromise.** It is said by our leaders that we cannot hurt the sacred Mother Earth without hurting ourselves. We cannot compromise, we can no longer **desecrate** the earth if we are to survive as a people. We see the kinds of tribal government that's allied with the special interests, with the corporations of Washington government. We see these people along with whites, destroying the three basic elements of life: earth, air and water. They walk the path of destruction. We are saying, walk the path of destruction with the white people if you want to. But there are a lot of white people who realize that it is a fact and the truth, and they no longer want to walk the path to destruction. These are the people that we are appealing to.

I would like the people to understand that the AIM is not [Anishinabe Ojibway activist and AIM cofounder and leader] Dennis Banks and [Lakota activist and AIM leader] **Russell Means** [see entry] and Vernon Bellecourt, or [Sioux medicine man and activist] Leonard Crow Dog, but the American Indian Movement is the thousands and thousands of traditional, grass-roots elders on the reservations, the poor people who have had no voice, the poor people for whom nothing changes, but conditions continue to deteriorate. The American Indian Movement is the youth of our nation who have now seen that we must survive as a civilization, for if the red-man is to perish, then, who deserves to live?...

Since Wounded Knee, all across the United States, on almost all reservations, and as I travel, people come up and tell me that almost every day the FBI has squads on reservations, interviewing and interrogating various people associated with the American Indian Movement in an effort to discourage these people from supporting our views. It is an effort to destroy the movement.

This is going on actively now and has been for two years on the Pine Ridge Reservation. The tribal chairman has his

compromise: agree to give up certain rights or privileges in the interest of reaching a settlement acceptable to a group of people.

desecrate: treat with contempt or lack of respect.

Clyde and Vernon Bellecourt

own vigilante squad, armed with automatic weapons most times, who have been spreading alcohol and drugs on the reservations. There have been up to forty unsolved murders of people who have been sympathetic or supporters of the American Indian Movement.... Known killers and rapists, who have assaulted people on the reservations have not been **indicted**, and this is the kind of harassment that takes place....

In order to put this into its proper perspective, we have to understand that the Bureau of Indian Affairs Police, along with the FBI, and we understand now that a State Highway Patrol Tactical Squad ... have mobilized probably a larger force than was even at Wounded Knee two years ago. The press for the most part has been censored. The information we have received is from direct sources.... Much of the press, which is only getting the reports from the FBI office, would indicate to the American people that agents Ron Williams and Jack Coler are, in fact, martyrs, that they were innocent FBI agents who during the course of their duty, were gunned down without provocation. This is totally ridiculous.

One has to look at the fact that these two men are only part of a massive FBI force, that since Wounded Knee, not only on Pine Ridge but on other reservations all across this country, have been systematically **interrogating**, harassing, intimidating and in many cases, assaulting any native people that might share the philosophies of self-determination of the American Indian Movement....

These two men are only part of a force that has been on the Pine Ridge Reservation for two years now (since Wounded Knee) in an effort to turn off any kind of support for the American Indian Movement by the poor people on that reservation. They are the same force that has kept the imposed leadership of Dick Wilson and kept him in office on that reservation....

At this time ... a state of **anarchy** exists [on the Pine Ridge Reservation]. It certainly has paved the way for the attorney general of [South Dakota] to move in with his state Tactical Riot Squad to assume **jurisdiction**.... We see it as another plot along with the FBI and the federal government to take control through state jurisdiction on those reservations.

indicted: formally charged with a crime.

interrogating: questioning.

anarchy: a state of political disorder and lawlessness.

jurisdiction: control, authority.

Shootout at Oglala

On June 26, 1975, near the town of Oglala on the Pine Ridge Reservation, a shootout took place. Two FBI agents—Ron Williams and Jack Coler—were found dead after they had gone to Pine Ridge and become involved in an exchange of gunfire. Later that day, more FBI agents and Indian police reinforcements arrived on the scene. Another gun battle erupted, this time resulting in the death of a Native American man.

The shootings came at a time of near-civil war on the reservation. Tensions between Indians and whites as well as between Indian activists and Indians who worked for, or sided with, the U.S. government were running extremely high. Conditions were even worse than they had been at the time of the Wounded Knee takeover two years earlier.

In the wake of the Oglala incident, government officials accused a group of Indians—including AIM member Leonard Peltier—of brutally ambushing the FBI agents after they had chased a suspect into a camp that served as the informal headquarters of AIM and other activist tribal groups. The Indians denied this version of the events. They insisted that they had heard some gunfire near their camp and went to investigate. They then spotted the FBI agents' cars and the agents themselves, wounded but still alive. But before they could reach the vehicles, someone else in a red pickup truck drove up, got out, and fired in the direction where the agents' bodies were later found. Both of the agents had been shot several times at point-blank range through the head.

Peltier fled to Canada but was arrested and brought back to the United States in early 1976 to face murder charges. (Two other Indians also stood accused of killing the agents but were later acquitted of the murders; charges against a fourth Indian were later dropped.) Peltier went on trial in Fargo, North Dakota, in the spring of 1977. The government's evidence against Peltier was questionable at best, and most of the testimony favorable to his case was not allowed to be presented. To his many supporters it seemed that he was not really being tried for murder. Instead, they felt he was a political prisoner—someone punished for his beliefs and for belonging to the "wrong" group.

Nevertheless, Peltier was quickly found guilty and sentenced to two life terms in prison, where he remains today. But his case attracted worldwide attention and renewed interest in the problems of Native Americans. Activists are still hard at work rallying for his release and trying to win him a new trial that they believe will end in a different verdict.

This is a threat not only to the nations of South Dakota but of tribal leadership across this country. If it is allowed to happen here then, next, the government will be moving in on their reservations. There is a state of emergency that exists....

Clyde and Vernon Bellecourt

I think one of the major enemies of Indian people today is ignorance. We have an American society that has been kept ignorant about the facts of history. The educational system has polluted the minds of their children, either portraying us in an image of the proud and noble savage without any concern for the human suffering that continues today, or on the other hand, the John Wayne mentality or frontier mentality prevails in the minds of most Americans. They don't even care about Indian people. They either feel that we don't exist or we are museum pieces. And the whole concept has brought about a dehumanization of Indian people.... [Whites] do not even know that they are, in fact, racist against Indian people.

Indian people have been brutalized and murdered on reservations and off reservations for 483 years. We have termed it America's longest undeclared war, and the first time that FBI agents are shot, there is a sudden outcry across the country that they become **martyrs.** They become heroes in a sense. Now it provokes the FBI and the police authorities in this country for a massive crackdown on the people of Pine Ridge. This is our fear right now, and unless the American people become aware of what the facts are ... it is never going to change, and they will remain unconcerned....

We are now tied up in five different courtrooms.... This has been a tactic of the government to divide our resources. In fact, they have forced us into running out of money in defending ourselves.

Real help right now could come through awareness. People should become aware of what is going on in Pine Ridge, become aware of the American Indian Movement as a traditional, spiritual movement. We need funds as a reality to continue to fund our defense in the courts, and we would ask those that want to contribute to please contribute to the Wounded Knee Committee....

As for Clyde Bellecourt, after the Wounded Knee takeover he began to devote more of his time to AIM's "survival school" program. These schools have two major goals. One

martyrs: people who sacrifice their lives or something else of great value to uphold certain ideas or causes.

Clyde Bellecourt speaking out against Indian mascots and racism in sports, 1992

is to help Indian youngsters adjust to white society while preserving important traditions of their own culture. The other is to counteract the **distorted** (and often negative) image of Indians common in many textbooks and in the popular media. Or, as Bellecourt himself once stated, "We wanted to teach our kids the truth about Indian people."

This feeling was at the heart of a speech Clyde Bellecourt gave in Washington, D.C., on July 15, 1978, during a protest march known as "The Longest Walk." The march had begun some five months earlier in San Francisco, California. By the time it reached the nation's capital, it had grown to include demonstrators from the entire continent of North America. (Many celebrity activists also took part, including comedian Dick Gregory and actor Marlon Bran-

distorted: twisted, misleading.

Clyde and Vernon Bellecourt

do.) A notably peaceful—and even spiritual—event, it also ranks as one of the strongest displays of Indian unity in United States history. Bellecourt's remarks are reprinted here from Native American Reader: Stories, Speeches and Poems, *edited by Jerry D. Blanche, Denali Press, 1990.*

99

We want you to know that we are attempting to call attention to and to gain your support in turning back the anti-Indian attitude, the anti-Indian legislation, and the John Wayne mentality that exists among the media today. We are asking you to help us to stop these **genocidal** practices that are taking place against my people.

We'll stop nuclear power! We'll stop nuclear warfare around this world! We have the capability and the spiritual power. It is here, with us today!

We want you who have gathered here today to hear our story to know that it hasn't been easy. I joined this Sacred Walk, this spiritual march, in ceremonies that were taking place in Topeka, Kansas. We were aware at that time that the FBI, in **collusion** with the Community Relations Service of the United States Justice Department, had been in front of us and in back of us, flashing phony mug shots of supposed fugitives, criminals, people who escaped from jails. They were telling our support groups in front of us and in back of us that these were the type of people that were on the Walk.

The FBI has worked in every way possible. It **parallels** their efforts to destroy Martin Luther King, to destroy Malcolm X, to destroy the Black Panther Party, and to destroy the black civil rights movement in this country. But we have been able to overcome that through these sacred pipes, the sacred drum, and the ceremonies.

This is all we have left here. Our way of life. And it was told to us that if our drum was ever stilled, you too would be through as a nation.

In the Mormon religion that we have come in contact with throughout this march, they say among one part of that church that it is the Native people that will stand up. It is

genocidal: characterized by deliberate and organized attempts to destroy a group of people.

collusion: collaboration, cooperation.

parallels: equals, matches.

Native people that will offer survival to the rest of the world. It is Native people that will inherit this part of the world, this island. And these Mormon people that I talked to said that they too, in their scripture and their philosophy and their prophesies, knew that a great march was coming from the West, travelling East. No different from the prophesies of our great medicine men, our great spiritual leaders and holy men, that have passed on before us. They too talked about this generation.

They even identified the young people who came down from the North—from the East and the South and the West—that they would run ten, fifteen, twenty miles, long distances, each day to carry these sacred pipes. It was said that from among this generation, these young people you see gathered here today would spring our leadership. The fifth generation is here among us. This is where our power is, and our strength. We are many great chiefs and great leaders, clan mothers, warriors, that have developed out of this spiritual walk and other occupations that have taken place for many, many years.

I would like to thank our younger brothers and sisters who have joined in to support our leadership. They support our chiefs that you see here among us. They support our women and they support our brothers and sisters who are in prisons and jails across this country....

We walk for our brothers and sisters and pray for our brothers and sisters who cannot be here with us today.

We walk also for our brother, Buddy Lamont, a Vietnam veteran who came home one of the most decorated warriors on the Pine Ridge Reservation. He came home and found the same armed forces that he fought with, surrounding his mother, his family, and his relatives on that reservation. We walk for this young warrior who came there and gave his life that we might live and that we might walk together again. [Buddy Lamont was killed by a sniper's bullet on April 26, 1973, during heavy gunfire exchange in the Wounded Knee takeover. He had recently joined forces with AIM.]

We walk for Pedro Bissonette, and Raymond Yellow Thunder, and the millions of Indian people who gave their lives that we might be given the opportunity to gather here to create, to build, to bring back the Old Ways, the ways of survival. [Pedro Bisonnette, an Ogala who organized the traditional people to work with AIM, was arrested after the Wounded Knee takeover, but charges against him were dismissed. He was then shot to death by BIA police on October 17, 1973. The police claimed he resisted arrest. Raymond Yellow Thunder was brutally murdered by two young white brothers in February 1972. When it appeared that local authorities were not going to prosecute the murderers, AIM was called in.]

One of the greatest things I have seen coming out of this march is that I have had whole families come up to me from the ghettos that they have pushed us into through these relocation programs. They told me that they could not go back home after being on this walk, holding these sacred pipes. There is a **deurbanization** coming along. It will be for the survival of our youth and the survival of our unborn generations.

We ask each and every one of you to pray with us for the next four days. We want to meet your community, we want to talk to your people, and we want to change the image that has been portrayed by John Wayne, the media, and the history books. We want to portray the truth. We the Indian people, the Red Man of the Western Hemisphere, are the truth of the Western Hemisphere!

Although the Bellecourts (especially Vernon) had slowed down by the mid-1990s due to battles with serious illness, they remained as active as possible in the movement to secure respect and justice for Native Americans. Some of their more common targets were sports teams that had Indian names or mascots (such as the Washington Redskins and the Atlanta Braves). They believed that this practice was racist and insulting to Native American people.

Sources

Books

Blanche, Jerry D., editor, *Native American Reader: Stories, Speeches and Poems,* Denali Press, 1990.

deurbanization: the process of getting rid of or backing away from the features, activities, behaviors, and so on that characterize life in a city.

Maestas, John R., editor, *Contemporary Native American Address,* Brigham Young University, 1976.

Matthiessen, Peter, *In the Spirit of Crazy Horse,* Viking, 1983, new edition, 1991.

Nabokov, Peter, editor, *Native American Testimony: A Chronicle of Indian-White Relations from Prophecy to the Present, 1492–1992,* Penguin Books, 1991.

Notable Native Americans, Gale, 1995.

Voices from Wounded Knee, 1973: In the Words of the Participants, Akwesasne Notes, 1974.

Periodicals

Minneapolis-St. Paul Magazine, "Blood Brothers," March 1996.

Sporting News, "NFL Comes Under Protest," February 3, 1992, p. 13.

Black Hawk

(Ma-ka-tae-mish-kia-kiak)
1767–1838

Chief of the Sauk (Sac) tribe

During the early 1800s, the young United States quickly began to expand westward from the original thirteen colonies. Black Hawk was one of a number of major Native American leaders who actively resisted this growth of white settlements into Indian lands. His Sauk homeland stretched out on both sides of the Mississippi River around what is now northwestern Illinois and southern Wisconsin. Like the Shawnee leader **Tecumseh** (see entry), he was convinced that the long-term survival of Indian nations depended on achieving unity among the tribes.

A Respected Warrior

Black Hawk himself was born in a village near the mouth of the Rock River in the vicinity of present-day Rock Island, Illinois. He first distinguished himself as a warrior at the age of only seventeen when he led his own war party against some other Indians. Later, during the War of 1812, he allied himself with Great Britain against the United States.

"THE WHITE MEN DO NOT SCALP THE HEAD; BUT THEY DO WORSE— THEY POISON THE HEART...."

Like many other Indians who supported the British, Black Hawk thought that by defeating the Americans he could stop or at least slow down white migration. But he also understood that individual tribes did not stand a very good chance of successfully challenging white settlers. He worked for many years to establish a loose **coalition** of other midwestern tribes threatened by America's rapid growth.

Black Hawk condemned each new treaty that allowed more settlers to move into Sauk territory. He claimed that Indians were usually pressured or tricked into signing away their lands, often while under the influence of alcohol furnished by whites. In fact, this was the case with the southern band of Sauk. They lived farther down the Mississippi River from Black Hawk's band, around what is now the state of Missouri. In 1804, they signed a treaty giving all tribal land east of the river to the United States.

Challenges Loss of Tribal Land to White Settlers

Black Hawk insisted that the southern band's tribal leaders did not speak for his band—which was a separate tribal group—and he refused to live by the terms of the treaty they had signed. But his strong opposition made little difference. By 1831, most of his people had been forced west across the Mississippi into Iowa. The less-fertile soil they found there made farming more difficult. After watching the Sauks struggle to grow enough food to feed themselves, Black Hawk decided it was time to take back the land.

On April 5, 1832, Black Hawk led his supporters east across the Mississippi River. Their goal was to plant corn, but they were prepared to fight any whites who tried to stop them. As it turned out, they did not have to wait long. A hastily assembled group of U.S. Army troops soon launched an attack against the Indians. But Black Hawk and his warriors fought back successfully and then headed north into Wisconsin. What later became known as the Black Hawk War had begun.

On July 21, the Indians again confronted some U.S. soldiers. This time, however, U.S. forces were much larger and better prepared. Over the next few weeks, they killed many of the Sauk warriors in a series of small skirmishes. With his

coalition: an alliance of different people or groups who come together to take action.

escape route down the Mississippi blocked, Black Hawk found himself trapped in northern Wisconsin. On August 27, after being captured by some members of the Winnebago tribe, he reluctantly agreed to surrender. It is believed he made the following speech at the time he was turned over to U.S. government authorities in the town of Prairie du Chien. The text is reprinted from Literature of the American Indian, *by Thomas E. Sanders and Walter W. Peek, Glencoe Press, 1973.*

99

You have taken me prisoner with all my warriors. I am much grieved, for I expected, if I did not defeat you, to hold out much longer, and give you more trouble before I surrendered. I tried hard to bring you into ambush, but your last general understands Indian fighting. The first one was not so wise. When I saw that I could not beat you by Indian fighting, I determined to rush on you, and fight you face to face. I fought hard. But your guns were well aimed. The bullets flew like birds in the air, and whizzed by our ears like the wind through the trees in winter. My warriors fell around me; it began to look dismal. I saw my evil day at hand. The sun rose dim on us in the morning, and at night it sank in a dark cloud, and looked like a ball of fire. That was the last sun that shone on Black Hawk. His heart is dead, and no longer beats quick in his bosom. He is now a prisoner to the white men; they will do with him as they wish. But he can stand torture, and is not afraid of death. He is no coward. Black Hawk is an Indian.

He has done nothing for which an Indian ought to be ashamed. He has fought for his countrymen, the squaws and papooses, against white men, who came, year after year, to cheat them and take away their lands. You know the cause of our making war. It is known to all white men. They ought to be ashamed of it. The white men despise the Indians, and

Black Hawk's words on surrender: "That was the last sun that shone on Black Hawk. His heart is dead, and no longer beats quick in his bosom. He is now a prisoner to the white men...."

drive them from their homes. But the Indians are not deceitful. The white men speak bad of the Indian, and look at him **spitefully**. But the Indian does not tell lies; Indians do not steal.

An Indian who is as bad as the white men, could not live in our nation; he would be put to death, and eaten up by the wolves. The white men are bad schoolmasters; they carry false looks and deal in false actions; they smile in the face of the poor Indian to cheat him; they shake them by the hand to gain their confidence, to make them drunk, to deceive them, and ruin our wives. We told them to let us alone, and keep away from us; but they followed on and **beset** our paths, and they coiled themselves among us like the snake. They poisoned us by their touch. We were not safe. We lived in danger. We were becoming like them, **hypocrites** and liars, **adulterers**. Lazy **drones**, all talkers, and no workers.

We looked up to the Great Spirit. We went to our great father. We were encouraged. His great council gave us fair words and big promises; but we got no satisfaction. Things were growing worse. There were no deer in the forest. The opossum and beaver were fled; the springs were drying up, and our squaws and papooses without **victuals** to keep them from starving; we called a great council and built a large fire. The spirit of our fathers arose and spoke to us to avenge our wrongs or die. We all spoke before the council fire. It was warm and pleasant. We set up the war-whoop, and dug up the tomahawk; our knives were ready, and the heart of Black Hawk swelled high in his bosom when he led his warriors to battle. He is satisfied. He will go to the world of spirits contented. He has done his duty. His father will meet him there, and **commend** him.

Black Hawk is a true Indian, and **disdains** to cry like a woman. He feels for his wife, his children and friends. But he does not care for himself. He cares for his nation and the Indians. They will suffer. He **laments** their fate. The white men do not scalp the head; but they do worse—they poison the heart; it is not pure with them. His countrymen will not be scalped, but they will, in a few years, become like white men, so that you can't trust them, and there must be, as in the white settlements, nearly as many officers as men, to take care of them and keep them in order.

spitefully: showing hatred or the desire to injure or annoy.

beset: attacked, harassed.

hypocrites: people who claim to have high moral standards but who do not really live by them.

adulterers: people who cheat on their spouses.

drones: people who live on work done by others.

victuals: food supplies.

commend: praise.

disdains: refuses out of a sense of contempt.

laments: mourns, grieves for.

Farewell, my nation! Black Hawk tried to save you, and avenge your wrongs. He drank the blood of some of the whites. He has been taken prisoner, and his plans are stopped. He can do no more. He is near his end. His sun is setting, and he will rise no more. Farewell to Black Hawk.

99

Held as a prisoner of war, Black Hawk was eventually taken to Washington, D.C. There he met with President Andrew Jackson, who scolded him for going to war against the whites. He was then sent on a tour of several major cities, including New York, Philadelphia, Pennsylvania, and Baltimore, Maryland. The purpose of these visits was to show him how big and powerful his enemy truly was. All this attention made him into a celebrity and led to the publication of his autobiography in 1833. But it also had the desired effect of convincing him how useless it was to struggle against the westward march of white civilization.

Eventually, Black Hawk and the rest of the Sauk people were relocated to a reservation near present-day Des Moines, Iowa. There he died in 1838, having been stripped of his rank as chief as a result of the disastrous Black Hawk War. Later, Black Hawk's bones were unearthed and put on display in a local museum that was destroyed by fire in the mid-1850s.

Sources

Books

Armstrong, Virginia Irving, compiler, *I Have Spoken: American History Through the Voices of the Indians,* Sage Books, 1971.

Black Hawk, *Life of Black Hawk* (reprint of 1833 autobiography), Dover, 1994.

Jones, Louis Thomas, *Aboriginal American Oratory: The Tradition of Eloquence Among the Indians of the United States,* Southwest Museum (Los Angeles), 1965.

McLuhan, T. C., *Touch the Earth: A Self-Portrait of Indian Existence,* Outerbridge & Dienstfrey, 1971.

Notable Native Americans, Gale, 1995.

Rosenstiel, Annette, *Red and White: Indian Views of the White Man, 1492–1982,* Universe Books, 1983.

Sanders, Thomas E., and Walter W. Peek, *Literature of the American Indian,* Glencoe Press, 1973.

Vanderwerth, W. C., *Indian Oratory: Famous Speeches by Noted Indian Chieftains,* University of Oklahoma Press, 1971.

Witt, Shirley Hill, and Stan Steiner, editors, *The Way: An Anthology of American Indian Literature,* Knopf, 1972.

Gertrude Simmons Bonnin

(Zitkala-Sa, Red Bird)
1876–1938

Activist and writer of the Sioux tribe

One of the most outspoken voices raised on behalf of Native Americans during the early twentieth century was that of Gertrude Simmons Bonnin. Her essays and short stories established her as an important writer of Indian literature. In addition, she was a reformer and activist devoted to improving the lives of Native Americans both on and off the reservation. That mission often led Bonnin to appear before government officials in Washington and at rallies comprised of ordinary citizens throughout the nation. In her speeches and lectures, she tried to give her audiences some idea of the poverty and despair many Indians faced daily.

Gertrude Simmons was born to an Indian mother and a white father at the Yankton Sioux Agency in South Dakota. (Some sources say she was a granddaughter of the famous Sioux Chief **Sitting Bull** [see entry].) She spent her early childhood on the reservation, where she followed the traditional Sioux ways. But when she was about eight, she left for Wabash, Indiana, to attend a Quaker missionary school

"THERE WAS A TIME, LONG AGO, WHEN INDIANS SHARED THEIR FOOD WITH THE HUNGRY, BUT THAT DAY IS PAST. NOW ALL INDIANS ARE TOO POOR. THEY HAVE NOTHING TO DIVIDE. THERE IS STARVATION."

for Indian children. Getting used to her new surroundings was difficult, and young Gertrude was very unhappy for quite some time. But she finally settled in and completed a three-year term. She then returned home for four years before heading to Santee Normal Training School in Nebraska, a teachers' college. Following her graduation in 1895, she went on to Earlham College in Richmond, Indiana. There she studied music (focusing on the violin) and earned recognition as the winner of a state-wide contest in public speaking.

Tries Her Hand at Writing

After leaving college in 1897, Bonnin accepted a teaching position at Pennsylvania's Carlisle Indian School. The time she spent there was not always pleasant. Carlisle founder Richard Henry Pratt believed that American Indian education should consist only of training in practical skills such as agriculture and homemaking, while Bonnin believed that Indian youth should be taught academic subjects. Nonetheless, during her time at Carlisle she took great pleasure in her music and also began writing. The contacts she made with some East Coast writers opened new doors for her, and before long she had published a collection of old Indian legends under her Sioux name, Zitkala-Sa, or Red Bird.

Around that time, Bonnin started contributing essays to well-known magazines such as Harper's and Atlantic Monthly. These soon brought her national attention as a harsh critic of white policy toward Native Americans, especially in the area of education. Like Carlisle, most Indian schools of that time concentrated on "practical" skills and often did not prepare students for advanced education or more fulfilling careers.

In 1899, Bonnin resigned from the Carlisle faculty and enrolled at the New England Conservatory of Music in Boston, Massachusetts, to study violin. The cultural atmosphere that surrounded her there made her happier than she had been in many years. But she still felt somewhat torn between two worlds—the Indian one and the white one. This had been a problem for her ever since she first went away to school as a child. It had even caused trouble between her and her mother through the years.

Determined to do something for those she had left behind on the reservation, Bonnin returned to South Dakota in late 1901. The following year, she married a fellow Yankton Sioux, Raymond T. Bonnin, who worked for the Indian Service. (The Indian Service—now known as the Bureau of Indian Affairs—was the name of the government agency responsible for carrying out most federal programs and policy concerning Native Americans.) The Bonnins soon moved to the Uintah and Ouray Reservation in Utah, where they spent the next thirteen years. Gertrude Bonnin worked mostly as a clerk and a teacher. Other than an opera she completed in 1913, she was not able to devote much time to her writing or her music.

Nationwide Reform Efforts

After living on the Utah reservation for several years, Bonnin's activities began to revolve around the Society of American Indians (SAI). An Indian reform organization founded in 1911 at Ohio State University, the SAI was the first group of its kind to be established and managed completely by Indians. The progress-minded members of the SAI felt that the only way to ensure a better life for their fellow Native Americans was to help them **assimilate into** mainstream white culture. Therefore, they supported changing the relationship between Indians and the federal government.

For example, the SAI urged that laws having to do with Indians be standardized. The organization also asked that the courts consider all reasonable claims regarding land settlements between Indians and the government. In addition, the SAI encouraged the government to hire more Indians to work for the Indian Service. It also **lobbied** for U.S. citizenship for Native Americans and took steps to preserve Indian history.

In 1916, Bonnin was elected secretary of the SAI. Not long after that, she and her husband moved to Washington, D.C.—the city she would call home for the rest of her life. She remained very active with the SAI and even edited

assimilate into: become absorbed into; adapt by becoming like the dominant social group.

lobbied: attempted to persuade legislators to push for a program or policy to become law.

its main publication, American Indian Magazine. *But increasing personal and political disagreements between members of the group sent the SAI into a slow decline. In 1920, Bonnin ended her association with the Society of American Indians.*

She then joined forces with a number of other organizations that were fighting for reform and Indian rights, including the American Indian Defense Association and the Indian Rights Association. In addition, she began lecturing extensively from coast to coast, speaking to women's clubs and other groups on Indian affairs. She also continued to lobby for Indian citizenship, finally meeting with success in 1924 with the passage of the Indian Citizenship Bill.

Both Bonnin and her husband devoted a great deal of their time to meeting with officials of the federal government as representatives of individual Indians and tribes. They also testified before congressional committees on a wide variety of issues that they themselves had investigated. The Bonnins regularly traveled throughout the country visiting reservations and noting the need for improvements in areas such as health care, education, conservation of natural resources, and preservation of Indian cultural traditions.

Forms the National Council of American Indians

In 1926, the Bonnins formed the National Council of American Indians (NCAI). Like the Society of American Indians (which by that time had completely fallen apart), the NCAI was made up exclusively of Native Americans; Bonnin served as its president. As head of the reform-oriented group, she directed her energies toward lobbying for Indian legislation in Congress and calling attention to the problems within the Indian Service.

These efforts finally did make some government officials take a closer look at the Indian Service. In 1928, U.S. Secretary of the Interior Hubert Work approached the Institute for Government Research about studying living conditions among Native Americans. (The Institute for Government Research is part of the Brookings Institution, a social science research organization based in Washington, D.C.) Work asked the Institute to focus in particular on economic activity, education, health, and the federal government's policies and practices.

Heading up the special group of scholars assembled for the task was Dr. Lewis Meriam, whose background was in economics and law. Under his direction, the Institute conducted a thorough investigation and published the results in a landmark report entitled The Problem of Indian Administration, *more commonly known as the* Meriam Report. *Its description of the "deplorable" state of life on the reservations—the high death rate among all age groups, the failure of the educational system, the widespread poverty and malnutrition—focused national attention on the plight of Native Americans. The U.S. government soon found itself under tremendous pressure to take immediate action.*

In mid-December of that year (1928), Bonnin voiced her thoughts on the findings of the Meriam Report *at a meeting of the Indian Rights Association in Atlantic City, New Jersey. The text of the following speech was furnished by the Harold B. Lee Library at Brigham Young University. The Library houses the Gertrude Simmons Bonnin Collection.*

99

The opportunity to speak today in a conference discussing the report of the Indian survey made by the Institute for Government Research is appreciated by this Indian speaker....

I have the honor to be president of the National Council of American Indians, an all-Indian organization based upon citizenship rights granted by Congress June 2, 1924.

Before that, Indians were jailed if they held meetings without permission from a superintendent....

The Indian's American citizenship has been dearly bought by repeated self sacrifices, until his unsurpassed loyalty and volunteer service in the World War [1917–18] won this recognition from Congress.

Many times, standing by the grave of the Unknown Soldier, I have felt that it may be an Indian boy, who bravely

Bonnin in tradional dress in 1926: "Indians are kept ignorant and 'incompetent' to cope with the world's trained workers, because they are not sufficiently educated in the government schools."

wards: people under the special protection of a government.

subordinate: occupying a position of lower class or less authority.

fought and heroically died for the principles of democracy, who lies there now.

Positively, no one on earth can honestly challenge the American Indian's loyalty to the government of the United States, though this government has waged more wars upon its Indian **wards** than any other nation against its own **subordinate** peoples.

Gertrude Simmons Bonnin

There is a distinction between "government" and "servants of the government." Whenever an Indian complains of unfaithful servants of the government and the **maladministration** of his affairs, he is heralded as "disloyal to the government" from certain quarters. This is untrue.

This **preliminary** is made necessary today in **refutation** of false charges uttered on the floor of the House by Congressman Crampton of Michigan on December 11, 1928, against the National Council of American Indians. Mr. Crampton inserted in the *Congressional Record* a portion of a letter, which he misquoted as follows:

> According to an Indian's statement and from my own personal observations, the Indians are very poor and hungry. They have no voice in their affairs. They are neglected. Whether sick or well, whether young or old, most of them or nearly all of them live in bad houses, wearing rags, and with little or no food. Their complaints to government officials go **unheeded**. Agents' offices are locked against the Indians most of the time.

And so forth **ad nauseam.**

Mr. Crampton described it as the "character of propaganda used to poison the judgment of the country against their own government." Yet before Mr. Crampton concludes his speech defending the Indian Bureau and the Budget Bureau for lack of adequate **appropriations**, and denying the disgraceful condition of Indian affairs, he contradicts himself. He agrees with me and with the report of the Institute for Government Research in their first sentence, which says: "An overwhelming majority of the Indians are poor, even extremely poor." Mr. Crampton falls into this agreement **unwittingly** in trying to **refute** the report that children in government schools are underfed.

He said:

> I have never seen any evidence of the children suffering from lack of food or from an undesirable character of food. Quite the contrary. It is true that oftentimes children will be seen in these schools who give evidence of lack of proper nutrition, but you must remember where these children have come from—the primitive sort of homes they come from to the schools.

maladministration: poor handling.

preliminary: introduction, opening statement.

refutation: proving something is wrong or false.

unheeded: ignored.

ad nauseam: to the point where one becomes sick and tired of hearing about something.

appropriations: money set aside for a specific purpose.

unwittingly: without knowing it.

refute: disprove, discredit.

The "primitive sort of homes"—that is exactly what I had in mind. The congressman admits these homes are bad and that food is lacking, and therefore, Indians young and old are hungry and sick.

The subcommittee of the Senate Indian Affairs Committee is holding hearings right now, and sworn testimony reveals horrible conditions—rotten meat, full of maggots, and spoiled flour which mice and cats had **defiled**, are fed to children in government schools. Sworn statements amply show that the report of the Institute for Government Research could all be transformed into the **superlative** degree and not begin to tell the whole story of Indian **exploitation**.

Had it been possible, these hearings of the Senate investigating committee should have been printed and read at this conference, together with this discussion of the report of the Institute for Government Research. We would all be convinced beyond any doubt as to the accuracy of this survey report under discussion. Printed reports of these hearings should be made available to the public—the American people. They have a right to know the facts if, as Mr. Crampton said, in justifying the Budget Bureau's cuts in Indian appropriations, increased appropriations would mean higher taxes upon the American people. Let the people know the facts, if this is a government "of the people, for the people, by the people."

As an Indian, speaking earnestly for the very life of my race, I must say that this report ... is all too true, although I do not always **concur** in their conclusions, which tend to minimize the responsibility of the Bureau.

On pages 11–12 the report says:

The survey staff finds itself obliged to say frankly and **unequivocally** that the **provisions** for the care of the Indian children in boarding schools are grossly inadequate.

The outstanding deficiency is in the diet furnished the Indian children, many of whom are below normal health. The diet is deficient in quantity, quality and variety.... At the worst schools the situation is serious in the extreme. The major diseases of the Indians are **tuberculosis** and **trachoma**. Tuberculosis unquestionably can best be combated by a preventive, **curative** diet and

defiled: made dirty, contaminated.

superlative: exaggerated, excessive.

exploitation: unfair use of another person for one's own profit.

concur: agree.

unequivocally: without any doubt whatsoever.

provisions: supplies.

tuberculosis: a contagious disease that usually affects the lungs, causing fever, weakness, loss of appetite, and coughing.

trachoma: a contagious infection of the eyelids that can lead to blindness.

curative: intended to cure.

Gertrude Simmons Bonnin

proper living conditions, and a considerable amount of evidence suggests that the same may prove true of trachoma. The great protective foods are milk and fruit and vegetables, particularly fresh green vegetables. The diet of Indian children in boarding schools is generally notably lacking in these preventive foods.... It may be seriously questioned whether the Indian Service could do very much better than it does without more adequate appropriations.

I do not agree with this concluding sentence, which minimizes the Bureau's actual responsibility by blaming Congress for inadequate appropriations.

For more than eleven years I have lived in Washington, D.C., and I have learned through attending congressional committee hearings and pending Indian legislation that it is the Indian Bureau that **drafts** these appropriations bills. In fact, all other bills affecting Indians are also referred to the Indian Bureau for its approval or disapproval. The American Congress is dependent for its information upon the Indian Bureau. What "**compromises**" are made in congressional committees behind closed doors is another chapter....

During the three last consecutive summers I have visited many Indian reservations, keeping my information on Indian conditions up to date. This past summer I went with Captain Bonnin, who was doing field investigation work for the Senate Indian Affairs Committee....

The Indian Bureau superintendents in the field have been holding meetings this summer, discussing this same report of the Institute for Government Research before us now. Their purpose was to refute and disprove the things contained in it! Subordinate employees have been approached and told they should be "loyal" to the government when asked to refute statements in the report. At **peril** of losing their jobs, some of them refused to deny the facts....

In addition to this **pernicious** activity among Indian Bureau superintendents trying to refute things told in the report of the Institute for Government Research, there are circulated misleading articles **emanating** from the Bureau. Recently I casually picked up from the reading table of a hotel a current magazine—the November 1928 issue of the *National Republic*. On page 34 is the caption "Education of the Indians"; the subhead states "Graduates of Government

drafts: draws up.

compromises: agreements that involve giving up certain rights or privileges in the interest of reaching a settlement acceptable to a group of people.

peril: risk.

pernicious: destructive, extremely harmful.

emanating: coming.

Indian Schools Are Doing Successful Work in All Walks of Life."

The pictures used are from the government Indian school, Haskell Institute. This is considered one of the best schools. But the article is upon the entire Indian field. The article, therefore, is entirely misleading....

This kind of a presentation of Indian matters is not **conducive** to having Congress make larger appropriations. Congress as a whole is dependent upon the Indian Bureau for its information, just as the American public is. Both Congress and the American people are wilfully misled about the actual conditions of Indian want and hopeless **destitution**....

In the printed hearings of the House Appropriations Committee in 1922, on page 328, [the assistant commissioner of the House Indian Affairs Committee] Mr. Meritt said: "We favor keeping **subsistence** down to the lowest possible point."

He was speaking of **rations** to old and **indigent** Indians and orphans.

I have visited Indian homes during my three summer visits. They are extremely poor. They have scarcely any food in their **hovels**. They complain to me of starving....

There was a time, long ago, when Indians shared their food with the hungry, but that day is past. Now all Indians are too poor. They have nothing to divide. There is starvation.

On page 262 of the report of the Institute for Government Research ... there appears the following: "It may be said in passing that the findings of the Red Cross report [of 1924] correspond very closely to those of the present survey as they relate to the same reservations."

This Red Cross survey of 1924 had been kept in the secret archives of the Indian Bureau these four years and has been refused to members of Congress who asked to see it. The evil conditions reported in the Red Cross survey remain unchanged, four years later.

Withholding reported facts of bad conditions in Indian affairs, the Bureau is broadcasting through the American press, and Congressman Crampton through the *Congressional*

conducive: tending to promote or help.

destitution: suffering from an extreme lack of food, clothing, shelter, and other resources and possessions.

subsistence: the minimum requirements of food, shelter, and so on needed to maintain life.

rations: supplies.

indigent: poor.

hovels: huts, shacks.

Gertrude Simmons Bonnin

Record, about *how much* the Indians have been helped and benefitted; how the Indian population has increased; how well they are fed and housed!...

If the high officials of the Indian Bureau continually fail to insist upon adequate congressional appropriations, are they ignorant of the actual suffering on the reservations? If not, they must be incompetent. If, on the other hand, these officials of the government prove unfaithful to their charge in "compromises" that would legislate away the wards' interests, knowing it means the ultimate destruction of helpless human beings—young and old—then they are criminals. In either case, a housecleaning is **imperative.**

I am desperately concerned for the life of my race while these countless investigations, revealing un-Christian exploitation of government wards, are made from time to time, only to lodge under lock and key in the Indian Bureau. How long—oh, how long!—shall this cruel practice continue?

Group of Omaha boys in cadet uniforms, Carlisle Indian School, Pennsylvania, 1880

The Indian race is starving—not only physically, but mentally and morally. It is a **dire** tragedy. The government Indian schools are not on a par with the American schools of today. The so-called "Indian Graduates from Government Schools" cannot show any **credentials** that would be accepted by any business house. They are unable to pass the Civil Service examinations. The **proviso** in Indian treaties that educated Indians, wherever qualified, be given preference in Indian Service employment is rendered meaningless. Indians are kept ignorant and "incompetent" to cope with the world's trained workers, because they are not sufficiently educated in the government schools.

Secretary [of the Interior Hubert] Work, in his annual report, 1928, page 13, states: "There is not an Indian school in the United States that is strictly a high school."

I quote this in refutation of the glowing propaganda in the

imperative: essential, urgently necessary.

dire: horrible, desperate.

credentials: references showing that a person has the right or the ability to do something.

proviso: condition, clause.

Gertrude Simmons Bonnin | 41

November 1928 issue of the *National Republic* and Mr. Crampton's speech in the *Congressional Record*, previously mentioned....

On page 15 of his report [Secretary Work] says:

As the inadequacy of the educational system for the Indians was one of the reasons for the department's request for the survey and report, the following summary of the findings of the investigators on this subject is of especial interest:

The survey staff finds itself obliged to say frankly and unequivocally that the provisions for the care of the Indian children in boarding schools are grossly inadequate.

The diet is deficient in quality, quantity and variety.

The great protective foods are milk and fruit and vegetables, particularly fresh green vegetables. The diet of Indian children is generally notably lacking in these foods.

The boarding schools are overcrowded materially beyond their capacities.

The medical attention rendered the boarding school children is not up to a reasonable standard.

The medical attention given children in day schools maintained by the government is also below a reasonable standard.

The boarding schools are supported in part by the labor of students.

The service is notably weak in personnel trained and experienced in educational work with families and communities.

Now these are some of the things of which I have complained in the past, and as a result I am referred to by Indian Bureau officials and congressmen as being an **agitator** and disloyal to the government; they even **infer** that I am dishonest and living off of the Indians. Such statements are grossly untrue and unjust. The sole purpose in making any criticism has been with a view that the evils pointed out by me might be corrected....

Indian funds might have been better used for higher education and colleges for Indians instead of building steel bridges, highways and expensive but worthless irrigation systems under Indian Bureau management....

In conclusion, I quote Major Frank Knox, who said at the close of his investigation of three reservations in Colorado

agitator: troublemaker.
infer: suggest, conclude.

42   Gertrude Simmons Bonnin

and Utah in 1925: "The reform which good business methods, efficient administration and an adequate protection of Indian rights requires cannot come from within the Bureau. It must come from without."

Too often employees in the Indian Service are Indian-haters and they are **discourteous** to Indians in their daily routine.

Above all things let there be this proviso written large in the government's new Indian policy—"That no expert or subordinate shall be employed who has racial prejudice against the Indian people."

The problem of Indian administration cannot be solved by mere increased appropriations unless coincidentally a new personnel is had in the Indian Service, and a new Indian policy which will provide court review of the guardian's handling of Indian funds and property....

The Meriam Report influenced the U.S. government's policy toward Native Americans during the presidential administrations of Herbert Hoover (1928–33) and his successor, Franklin D. Roosevelt (1933–45). Hoover, for example, appointed two leading members of the Indian Rights Association as commissioner and assistant commissioner of the Bureau of Indian Affairs. Roosevelt's Depression-era reforms included the Indian Reorganization Act of 1934 and its promised "Indian New Deal." These acts, though rejected by many tribal groups, gave Indians a form of self-government and the right to observe their own cultural traditions.

As for Bonnin, she remained active in the reform movement throughout the 1930s. She continued lobbying Congress (especially on behalf of the Sioux and the Utes) and gave frequent lectures across the United States. To dramatize her message, she often appeared on stage in native dress. After her death in 1938 at the age of sixty-one, Bonnin was buried in Arlington National Cemetery.

discourteous: rude.

Sources

Books

Bonnin, Gertrude Simmons, *Old Indian Legends* (reprint of original 1901 edition), University of Nebraska Press, 1985.

Bonnin, Gertrude Simmons, *American Indian Stories* (reprint of original 1921 edition), University of Nebraska Press, 1985.

Gridley, Marion E., *American Indian Women,* Hawthorn Books, 1974.

Jones, Louis Thomas, *Aboriginal American Oratory: The Tradition of Eloquence Among the Indians of the United States,* Southwest Museum (Los Angeles), 1965.

Notable Native Americans, Gale, 1995.

Periodicals

American Indian Quarterly, "Gertrude Simmons Bonnin, 1876–1938: 'Americanize the First Americans,'" winter 1988, pp. 27–40.

Journal of the West, "Twentieth Century Indian Leaders: Brokers and Providers," July 1984, pp. 3–6.

New York Times, January 27, 1938, p. 21.

Other

Gertrude Simmons Bonnin Collection, Harold B. Lee Library, Brigham Young University.

Joseph Brant

(Thayendanega)
1742–1807

Chief of the Mohawk tribe

One of the best-known Indian leaders of the American colonial period was Joseph Brant. He was a Mohawk chief and major spokesperson for the Iroquois Confederacy, also called the Six Nations of the Haudenosaunee (which means People of the Longhouse). This confederation of Iroquois tribes—the Mohawk, Oneida, Onondaga, Cayuga, Seneca, and Tuscarora—along with other Iroquoian allies, had for years maintained a strong position throughout a territory that included most of present-day New York State and southeastern Ontario, Canada.

Brant was the son of a full-blooded Mohawk chief and a woman who some historians believe might have been half European. Brant lost his father at an early age and took the English surname (last name) of his stepfather—who was also a Mohawk—when his mother remarried. He spent his childhood in a long-established Mohawk community, Canajoharie, near the Ohio River. There he had frequent contact with white settlers to the east, but life to the west along the

"WE ARE OF THE SAME OPINION WITH THE PEOPLE OF THE UNITED STATES; YOU CONSIDER YOURSELVES AS INDEPENDENT PEOPLE; WE ... LOOK UPON OURSELVES AS EQUALLY INDEPENDENT."

Colonial Alliances of the Haudenosaunee

In the seventeenth and eighteenth centuries there were four European colonial powers competing for domination in North America: Britain, France, Spain, and the Netherlands. At the same time, great tribal confederacies—such as the Six Nations of the Haudenosaunee—controlled the Great Lakes, the Ohio Valley, and the Mississippi. The Europeans, who were still vastly outnumbered by Indians, usually staked their territorial claims in the New World by making alliances with Indians in a particular territory. European rivalries gradually evolved into a system of spheres of influence. France established trading posts on the St. Lawrence and Mississippi river, and Britain and the Netherlands began to colonize the Atlantic seaboard. Each European nation tried to build a competing network of Indian allies surrounding its own colonies. Frequently, at first, Indians and Europeans mutually sought the advantages of trade and military coalitions.

The well-established Haudenosaunee confederacy allowed the Iroquois groups to maintain a strong political and economic position in the Northeast, as they had for centuries before the Europeans arrived. They maintained extensive fur trading with the French in the seventeenth century and later managed to remain neutral as France and Britain competed as colonial powers in the "New World". The Haudenosaunee were careful to make treaties with all of the rival European powers, favoring none. Eventually, however, the long-standing conflicts between Britain and France came to a head, and the French and Indian War (1754–63) began. Although many Indians fought with the French against the British, both European powers had allies among the tribes. Many Iroquois, primarily the Mohawk, fought alongside the British, while other groups, such as the Wyandotte, Shawnee, Chippewa, Ottawa, Miami, Abenaki, and Lenape, sided with the French. Although France did well in the early battles of the war, Britain ultimately defeated France at Montreal.

Britain then worked to establish treaties with France's former tribal allies across the

Ohio was still largely untouched by Europeans. This offered Brant freedom to hunt, fish, swim, trap, and canoe in preparation for his role as an adult hunter and warrior.

Later, Brant's half-sister Molly married Sir William Johnson (see box above for more information), the British Superintendent of Indian Affairs in colonial America, and twelve-year-old Joseph went to live with them at Fort Johnson in upstate New York. The couple later arranged for him to attend school in Lebanon, Connecticut, where he learned to express himself well in both spoken and written English. He colonies. Sir William Johnson, British Superintendent of Indian Affairs, was a great admirer of the Haudenosaunee and involved them as go-betweens in expanding the British alliance system. Johnson adopted Haudenosaunee forms of diplomacy, exchanging medals and "wampum" with the Indians, who came to regard the British king as a distant leader of the allied tribes. Treaties were renewed every few years, in accordance with Indian practices. By the 1770s, Johnson had succeeded in linking nearly half the continent under British rule with the Haudenosaunee acting as informal leaders of this broad coalition of Indian nations. However, the Six Nations increasingly came to be seen as puppets of the British and lost power among other Indian groups, who formed their own coalitions without Iroquois leadership.

When the American colonists fought for independence from the British in the Revolutionary War in 1776, Native Americans allied themselves on both sides of the conflict. For the Haudenosaunee this meant a bitter internal division in their centuries-old confederacy. At the beginning of the war, many Iroquois, especially the Seneca and Onondaga, preferred neutrality. Some of the Mohawk, led by Joseph Brant, fought alongside the British. The Oneida and the Tuscarora—because of trade and friendship ties with settlers—sided with the United States. The Iroquois League's Confederate Council, which operated only when there was agreement among all six nations, could not arrive at a plan of action. Since there was no agreement among the tribes, individual nations, villages, and even families had to make their own decisions about alliance or neutrality. The division in the confederacy never fully healed. After the revolution, the pro-British Iroquois moved to Canada to form their own confederacy and the Iroquois remaining in New York formed a separate coalition.

also converted to Christianity as a member of the Episcopal Church (Church of England).

At Ease in Two Worlds

As a young adult, Brant moved easily between the white and Indian worlds. He prepared translations into the Mohawk language of various religious texts (including parts of the Bible) and served as a missionary to the Mohawk people. He also served as an interpreter and diplomat for the British in their dealings with various Iroquois tribes. In fact, he supported Great Britain during the French and Indian War (1754–63) and immediately after that when the British battled the Ottawa chief Pontiac. This alliance helped expand the Iroquois confederation's influence over a larger territory for many years. At the same time, it helped maintain the delicate balance of power between British and French interests in the colonies.

In 1774, Brant became secretary to the British superintendent of Indian affairs. The following year, he made his first trip to England, where he was taken to meet the king and other members of the royal court. He also posed in traditional dress for formal portraits by the painters George Romney and Benjamin West.

By the time of the Revolutionary War (1775–83), Brant had been commissioned a British colonel. (He is often referred to as "Captain Brant" in historical records from that period.) His forces during the war were composed of members of the fragmented Iroquois League, British soldiers, and Tories (colonists who supported the British). Brant's troops carried out raids as far west as the Ohio Valley with the intention of depleting (using up) the food and supplies of the American soldiers. His company also fought in several key battles. Brant served the British Army with distinction as both a soldier and a diplomat. He was also useful in persuading as many fellow Iroquois as possible to fight for the British against the American colonists.

Settles in Canada

After the war was over, the British rewarded Brant's service with a land grant at Anaquaqua, along the Grand River in Ontario, Canada. There he retired as a British officer on half pay. Many Mohawk and other Indians from the Iroquois League followed him to Anaquaqua and the area eventually became the Six Nations Reserve. Brant spent the rest of his life acting as a **mediator** between the Indians, the British, and the Americans as they struggled to find a way to live together in peace.

On April 21, 1794, a special council meeting between Indians and whites took place in an Onondaga village on Buffalo Creek in New York. Joseph Brant spoke for the Iroquois confederation, Colonel John Butler represented Great

mediator: negotiator; go-between.

Britain's King George III, and General Israel Chapin appeared on behalf of the new American government. In a speech to his fellow negotiators, Brant asked them to be open and honest in their dealings with the Indian people as they tried to settle arguments over the various peace terms and territorial boundaries that had been proposed since the end of the Revolutionary War. His remarks are reprinted from W. C. Vanderwerth's Indian Oratory: Famous Speeches by Noted Indian Chieftains, *University of Oklahoma Press, 1971.*

99

Brothers: You, of the United States, listen to what we are going to say to you; you, likewise, the King.

Brothers: We are very happy to see you, Colonel Butler and General Chapin, sitting side by side, with the intent of hearing what we have to say. We wish to do no business but what is done open and **aboveboard.**

Brother: You, of the United States, make your mind easy, on account of the long time your president's speech has been under our consideration; when we received it, we told you it was a business of importance, and required some time to be considered of.

Brother: The answer you have brought us is not according to what we expected, which was the reason for our long delay; the business would have been done **with expedition,** had the United States agreed to our proposals. We would then have collected our associates, and **repaired** to Venango, the place you proposed for meeting us.

Brother: It is not now in our power to accept your invitation; provided we were to go, you would conduct the business, as you might think proper; this has been the case at all the treaties held, from time to time, by your commissioners.

Brother: At the first treaty, after the conclusion of the war between you and Great Britain, at Fort Stanwix, your commissioners conducted the business as it to them seemed best; they pointed out a line of division, and then confirmed it; after this, they **held out** that our country was **ceded** to them

aboveboard: honestly, without any intention to deceive.

with expedition: quickly.

repaired: returned.

held out: suggested.

ceded: granted or transferred (usually by treaty).

Brant, representing the Iroquois, proclaimed: "This country was given to us by the Great Spirit above; we wish to enjoy it, and have our passage along the lake...."

by the King; this confused the chiefs who attended there, and prevented them from making any reply to the contrary; still holding out, if we did not consent to it, their warriors were at their back, and that we would get no further protection from Great Britain. [Brant is referring here to a treaty that members of the Iroquois confederation had signed in

1784 at Fort Stanwix, New York. This treaty granted all of the Indian land west of the Niagara River to the United States.]

This has ever been held out to us, by the commissioners from Congress; at all the treaties held with us since the peace, at Fort McIntosh, at Rocky River, and every other meeting held, the idea was still the same.

Brother: This has been the case from time to time. Peace has not taken place, because you have held up these ideas, owing to which much mischief has been done to the southward.

Brother: We, the Six Nations, have been exerting ourselves to keep peace since the conclusion of the war; we think it would be best for both parties; we advised the confederate nations to request a meeting, about halfway between us and the United States, in order that such steps might be taken as would bring about a peace; this request was made, and Congress appointed commissioners to meet us at Muskingum [in eastern Ohio], which we agreed to, a boundary line was then proposed by us, and refused by Governor [Arthur] St. Clair [of the Northwest Territory], one of your commissioners. The Wyandots, a few Delawares, and some others, met the commissioners, though not authorized, and confirmed the lines of what was not their property, but a common to all nations.

Brothers: The idea we all held out at our council, at Lower Sandusky [in Ohio], held for the purpose of forming our confederacy, and to adopt measures that would be for the general welfare of our Indian nations, or people of our color; owing to those steps taken by us, the United States held out, that when we went to the westward to transact our private business, that we went with an intention of taking an active part in the troubles **subsisting** between them and our western **brethren**; this never has been the case. We have ever wished for the friendship of the United States.

Brother: We think you must be fully convinced, from our **perseverance** last summer, as your commissioners saw, that we were anxious for a peace between us. The **exertions** that we, the Six Nations, have made towards the accomplishing this desirable end, is the cause of the western nations being somewhat **dubious** as to our sincerity. After we knew their doubts, we still persevered; and, last fall, we pointed out

subsisting: existing.

brethren: brothers (in the sense of fellow Indians, not actual relatives).

perseverance: continuing to do something despite opposition from others.

exertions: efforts.

dubious: doubtful.

methods to be taken, and sent them, by you, to Congress; this we certainly expected would have proved satisfactory to the United States; in that case we should have more than ever exerted ourselves, in order that the offers we made should be confirmed by our confederacy, and by them strictly **adhered to.**

Brother: Our proposals have not met with the success from Congress that we expected; this still leaves us in a similar situation to what we were when we first entered on the business.

Brother: You must recollect the number of chiefs who have, at **divers** times, waited on Congress; they have pointed out the means to be taken, and held out the same language, uniformly, at one time as another; that was, if you would withdraw your claim to the boundary line, and lands within the line, as offered by us; had this been done, peace would have taken place; and, unless this still be done, we see no other method of accomplishing it.

Brother: We have borne everything patiently for this long time past; we have done everything we could consistently do with the welfare of our nations in general—notwithstanding the many advantages that have been taken of us, by individuals making purchases from us, the Six Nations, whose **fraudulent** conduct towards us Congress never has taken notice of, nor in any wise seen us **rectified**, nor made our minds easy. This is the case to the present day; our patience is now entirely worn out; you see the difficulties we labor under, so that we cannot at present rise from our seats and attend your council at Venango, agreeable to your invitation. The boundary line we pointed out, we think is a just one, although the United States claim lands west of that line; the **trifle** that has been paid by the United States can be no object in comparison to what a peace would be.

Brother: We are of the same opinion with the people of the United States; you consider yourselves as independent people; we, as the original inhabitants of this country, and **sovereigns** of the soil, look upon ourselves as equally independent, and free as any other nation or nations. This country was given to us by the Great Spirit above; we wish to enjoy it, and have our passage along the lake, within the line we have pointed out.

adhered to: followed.

divers: various.

fraudulent: misleading, dishonest.

rectified: corrected, improved.

trifle: small amount.

sovereigns: people who have authority over a certain area.

Joseph Brant

Brother: The great exertions we have made, for this number of years, to accomplish a peace, and have not been able to obtain it; our patience, as we have already observed, is exhausted, and we are discouraged from persevering any longer. We, therefore, throw ourselves under the protection of the Great Spirit above, who, we hope, will order all things for the best. We have told you our patience is worn out; but not so far, but that we wish for peace, and, whenever we hear that pleasing sound, we shall pay attention to it.

Sources

Books

Jones, Louis Thomas, *Aboriginal American Oratory: The Tradition of Eloquence Among the Indians of the United States,* Southwest Museum (Los Angeles), 1965.

Kelsay, Isabel Thompson, *Joseph Brant, 1743–1807: Man of Two Worlds,* [Syracuse], 1984.

Notable Native Americans, Gale, 1995.

Rosenstiel, Annette, *Red and White: Indian Views of the White Man, 1492–1982,* Universe Books, 1983.

Vanderwerth, W. C., *Indian Oratory: Famous Speeches by Noted Indian Chieftains,* University of Oklahoma Press, 1971.

Van Every, Dale, *A Company of Heroes: The American Frontier, 1775–1783,* Ayer, 1976.

Witt, Shirley Hill, and Stan Steiner, *The Way: An Anthology of American Indian Literature,* Knopf, 1972.

Ben Nighthorse Campbell

1933–

Artist, businessman, and U.S. Senator of the Northern Cheyenne tribe

"I NEVER LET AN OPPORTUNITY GO BY WITHOUT ENCOURAGING INDIAN PEOPLE TO GET INVOLVED IN THE POLITICAL SYSTEM. I AM CONVINCED THAT AMERICA ... *IS READY* TO LEARN VALUES OF TRADITIONAL NATIVE AMERICAN WAYS. NATIVE AMERICANS CANNOT CONTINUE TO LIVE OUR INSULATED LIFESTYLES IF WE ARE GOING TO HELP LEAD THIS NATION."

In both his personal and professional life, Ben Nighthorse Campbell is colorful and free-spirited. The pony-tailed politician usually wears a cowboy hat and boots, a bolo tie, and distinctive jewelry he designs and makes himself. His preferred means of transportation is his Harley-Davidson motorcycle—except when he is back home on his ranch, where he enjoys riding his beloved horse, War Bonnet. On the floor of the U.S. Senate, Campbell has angered some of his colleagues by crossing party lines when it comes time to vote on certain issues. In his typically blunt and outspoken fashion, however, Campbell brushes aside any criticism. "I always say that if I have the right and the left both mad at me," he once remarked to a People *magazine reporter, "then I must be doing something right."*

Early Life

Campbell was born in Auburn, California. His mother had immigrated to the United States from Portugal, and his father was of Cheyenne, Apache, and Pueblo Indian ancestry. (Campbell himself is an enrolled member of the Northern Cheyenne tribe but thinks of himself as a representative of all Native American people in his role as a U.S. senator.) The family was extremely poor, and Campbell's parents battled illness and other problems while he was growing up. As a result, he had a difficult and unsettled childhood; occasionally, he had to live for a while in foster homes and orphanages. However, young Ben found some comfort in art. Using scrap materials he found in the garbage, he learned to work with metal and wood. By the age of twelve, he was creating pieces of jewelry.

As a teenager, Campbell was a below-average student who spent most of his time hanging out with fellow members of a local gang. He dropped out of high school during his junior year and joined the Air Force. His two-year hitch—half of which he spent in South Korea—gave Campbell a chance to turn his life around. Not only did he earn his high school diploma, he also developed a passion for the sport of judo.

Achieves World-Class Ranking in Judo

Upon his return home in 1953, Campbell attended San Jose State University. He graduated from there in 1957 with a bachelor's degree in physical education and fine arts. In addition, he served as captain of the judo team, winning the Pacific Coast championship and becoming the youngest American ever to reach the rank of fourth-degree black belt.

Campbell spent the next two years as an elementary school teacher. He then quit to move to Tokyo, Japan, so that he could continue his judo training and prepare to compete on an international level. Four **grueling** years of training helped him reach sixth-degree black belt status and capture a gold medal in the 1963 Pan American Games in Brazil. The following year, he earned a spot on the U.S. Olympic judo team, but an injury destroyed his hopes of winning any medals.

Shortly after that, Campbell decided to call an end to his competitive career. (At the time, he was ranked number

grueling: demanding to the point of exhaustion.

four in the world.) He returned to teaching but remained active in judo as an instructor and promoter until the early 1970s. He then withdrew from the sport to pursue another love—raising and training championship quarter horses.

Creates Award-Winning Jewelry

Around the same time, Campbell also went into the jewelry business. Using metalworking techniques he had learned in Japan, he began creating unique necklaces, bracelets, rings, and other pieces that feature traditional Native American designs. Since then, his artistic skills have earned him more than two hundred awards. His "Painted Mesa" line of jewelry is available nationally at prices ranging from a couple of hundred dollars to well over twenty thousand dollars.

Campbell entered politics in 1982 when Democratic party leaders in his district asked him to challenge a popular Republican for a seat in the Colorado house of representatives. His tireless campaigning led to victory that year and in two later elections. In 1986, Campbell traded on his success in the Colorado state legislature to run for a seat in the U.S. House of Representatives and once again was victorious. He remained in Washington, D.C., for the next six years, easily winning reelection twice in a district made up of large groups of Republican voters as well as Democratic-leaning Hispanic Americans.

*Very early on, Campbell showed that his **agenda** reflected the concerns of his **constituents** and not necessarily those of his party. In fact, he has described himself as a **liberal** on social issues and a **conservative** on money matters. For example, he was a member of the committees that drafted legislation regarding small businesses, national parks and tourism, agriculture, and mining—all of great interest to Coloradans. But he often voted in ways that did not please his fellow Democrats, such as when he came out against gun control and in favor of a constitutional amendment to ban flag-burning. On the other hand, his pro-choice beliefs on abortion did not please conservative Republicans.*

In the House of Representatives Campbell tackled issues of particular interest to Native Americans. For instance, he

agenda: program or plan of things to be considered or done.

constituents: the people who elect someone to public office to represent them.

liberal: broad-minded; open to reform; not bound by tradition.

conservative: moderate, cautious, inclined to follow tradition and reject or be suspicious of change.

supported efforts to establish a Smithsonian-affiliated National Museum of the American Indian in Washington, D.C. He also helped draft and served as co-sponsor of the Indian Arts and Crafts Act of 1990. Its goal is to help protect Indian artists and their customers from fake "Indian" art. And he played a major role in the fight to change the name of Montana's Custer National Battlefield Monument—"the only battlefield I've ever heard of being named after the loser," as he put it—to the Little Bighorn National Battlefield Monument.

Elected to the United States Senate

In 1992, Campbell decided to run for the U.S. Senate. His victory in the November election made him the first Native American to serve in the Senate since 1929. There he continued to display an independent streak.

Along with the Republicans, he backed legislation to develop natural gas resources underneath land within his district. He opposed the efforts of President Bill Clinton's administration to raise fees for grazing, mining, and logging on federal property. On other issues, however, Campbell has sided with the Democrats. Despite his past opposition to gun control, for example, he cast the deciding vote in 1993 in favor of the controversial crime bill that banned most assault weapons. His support for the ban prompted hundreds of negative calls to his office, including some two dozen death threats.

Campbell has also tackled one of the major problems of the Indian community with his sponsorship of a Senate bill to increase the public's awareness of Fetal Alcohol Syndrome and Fetal Alcohol Effect. Both are incurable conditions that can severely damage the mental and physical health of children whose mothers drink large amounts of alcohol while they are pregnant. In addition, Campbell introduced a bill that would force the Washington Redskins football team to change their name (which many Native Americans find offensive) in exchange for the privilege of leasing federal land for a new stadium in the nation's capital.

In March 1995, Campbell shocked and angered many of his Democratic colleagues when he announced that he was *switching political parties. According to the senator, he decided to join the Republicans for a variety of reasons. Among them were differences with the Democrats over the balanced-budget amendment to the constitution, federal land-use policies, and term limits. He also complained about the shabby treatment he had received from Colorado party officials. Changing parties was something he had been thinking about doing for months, he said. "I can no longer represent the agenda that's put forth by the party, although I certainly agree with many of the things that Democrats stand for."*

Through the years, Campbell has often been called upon to give speeches in honor of one occasion or another. In May 1991, for instance, he was asked to address the graduates of Haskell Indian Nations University in Kansas on the topic of achieving success. The following speech is similar to ones he has delivered on many other occasions to Native American youth. Campbell's Senate office provided a copy of his remarks.

99

Today is the day you and your families have long looked forward to and is a turning point in your lives. For me it is particularly rewarding to know the dreams of the elders are being fulfilled. The [German] philosopher [Johann Wolfgang von] Goethe once said, "Whatever you dream, follow it with action, because the boldness of action in making dreams come true has a magic, a power, and a genius in itself." Literature and philosophy were not my strong suits, but people of all races have recognized the importance of dreams—American Indians more than most.

Today is the day on which you begin making your dreams come true. What you dream, so once did I. In years to come, you will look back to a very special person in your lives (or perhaps several) who you will always remember as the person who encouraged those dreams. They may take credit for your successes, but blame the failure on no one.

To our graduating class today, I would suppose you have been **deluged** by time-worn phrases such as "commence-

deluged: flooded, swamped.

ment is the beginning" or "the future belongs to you" or equally **abstract** comments on your new venture. But no matter how many times your friends and teachers said the same thing to other graduating classes, they are sincere. They love you and are proud of you.

As a former teacher, I am proud of you, too. In part you are a product of the story of the American education system. That story is one of the great **epochs** of human learning. It is the story of goodness and sharing as well as greatness that has been heard around the world.... Our educational system has become the most important link in a world that grows ever smaller. The strength of our education system will determine whether this world will face a future of enlightenment or darkness.

Nighthorse in 1992: "From medicine to nutrition to the founding of our U.S. Constitution, our native people provided the source material and often the inspiration for this nation."

abstract: not connected to anything concrete or real.

epochs: extended periods of time marked by a memorable series of events or distinctive developments.

If ever in the coming years you grow **disillusioned** with this nation, if ever you doubt that America holds a special place in all the long history of humankind, remember that we are still the center of the world for new skills and new ideas. We are still the stronghold for **dissent**, challenge, and experiment. We are a nation in which questioning is encouraged and protest is a constitutional right, and even though our national policy has a terrible record in dealing with American Indians, we must strive to improve.

Remember with pride that many of America's greatest accomplishments had their roots in traditional Indian life. From medicine to nutrition to the founding of our U.S. Constitution, our native people provided the source material and often the inspiration for this nation. Our institutions do not control us, and although your college days may be over, your education is not, nor will it ever be.

That time has come to move forward and take both the human and economic skills you have learned with you. Full well, you must remind yourselves that real success is not **gauged** by **monetary** measurements but by human measurements. It is the size of your heart that really counts, not the size of your wallet. Just as the history of a nation is not measured by its wealth but by its goodness. Let us hope that when you return to this institution for the graduation of your own son or daughter, you will not only do so in a world at peace, but will have been judged successfully by those human measurements that we commonly call "the Indian way" that is our cultural heritage to pass on to our children. Let us not forget that this good fortune has come to you because our elders have suffered and sacrificed, and that to preserve it, there will come times when you, too, must sacrifice.

We see in you such strength and hope, such buoyancy, such good will. Such straightforward and uncomplicated happiness that our Creator has already blessed you and that our people have already imprinted the love of peace and freedom in your hearts. Perhaps Thomas Jefferson would have agreed with Indian dreamers when he said, "I like the dreams of the future better than the history of the past."

As I think back to my own experiences since I graduated San Jose State about a hundred years ago, I can tell you that

disillusioned: disappointed after becoming aware of being tricked or misled.

dissent: protest, disagreement.

gauged: measured, judged.

monetary: having to do with money.

Ben Nighthorse Campbell

nothing is without risk. Success does not come through simplicities but through hard work and **perseverance.** You have been educated but not **indoctrinated.** Now you must go forward with equal shares of confidence and **skepticism,** full well knowing that you may pursue a profession not yet created.... What you have trained for, you may not do. Look at me; I majored in physical education and ended up making my living as an artist who raises cattle and is occasionally distracted by public office....

We have confidence you will rank wisdom ahead of book knowledge, truth ahead of technology. You will maintain high standards without being **snooty** and have convictions without being crabby. You will be **principled** without being **prudish** and show sympathy without being **saccharine....**

For most of you, the grades you worked so hard for are now **moot.** Few people you meet will care.... In the professional world, no one will ask you what grade you made in Psychology 1A or Accounting 302. What they will ask you is, "Can you do the job?" "How active are you in the community?" "To what associations do you subscribe?" And, "Do you get along with your fellows?" Those are now the goals on which you must concentrate.

No one can **mandate** success. No one can legislate that you reach your goals. There are no laws to make you excel, and to everything there is a cost. The cost of excellence is discipline; the cost of **mediocrity** is disappointment. But the cost of **apathy** is by far the greatest—the cost of apathy is failure.

I am convinced that what you do with your life is secondary to how well you do it. As a former Olympic team member, I used to think my goal should be how much weight I should lift up. Now I know it should be how many humans I can uplift. Surely, we all make mistakes. I've made more than I can remember. To that end I would say, remember the words of President [Abraham] Lincoln, who said, "I am not concerned that you fall, I am concerned that you arise." Arise you can, lead you must. Succeed you will, because this land is your future. Your decisions will determine the world's future as well as the future of our Indian people.

Even though my age group has not done a very good job of finding common goals, we have confidence in your ability

perseverance: continuing on despite opposition, setbacks, and discouragement.

indoctrinated: influenced to believe a certain way while being taught something.

skepticism: doubt.

snooty: snobbish.

principled: devoted to acting according to high standards.

prudish: excessively proper to the point of being irritating.

saccharine: overly sweet or agreeable, often to the point of being distasteful.

moot: without meaning.

mandate: order, command.

mediocrity: the state of being of ordinary or low quality.

apathy: lack of feeling or concern; indifference.

to learn from our mistakes and do better. Don't settle for doing as well, do better. Think of the mistakes we have made in caring for our air, our water, our Earth Mother. You must strive for a peaceful world and recognize in the great scheme of things that, although any darn fool can kill, not even the wisest man can give life back. We would have done better, but did not. You will do better because our failures have brought your goals into focus.

Think of what people can do with a focus and a goal. A poor girl becomes one of America's greatest educators and is given the Presidential Medal of Freedom—[Navajo activist] Annie Wauneka. A youngster born on the Pine Ridge Reservation who was given no chance to win becomes a world-famous Olympian—[Oglala Sioux track star] Billy Mills. A young Pueblo Indian blinded by an explosion in Vietnam becomes a world-famous sculptor—Michael Naranjo. They prove there are no secrets to success, but the common denominator is simply be the best you can be.

My friends, as I stand here as the last obstacle you must endure before going forward to your life's work, I want to describe the place in which some of the world's most meaningful decisions have been made. A place that most Americans know as the Hall of the People. A place where each person is heard, a process patterned after Indian council fires.

When I was elected to Congress, I had never been inside our Capitol building. When I was traveling with the U.S. Olympic team, I saw the Great Pyramids of Egypt and the Taj Mahal in India. I marvelled at the Coliseum in Rome and the Eiffel Tower in Paris. I saw people **pay homage** to the great Buddha in Kamakura and to the Christ on the mountain above Rio de Janeiro. I tell you truthfully that what you own in your Capitol easily equals any and all of the manmade treasures on this earth. And the reason it does is because all the brilliance, all the imagination and all the **cumulative** wisdom of mankind has a hand in developing our institutions. They are only two hundred years old, but they meld thousands of years of experience.

As you look around the chamber of the House, you realize how many human beings in history sowed and nurtured the seeds of freedom that have grown to maturity in this

pay homage: show great respect and devotion.

cumulative: building up or increasing by adding new things.

Ben Nighthorse Campbell

nation.... I must admit that sometimes our decisions in Congress fly in the face of collective, conventional, or any other kind of wisdom, but we are still young as nations go.

I compare it to the magic place where I live near the ruins of Mesa Verde National Park in Colorado, where the ancient ones settled before Christ walked this earth and where they lived in harmony for nine hundred years.... Surely if they could do it, we can, too.

And that, my brothers and sisters, must be your objectives as you leave this place. I cannot tell you how much I believe that as we go into 1992, ... the coming decade will be a major turning point in the history of our people. As my friends know, I never let an opportunity go by without encouraging Indian people to get involved in the political system. I am convinced that America, which has failed so miserably in fighting social evils from drugs to crime, from prostitution to hunger, *is ready* to learn values of traditional Native American ways. Native Americans cannot continue to live our insulated lifestyles if we are going to help lead this nation. We need to help lead this nation. We need not abandon our traditional values—that's what makes our people so unique in this nation—we need to affect public policy to recognize those values, and to do that, we must be involved in city, school board, county, state, and federal government. Run, help, question.

In closing, let me leave you with a Daniel Webster phrase that is inscribed in marble behind the speaker's chair in the House chamber and boldly proclaims to all who enter that chamber: "Let us develop the resources of our land, call forth its powers, build up its institutions, promote all its great interests and see whether we, also, in our day and generation, may not perform something worthy to be remembered." Young friends, do something to be remembered. Go forward, make your mark. Win some and lose some. Fight the good fight. Be proud of being Indian. But above all, do something to be remembered for.

Sources

Books

Congressional Record, 103rd Congress, 1st session, July 22, 1993, p. S9261.

Notable Native Americans, Gale, 1995.

Viola, Herman J., *Ben Nighthorse Campbell: An American Warrior,* Orion Books, 1993.

Periodicals

Detroit Free Press, "Second Senator Defects to GOP," March 4, 1995, p. 5A.

Grand Rapids Press, "Colorado Senator Makes Switch to GOP," March 4, 1995, p. A2.

Indian Country Today, "Campbell Discusses Issues of Today," August 18, 1993.

Life, "A Gem of a Lawmaker," June 1994, p. 108.

Newsweek, "How the West Was Lost," March 20, 1995, p. 31.

New Yorker, "Silver Lining," November 23, 1992, pp. 49–50.

People, "Rites of Victory," November 30, 1992, pp. 50–52.

Ada Deer

1935–

Social worker, activist, and U.S. government official of the Menominee tribe

As the first woman ever to head the Bureau of Indian Affairs (BIA), Ada Deer promised to "shake things up." The task before her was a major one, for the BIA has often been criticized as one of the U.S. government's most poorly managed and corrupt agencies. Deer brought a new sense of energy and commitment to the job. She declared that "the days of federal paternalism are over" and that she intends to create a new administration "based on the Indian values of caring, sharing, and respect."

Early Life

Deer was born and raised on the Menominee Reservation in northeastern Wisconsin. She credits her mother with teaching her that it was her duty to do whatever she could to correct injustice in the world. This eventually influenced her to study social work at the University of Wisconsin in Madison. In 1957, she became the first member of her tribe to earn a bachelor's degree from the university. She

"In order to overcome media stereotypes of Indians, we must become pro-active in educating the press and public about the 'true history' and current conditions of native people...."

then went on to achieve another milestone in 1961 when she became the first Native American to obtain a master's degree in social work from New York City's Columbia University.

Throughout the late 1950s and 1960s, Deer held several different jobs in her field. Her first ones were in New York City while she was still in graduate school. Later, she moved to Minneapolis, Minnesota. It was there, in 1964, that she accepted a post as community service coordinator with the BIA's local office. But she resigned just a few years later in frustration over the lack of interest BIA officials showed toward her many suggestions for improvement.

Deer spent the rest of the 1960s and early 1970s in a variety of other social work positions. Most of them were in Minnesota and Wisconsin except for a brief period in 1968 when she helped train Native American Peace Corps volunteers in Puerto Rico. In addition, Deer was active in the fight for women's rights and environmental protection.

Deer's interests also led her to return to school. Beginning in 1971, she enrolled in the University of New Mexico's American Indian Law Program. Later, she continued her law studies at the University of Wisconsin in Madison.

Leads Drive to Restore Federal Recognition to the Menominees

Around this same time, however, Deer was becoming increasingly busy with a far more urgent matter—restoring federal recognition to the Menominee tribe, which had lost its official status as an Indian tribe in 1953 under a congressional act known as the Termination Resolution. (See box for more information.) By the end of the 1960s, the sudden end to federal benefits due to termination, along with poverty, health problems, racism, and mismanagement had left the Menominees economically, politically, and culturally on the brink of extinction as a group.

Into this desperate situation stepped Deer and several other activists, mostly women. They felt that the only way to save the Menominees was to restore their status as a federally-recognized tribe. In 1970, they established a

The Termination Resolution of 1953

In 1953, Congress passed a law that ended (or terminated) the trust relationship between the U.S. government and native nations. Under the policy of termination, Indians were to lose the special status guaranteed to them by the Constitution and by hundreds of treaties, and be treated the same as any U.S. citizens. In 1954, Con-gress began terminating tribes; the Klamath of southern Oregon; four Paiute bands and the Uintah and Ouray of Utah and the Alabama and Coushatta of Texas all lost their tribal recognition. Other terminations followed, including that of the Menominee. Termination was devastating for most tribes, resulting in extreme poverty and near-loss of community for tribal members.

political organization known as *Determination of Rights and Unity for Menominee Shareholders*, or DRUMS. The group's goal was to take action on the short-term as well as the long-term needs of the community, including the repeal of the Termination Resolution.

Deer also served as vice president and chief lobbyist of a DRUMS-affiliated group called the National Committee to Save the Menominee People and Forest. In this role, she spent the next few years relentlessly arguing the case for restoration before state and national legislators. Her efforts were finally rewarded in December 1973 when President Richard Nixon signed the Menominee Restoration Act into law. This event was a tremendous accomplishment for Deer and the Menominee, marking the first time a Native American tribe had succeeded in convincing the federal government to reverse its Indian policy.

Afterwards, Deer was elected chief of the Menominee Restoration Committee, a temporary government in charge of carrying out the tribe's transition back to reservation status and setting the course for its future. In 1977, believing that she had accomplished her goals and it was time for others to take over, she resigned from the committee. Deer then joined the faculty of the University of Wisconsin in Madison, where she taught in both the School of Social Work and in the American Indian Studies Program.

In 1978, Deer entered politics with an unsuccessful bid to become the Democratic party's nominee for Wisconsin secretary of state. She tried for the same office in 1982 and

Early Developments in BIA Administration

The Bureau of Indian Affairs, or the BIA, is the agency of the United States government that carries out most federal policy and manages and distributes federal funds designated for Native Americans. Since 1849 it has been a part of the Department of the Interior, which also oversees land and water use as well as the national park system. The BIA originated in the second half of the nineteenth century, when the federal government realized that American expansion onto Indian lands could not be held back. All Indians were to be relocated onto reservations and then "civilized," or assimilated into American culture. The Office of Indian Affairs was established to serve as the administrator of the new reservations. (Before 1849, the Department of War handled all types of relations with the Indians, including trade and land purchases.)

Most Indian groups arrived at the reservations with their own traditional forms of law and government. The policy of the Office of Indian Affairs, however, was to replace traditional leaders with hand-picked Indians to carry out its own legal and administrative systems on the reservations. The Indian Office also enacted the Code of Indian Offenses, which prohibited many traditional cultural and religious practices, including the Ghost Dance. From the start, the Indian Affairs office held great power over the Indian groups moving onto reservations—with their own tribal economies destroyed by the move—because it controlled the necessities of life, such as food and shelter. Tribes ended up with little say in the policies that determined their economies, governments, religion, law, education, or health.

again met with failure. Ten years later, she decided to give politics another chance. This time she ran for a seat in the U.S. House of Representatives. She scored a surprising come-from-behind victory in the primary over her well-known Democratic opponent. In the November 1992 general election, however, she lost to her Republican challenger.

Heads Bureau of Indian Affairs

Six months later, in May 1993, President Bill Clinton nominated Deer to head the Bureau of Indian Affairs. She was a popular choice among Native Americans as well as in the halls of Congress, and she was easily **confirmed.** Deer hit the ground running, visiting many BIA offices and reservations throughout the country over the following months. At every stop, she challenged BIA employees and

confirmed: approved.

Perhaps the greatest injustice in the administration of Indian affairs was the government's ulterior purpose of acquiring Indian land and natural resources for white settlers while it was supposed to be working toward the best interests of Indians. Within the reservations, BIA agents had appointed many "Americanized" leaders who were often manipulated to serve U.S. policy rather than the interests of the tribe. Indian land and resources were sold or leased at tiny fractions of their worth.

The Office of Indian Affairs was also inefficient in administering the needs of the reservations because of widespread corruption that developed in its early days. By the late 1800s, Indian agents were generally professional politicians who had their own followers and patrons. People received jobs in the Indian office by doing political favors, not because of concern or expertise. Once appointed, Indian agents and their subordinates (people who worked for them) often controlled large amounts of money—usually meant for the purchase of supplies for the reservations—with little supervision from Washington. The best interests of the people living on reservations were often neglected, while scandals and corruption within the Indian service were widespread and well known.

Impoverishment and inadequate means of supporting themselves caused Indians to become dependent on government funds for survival. But because of BIA manipulations, Native Americans were frequently unable to trust the leadership of their reservations and thus were virtually powerless to protect themselves and their cultures from the government's shifting policies.

tribal leaders to contact her directly her about the problems they were facing and to pass along any solutions they had considered. As she often tells people, she lives by the motto "one person can make a difference."

As head of the BIA, Deer's goals included seeing to it that Indians finally have the things she says "are basic to every human being"—namely, jobs, food, shelter, health care, and education. She also supported teaching young Native Americans their own languages and allowing them to observe their own cultural practices if they wish. A strong proponent of **self-determination,** she has pledged to continue the push toward shifting more power from the federal government to the tribes in an effort to help them gain self-sufficiency.

Deer also expects to tackle a number of other major issues facing the BIA. Among them are expanding reserva-

self-determination: freedom to choose one's own political future.

tion gambling, granting mining and grazing rights on trib-al lands, regulating the disposal of hazardous waste on tribal lands, and extending federal recognition to certain tribes. Perhaps most important of all, she wants to reorga-nize the BIA itself to improve its efficiency and keep better track of the money it spends.

In late July 1994, Deer was the featured speaker at an awards dinner held during the tenth annual conference of the Native American Journalists Association in Atlanta, Georgia. (The conference was part of a larger gathering of minority journalists called Unity '94 Alliance.) At a series of workshops, lectures, and discussion groups, people voiced their opinions on a variety of topics of professional interest. One of those topics was the problem of ethnic stereotyping in the media. As a longtime social worker, Deer was all too familiar with the damage done to Indian self-esteem by dis-torted images of Native Americans in print and on film. Thus, she used her speech to urge her listeners to do every-thing possible to fight against such images and present a more realistic view of Indians and their accomplishments. Her remarks are reprinted here from a copy of the speech furnished by Deer's office.

As we gather at this banquet awards program ... to com-memorate a decade of progress in the communications field for American Indians and other people of color and to pay tribute to past or current reporters who gave their life or lost a job so that the "truth" could be told, I'd like to share with you my thoughts about the problem of media stereotypes and what can be done about it.

Earlier this month, on July 4, the United States of America observed its 218th birthday. At such times, we think about the Founding Fathers such as Benjamin Franklin, Thomas Jef-ferson, and Thomas Paine. But rarely does one read news sto-ries in daily papers [or] hear or see any mention on radio or television about the major contributions American Indians made to democracy and the federal government system we know today. This, my friends, is the type of uplifting and true story you as reporters can help to tell, not only to our own people, but to everyone. And I'm not talking about "**advocacy journalism.**" What I am talking about is simply good factual reporting.

Let me elaborate. American democracy owes its distinctive character of debate and **compromise** to the principles and structure of American Indian civil government. You see, the Founding Fathers faced a major problem when it came time to invent a "new" nation, for they really had no blueprint for the type of government they envisioned. Many of them, however, had come to admire the Iroquois League, particularly Thomas Jefferson, Thomas Paine, and Benjamin Franklin.

Jefferson, author of the Declaration of Independence and **framer** for the U.S. Constitution, was so fascinated by the Indians and their form of self-rule that he advocated the University of Virginia (of which he was the founder) offer Indian studies. He was the first to propose a systematic, **ethnological** study of American Indians. Jefferson noted that Indian political leaders did not acquire their positions by **heredity**, but by election, although "outsiders" could be naturalized or adopted into the Indian nation. In such cases, even they could then be elected to tribal office. This was not the case in Europe, with its rigid class system based on family lines and nobility.

As for Thomas Paine, a Quaker and radical **proponent** of democracy, he, too, developed an interest in Indians. Paine viewed the Indians as models for how society might be organized....

At the time the Europeans arrived in America, the Iroquois League was the most extensive [and] important political unit north of the Aztec civilization. Its beginnings predated the arrival of Columbus by hundreds of years. The **sovereign** nations represented in the League were the Mohawk, Onondaga, Seneca, Oneida, and Cayuga.

It was Iroquois Chief Canassatego in July of 1744 who suggested the colonists of Pennsylvania form a "union" much like the Iroquois had done. They would then be able to speak with one voice. Under the Iroquois form of government, certain chiefs were nominated by the women and confirmed by the tribal and league councils. No action could be taken without **unanimous** consent. This structure influenced

advocacy journalism: a type of reporting that tries to promote or support a certain cause or point of view.

compromise: an agreement to give up certain rights or privileges in the interest of reaching a settlement acceptable to a group of people.

framer: a person who draws up a document and shapes its content.

ethnological: cultural.

heredity: inheritance.

proponent: supporter.

sovereign: free from control by others.

unanimous: having the agreement of everyone.

many of the Founding Fathers, like Benjamin Franklin, who sought a plan of representative government for the colonies....

Prior to the War of 1812, some Indians and tribes were highly regarded by the early settlers. In fact, a large number of whites at this time traded their European lifestyles in to "go native." They were referred to as "Squaw Men." Only a few years after Virginia was settled, for example, more than forty male colonists and several Englishwomen had married Indians and gone off to live with the tribes....

But after the American Revolution relations became strained, especially when some Indian nations sided with the British during the War of 1812. In the years to follow, various Indians for different reasons fought against the Americans on the side of the Dutch, French or British. It's interesting that the change in perception of Indians from nobles to savages coincided with the start of the great trek westward and the opening of the plains and Pacific areas to settlers by the 1880s.

Since Hollywood or the film industry has played such a big role in promoting ethnic stereotypes and **caricatures**, mostly through Western cowboy pictures, it's interesting to note that actor John Wayne, who was a famous **celluloid** Indian fighter, once told an interviewer, "I don't feel we did wrong in taking this great country away from them. There were great numbers of people who needed new land, and the Indians were selfishly trying to keep it for themselves."

Also, I find it interesting that on holidays like Memorial Day, we seldom (if ever) hear about the major significant contributions American Indians have made to this country through the military. American Indians have fought in every war, including the American Revolutionary War. In fact, this demonstration of patriotism was one of the reasons that Congress decided to pass the Indian Citizenship Act of 1924. More than eight thousand Indians served in the Army during World War I. Most recently, we once again saw brave American Indian men and women participate in the Persian Gulf War. American Indians have received every award possible, including Congressional Medals of Honor. And it was the Navajo Marines, later called the CodeTalkers, who managed to out-

caricatures: images of someone or something presented in a distorted manner.

celluloid: motion-picture film.

The BIA in the 1990s

In the 1960s and 1970s, the government's authoritative treatment of Native Americans came under fire for being inhumane, unjust, and economically unsound. Today tribal government relations with federal, state, and local governments in the United States are frequently characterized as government-to-government relationships in which tribes are treated as self-determining entities. Some reservations in the United States are now prospering—running their own programs and businesses effectively. But there are many reservations in the United States that remain impoverished. Remote locations, poor training, inadequate land or equipment, lack of resources, and a variety of other factors on many reservations have perpetuated dependence on federal funds and the BIA. Unfortunately, after years of mismanagement, the BIA itself is considered one of the U.S. government's worst bureaucratic nightmares. Efforts have been made to bypass it altogether by giving federal money directly to tribes.

In bookkeeping alone, the BIA is in a disastrous state. Although the BIA received $1.8 billion in 1994, only an estimated 10 to 20 cents of every dollar of that money actually reached Indian tribes. A 1991 audit showed $485 million in accounting errors for the years 1990 and 1991. Although the BIA claimed to have spent $25 billion on education, housing, employment, resource management, and community development in the last 20 years, the conditions on many reservations severely deteriorated. Schools were falling apart and lacked adequate plumbing, heating, and electricity. Many reservations with natural resources claim that the BIA has habitually mismanaged leasing and development.

The problems facing the BIA in the mid-1990s were great, as were the needs of many Native Americans. According to the 1990 census, one third of American Indians earned incomes below the poverty line. *Time* reported in September 1995: "On the reservations, where per capita income averages $4,500, half of all children under age six live below the line; 1 out of every 5 Indian homes lacks both a telephone and an indoor toilet." At Pine Ridge reservation in South Dakota, Delbert Brewer, a local Oglala BIA official told the *New York Times*, "The biggest employers here are the Federal agencies. The reservation is 90 percent dependent on the Federal Government—and if that dries up, we are dead as a nation."

smart the Japanese using their native language as a secret code in World War II. But again, this positive image of American Indians and their invaluable contributions to America remain "invisible" in the mainstream media channels of this country. In order to overcome media stereotypes of Indians, we must become pro-active in educating the press and public about the "true history" and current conditions of native people....

Examples of positive media accounts [show] that the press is capable of being fair and factual. I think a great organization like yours could help **expedite** the media educational process by perhaps publishing a reporter's stylebook (along the lines of the Associated Press version) giving backgrounders on Indian issues, a historical timeline, and a list of terms **deemed** offensive to Indians. Certainly the more Indian reporters, editors, publishers, and filmmakers we can get placed in meaningful positions in the media industry, the better off we will be....

In my position as Assistant Secretary for Indian Affairs [in the] Department of Interior, I find myself having to constantly "educate" reporters—and elected officials—about Indian history and contemporary issues, which, naturally, are always linked to the past. Therefore, I'm very aware of the need for us to tell our story to the non-Indian community in order to keep things in perspective and create better understanding. Certainly using all forms of media to do this is of **paramount** importance.

It is a time for "reconciliation and diversity" in our world. In the middle of an "Information Age," we can no longer afford the luxury of misinformation or mean-spirited ethnic stereotypes. In order to survive in our "new world order," we must seek to live together in harmony and peace, more so now than ever....

99

Because of Deer's background as well as the respect she enjoys among Native Americans, many were hopeful that she would succeed where others have tried and failed to clean up the BIA. It was clearly a job filled with tremendous challenges. Reviews of her efforts after her first couple of years in office were mixed at best. Drastic budget cuts in federal funding for Indian affairs made it impossible for her to carry out major reorganization plans and there were rumors that she did not get along well with her boss, Secretary of the Interior Bruce Babbitt. While most Native Americans have the utmost respect for her as a leader and activist within their community, some expressed concern

expedite: speed up.
deemed: considered.
paramount: supreme.

that she had not shown as much strength and ability in her government post.

As for Deer, she admitted that "it's been really hard. People told me when I came in that it's the worst job in the government. I didn't really understand quite what they meant, but now I do." Yet she refused to give up, even in the face of criticism from a number of prominent tribal leaders. "I am a very determined person...," she declares. "Most people who succeed in making a difference in this world are controversial. I am!"

Sources

Books

Deer, Ada, and R. E. Simon, Jr., *Speaking Out,* Children's Press Open Door Books, 1970.

Hardy, Gayle J., *American Women Civil Rights Activists: Biobibliographies of 68 Leaders, 1825–1992,* McFarland, 1993.

Katz, Jane B., editor, *I Am the Fire of Time: The Voices of Native American Women,* Dutton, 1977.

Nomination of Ada Deer: Hearing Before the Committee on Indian Affairs, United States Senate, 103rd Congress, 1st Session, July 15, 1993, U.S. Government Printing Office, 1993.

Notable Native Americans, Gale, 1995.

Peroff, Nicholas C., *Menominee Drums: Tribal Termination and Restoration, 1954–1974,* University of Oklahoma Press, 1982.

Periodicals

Anchorage Daily News, "First Woman to Lead BIA Calls for Vision," August 31, 1993, p. B2.

Capital Times (Madison, Wisconsin), "Ada Deer Is Finally Given 'Heroine' Status," March 18, 1985, p. 2; "Ada Deer for Congress," August 27, 1992; "Deer Brings Fresh Outlook," August 10, 1993.

Chicago Tribune, "Woman Picked to Lead Indian Bureau," May 20, 1993, p. A1.

Christian Science Monitor, "Aiming to Make Electoral History," October 21, 1992.

Denver Post, "Female BIA Chief 'Shaking Agency Up,'" September 2, 1993, p. B2.

Grand Rapids Press, "Deer Not Running for Cover As Critics Blast Her Work," April 28, 1996, p. A13.

Indian Country Today, "Standing Ovation for Deer," July 21, 1993, p. A1; "Deer Calls for Help in BIA Shake-Up," September 8, 1993, p. A1.

Star Tribune (Minneapolis), "Dauntless Deer Shaking Up BIA," March 6, 1994.

Sunday Oregonian, "Woman Tapped to Lead BIA May Gain Fame but Enters Tough Game," May 23, 1993, p. A20.

Tundra Times, "Ada Deer: Native Values for BIA Management," September 8, 1993, p. 1.

Geronimo

(Goyathlay)
c. 1829–1909
Chief of the Apache tribe

    Now regarded as a legendary symbol of Indian resistance to the invasion of white people, Geronimo was the war chief of the Chiricahua Apaches, whose homeland was in what is now southwestern Arizona. The Apaches were primarily a nomadic tribe that hunted buffalo and did a little farming in the desert climate. The first major threat to their way of life surfaced in the late 1500s, when the Spanish arrived in Mexico and began to expand their influence north. Clashes between the two groups were still very common by the time the United States acquired the territory during the mid-1800s. Squeezed in between the Mexicans and an ever-growing population of American settlers, the Apaches—well known for their skill and ferocity as warriors—did what they could to repel the invaders of their lands on both sides of the border.

    Geronimo was born into this hostile atmosphere in 1829, near the headwaters of New Mexico's Gila River. He began taking part in battle in his late teens. In 1858 he

"I THINK I AM A GOOD MAN, BUT IN THE PAPERS ALL OVER THE WORLD THEY SAY I AM A BAD MAN; BUT IT IS A BAD THING TO SAY SO ABOUT ME. I NEVER DO WRONG WITHOUT A CAUSE."

77

experienced a great personal tragedy. While on a peaceful trip to Old Mexico with a group of Apaches, Geronimo returned to camp after a day of trading. He and his companions found that Mexican troops had attacked the camp in their absence, killing all the warrior guards, capturing the ponies, stealing the guns and supplies, and killing many of the women and children. Geronimo's mother, wife, and three children had all been massacred. Geronimo vowed vengeance, and afterwards engaged in many bloody battles with Mexican soldiers. He fought so hard that other Apaches often refused to join him on his raids, which continued year after year and often provided the Apache with stolen livestock and supplies.

Guerrilla Warfare against Mexicans and Americans

In 1876, the U.S. government decided to move the Chiricahua Apaches to the San Carlos agency in the White Mountain reservation in Arizona. About half of the band went voluntarily to San Carlos; many of the rest—Geronimo among them—fled across the border to Mexico and then moved on to a hideout near an agency in New Mexico. Over the next ten years, Geronimo and his followers—despite being vastly outnumbered by the Army troops sent in to control them—effectively waged **guerrilla warfare** against both the Mexicans and the Americans.

Geronimo was captured and imprisoned several times during this period. Sometimes he was released and at other times he escaped. He and his band of warriors would then vanish into the safety of the mountains. Occasionally, the small group would settle down and farm or ranch on reservation land for a season. But soon they would move on to territory outside the reservation, often taking with them their livestock and other supplies. The government and newspapers called Geronimo's travels outside the reservations "escapes," but Geronimo did not think of it as breaking laws. He was on land that Apaches had inhabited for many years. As food provisions diminished in one area, it was only customary that a nomadic Apache group would relocate to a more bountiful area. Once, when he was arrested by soldiers and put in chains, Geronimo demanded

guerrilla warfare: a type of war characterized by small, independent groups of people carrying out acts of harassment and deliberate destruction.

to know why they treated him this way: "I do not think that I ever belonged to those soldiers at Apache Pass, or that I should have asked them where I might go."

Apache leaders continued to fight against U.S. troops, and in 1881 rumors reached the San Carlos agency that all Apache leaders were about to be arrested. In response, a Chiricahua group that included Geronimo traveled to San Carlos and led many Chiricahua and Warm Springs Apaches off the reservation and down to Mexico. U.S. troops chased them to the border. As the warriors protected the group from the soldiers at their rear, Mexican soldiers who happened to be positioned on the other side of the border killed the women and children at the front of the group. Geronimo, once again, escaped.

During these years, Geronimo spoke with many U.S. military officials. Many different stories exist about these dealings, but there is little certainty about the exact sequence of events. It is clear, though, that the Apache chief felt he could not trust the U.S. spokesmen, who often gave him false promises and lies. In 1883, however, General George Crook, who after many years of battling Indians had evidently come to respect them, went to Mexico to negotiate with Geronimo. The two men achieved some mutual trust and respect. Geronimo agreed to go back to the San Carlos agency, where Crook had recently taken command. The Apache leader voluntarily gathered up his people and returned to the White Mountain reservation without escort. Crook removed most of the soldiers from the agency and allowed the people in San Carlos agency more freedom to govern themselves. For a year the agency was at peace.

But in 1885, Geronimo led a group of 134 Indians— mostly women and children—off the reservation and back down to Mexico. Apparently word had once again reached him that soldiers were about to arrest and hang him. Meanwhile, the newspapers and magazines of the day took advantage of the situation to thrill readers with distorted accounts of Geronimo and the Apaches that portrayed them as nothing more than brutal savages. They made much out of Geronimo's "escape" and incited local panic. The press also blamed Geronimo—who had headed *straight for Mexico—for acts committed in the region by lesser-known Indians. The military, under pressure from a near-hysterical public, sent General Crook to Mexico with orders to kill Geronimo or take him in an unconditional surrender.*

A Time to Surrender

With Apache scouts, Crook located Geronimo in Mexico in March of 1886. Crook asked Geronimo why he had left the reservation and the chief replied: "You told me that I might live in the reservation the same as white people lived. One year I raised a crop of corn, and gathered and stored it, and the next year I put in a crop of oats, and when the crop was almost ready to harvest, you told your soldiers to put me in prison, and if I resisted to kill me." According to Geronimo, the general denied that he had given these orders. But he also explained to Geronimo that he must surrender unconditionally, which would probably mean being sent to Florida. Geronimo negotiated, saying that he would not surrender unless Crook could promise him that he would only have to stay in Florida for two years, after which time he could go back to his people at San Carlos. Crook promised Geronimo this, but soon afterwards found that Washington would not agree to any terms. Geronimo once again escaped and remained in Mexico, where he and his followers battled with Mexican troops, attacking and killing many people. Crook then resigned and Brigadier General Nelson Miles took his post in Arizona, bringing with him five thousand soldiers to police the White Mountain reservation.

American troops were close on Geronimo's trail in Mexico; it was Lieutenant Charles B. Gatewood who first encountered him face to face in 1886. Peace talks did not flow smoothly, even after General Miles arrived. Geronimo felt he could not trust the white men to tell him the truth after so many years of lies. During the negotiations of the terms of his surrender, the famous war chief delivered the defense of himself and his actions that follows. As the speech makes clear, communication was difficult for many reasons. Geronimo was concerned that officials would believe the horrible things that had been said about him in

the newspapers. Rumors had long been a problem; know-
ing what to believe and what not to believe was nearly
impossible. And when dealing with interpreters and mes-
sengers, it was difficult to know if he was hearing the actu-
al messages sent by the military commander or Washing-
ton. (Geronimo, like the military officials, may have played
a little fast and loose with the truth; according to some his-
torians, Geronimo's claims of innocence were quite a
stretch from what actually happened.) His speech is reprint-
ed from W. C. Vanderwerth's Indian Oratory: Famous
Speeches by Noted Indian Chieftains, *University of Okla-*
homa Press, 1971.

I want to talk first of the causes which led me to leave the
reservation. I was living quietly and contented, doing and
thinking of no harm, while at the Sierra Blanca [the White
Mountain reservation].... I was living peaceably and satisfied
when people began to speak bad of me. I should be glad to
know who started those stories. [Geronimo was referring here
to rumors he had heard that the Americans wanted to arrest
him and then hang him, making him feel the need to escape
from the agency.] I was living peaceably with my family, having plenty to eat, sleeping well, taking care of my people, and
perfectly contented. I don't know where those bad stories
first came from. There we were doing well and my people
well. I was behaving well. I hadn't killed a horse or man,
American or Indian. I don't know what was the matter with
the people in charge of us. They knew this to be so, and yet
they said I was a bad man and the worst man there; but what
harm had I done? I was living peaceably and well, but I did
not leave on my own accord. Had I left it would have been
right to blame me; but as it is, blame those men who started
this talk about me....

I would like to know now who it was that gave the order to
arrest me and hang me. I was living peaceably there with my
family under the shade of the trees, doing just what General
[George] Crook had told me I must do and trying to follow his
advice. I want to know now who it was ordered me to be
arrested. I was praying to the light and to the darkness, to God

Geronimo in 1886: "I don't want that we should be killing each other."

and to the sun, to let me live quietly with my family. I don't know what the reason was that people should speak badly of me. I don't want to be blamed. The fault was not mine.... Find out who it was that began that bad talk about me.

I have several times asked for peace, but trouble has come from the agents and interpreters. I don't want what has passed to happen again. Now, I am going to tell you something else. The Earth-Mother is listening to me and I hope that all may be so arranged that from now on there shall be no trouble and that we shall always have peace. Whenever we see you coming to where we are, we think it is God—you must come always with God. From this on I do not want that anything shall be told you about me even in joke. Whenever I have broken out, it has always been on account of bad talk. From this on I hope that people will tell me nothing but the truth. From this on I want to do what is right and nothing else and I do not want you to believe any bad papers about me. I want the papers sent you to tell the truth about me, because I want to do what is right. Very often there are stories put in the newspapers that I am to be hanged. I don't want that any more. When a man tries to do right, such stories ought not to be put in the newspapers.

There are very few of my men left now. They have done some bad things but I want them all rubbed out now and let us never speak of them again. There are very few of us left. We think of our relations, brothers, brothers-in-law, father-in-law, etc., over on the reservation, and from this on we want to live at peace just as they are doing, and to behave as they are behaving. Sometimes a man does something and men are sent out to bring in his head. I don't want such things to happen to us. I don't want that we should be killing each other.

What is the matter that you don't speak to me? It would be better if you would speak to me and look with a pleasant face. It would make better feeling. I would be glad if you did. I'd be better satisfied if you would talk to me once in a while. Why don't you look at me and smile at me? I am the same man; I have the same feet, legs, and hands, and the sun looks down on me a complete man. I want you to look and smile at me.

I have not forgotten what you told me, although a long time has passed. I keep it in my memory. I am a complete man. Nothing has gone from my body. From here on I want to live at peace. Don't believe any bad talk you hear about me. The agents and the interpreter hear that somebody has done wrong, and they blame it all on me. Don't believe what they say. I don't want any of this bad talk in the future. I don't want those men who talked this way about me to be my agents any more. I want good men to be my agents and interpreters; people who will talk right. I want this peace to be legal and good. Whenever I meet you I talk good to you, and you to me, and peace is soon established; but when you go to the reservation you put agents and interpreters over us who do bad things. Perhaps they don't mind what you tell them, because I do not believe you would tell them to do bad things to us. In the future we don't want these bad men to be allowed near where we are to live. We don't want any more of that kind of bad talk. I don't want any man who will talk bad about me, and tell lies, to be there, because I am going to try and live well and peaceably. I want to have a good man put over me.

While living I want to live well. I know I have to die some-time, but even if the heavens were to fall on me, I want to do what is right. I think I am a good man, but in the papers all over the world they say I am a bad man; but it is a bad thing to say so about me. I never do wrong without a cause. Every day I am thinking, how am I to talk to you to make you believe what I say; and, I think, too, that you are thinking of what you are to say to me. There is one God looking down on us all. We are all children of the one God. God is listening to me. The sun, the darkness, the winds, are all listening to what we now say.

To prove to you that I am telling you the truth, remember I sent you word that I would come from a place far away to speak to you here, and you see us now. Some have come on horseback and some on foot. If I were thinking bad, or if I had done bad, I would never have come here. If it has been my fault, would I have come so far to talk to you? I have told you all that has happened. I also had feared that I should never see Ka-e-te-na again, but here he is, and I want the past to be buried. I am glad to see Ka-e-te-na. I was afraid I should never see him again. That was one reason, too, why I left. I wish that Ka-e-te-na would be returned to us to live with his family. I now believe what I was told. Now I believe that all told me is true, because I see Ka-e-te-na again. I am glad to see him again, as I was told I should. We are all glad. My body feels good because I see Ka-e-te-na, and my breathing is good. Now I can eat well, drink well, sleep well, and be glad. I can go everywhere with good feeling. Now, what I want is peace in good faith. Both you and I think well and think alike.

Well, we have talked enough and set here long enough. I may have forgotten something, but if I remember it, I will tell you of it tonight, or tomorrow, or some other time. I have finished for today, but I'll have something more to say bye and bye.

Several months went by before Geronimo officially surrendered to U.S. troops. Accounts of what he understood the terms to be vary according to the source of the information. Apparently Geronimo was under the impression that he and his followers—who by this time numbered only a few dozen men, women, and children—would be reunited with other Apaches and given good reservation land and supplies. Instead, when they finally gave themselves up in September 1886, they were treated as prisoners of war. Army troops put the Apaches on a train and sent them to live at a series of military bases.

Their first stop was in Texas, where Geronimo was nearly put on trial for murder in a civilian court in San Antonio. The government then hurried the Apaches off to Florida. Many of them died there in the humid climate from diseases they had never been exposed to in the desert heat of the Southwest. Although the Apaches begged for years to be allowed to return to their homeland, they were never allowed to go home. In 1894, they were finally moved to Fort Sill in Oklahoma Territory. There they turned to farming to support themselves.

Geronimo remained a prisoner of war for the rest of his life. But the public that had feared his name for so many years was strongly drawn to him after his surrender. He became a celebrity and a tourist attraction. He was even given permission to leave the reservation now and then to attend fairs and exhibitions at which he sold his autograph as well as pictures of himself. In 1905, he visited Washington, D.C., and attended the inauguration ceremonies of President Theodore Roosevelt. He died of pneumonia in 1909 at Fort Sill and is buried on the grounds there.

Sources

Books

Brown, Dee, *Bury My Heart at Wounded Knee: An Indian History of the American West,* Holt, 1970.

Debo, Angie, *Geronimo: The Man, His Time, His Place,* University of Oklahoma Press, 1982.

Dugan, Bill, *War Chiefs: Geronimo,* HarperCollins, 1991.

Falk, Odie B., *The Geronimo Campaign,* Oxford University Press, 1969.

Geronimo, *Geronimo, His Own Story,* edited by S. M. Barrett, Dutton, 1970.

McLuhan, T. C., *Touch the Earth: A Self-Portrait of Indian Existence,* Outerbridge & Dienstfrey, 1971.

Notable Native Americans, Gale, 1995.

Roberts, David, *Once They Moved Like the Wind: Cochise, Geronimo, and the End of the Indian Wars,* Simon & Schuster, 1993.

Rosenstiel, Annette, *Red and White: Indian Views of the White Man, 1492–1982,* Universe Books, 1983.

Schwartz, Melissa, *Geronimo,* Chelsea House, 1992.

Sonnichsen, C. L., editor, *Geronimo and the End of the Apache Wars,* University of Nebraska Press, 1990.

Vanderwerth, W. C., *Indian Oratory: Famous Speeches by Noted Indian Chieftains,* University of Oklahoma Press, 1971.

Witt, Shirley Hill, and Stan Steiner, *The Way: An Anthology of American Indian Literature,* Knopf, 1972.

Suzan Shown Harjo

1945–

*Activist and poet of the
Cheyenne and Arapaho tribes*

"MANY OF THE PEOPLE IN THE WORLD THINK THEY KNOW ABOUT NATIVE PEOPLES. AND MOST OF THE THINGS THEY KNOW ARE WRONG."

As president and executive director of the Washington, D.C.-based *Morning Star Institute*, Suzan Shown Harjo works to defend and preserve Native American culture. These activities have taken her in many different directions. For example, she has lobbied (attempted to influence legislators) for religious freedom and the reburial of Indian remains and sacred objects. She has also challenged the right of sports teams to use names or mascots that ridicule or degrade Indians. Underlying all that Harjo does is the belief that existing prejudices or stereotypes about native peoples make it easier to deny that they are human beings. This in turn, she says, makes it easier to ignore them. As she explained to an interviewer for the Los Angeles Times, "Public policy is not done in any positive way for cartoons, or for people who are already dead, or people who don't have a future."

Harjo was born in Oklahoma and spent most of her childhood there. Her family farmed a small plot of reservation land, but what little they could grow on it was barely enough for them to get by on. During the 1950s, however, her father—a disabled veteran of World War II—reenlisted in the U.S. Army. When he was sent to serve in Naples, Italy, the family moved there with him. While life there was very different from what she had known back home, Harjo was able to relate to the warm, tribal-like relationships she observed between the Italian families she came to know.

The roots of Harjo's activism date back at least to the struggles for Indian religious freedom during the mid-1960s. She also fought for Indian cultural rights during the late 1960s and early 1970s. During that time of upheaval, she and her late husband, Frank Ray Harjo, coproduced a biweekly radio program called "Seeing Red" on WBAI-FM in New York City. It was the first regularly scheduled Indian news and analysis show in the United States.

In addition to her duties as a journalist, Harjo served as the station's director of drama and literature and produced a number of plays for broadcast. She also took to the stage herself on occasion as an actress and singer, sometimes in connection with an **improvisational troupe** she founded called the Spiderwoman Theatre Company.

Leads Fight for Native American Rights from Nation's Capital

In 1974, Harjo moved to Washington, D.C., which has since then served as the base of operations for her activism. One of her first jobs was with the National Congress of American Indians (NCAI). The largest group of its kind in the United States, the NCAI was established in 1944 by members of many different tribes who shared a common interest in safeguarding the rights of Native Americans and preserving their culture. Harjo served as the organization's communications director, legislative assistant, and coordinator of the National Indian **Litigation** Committee.

In 1978, Harjo joined the administration of President Jimmy Carter as special assistant in the Office of the Secretary of the Interior. In this role, she planned and **drafted** legislation concerning issues of interest to Native Americans. She also served as one of the administration's links to Congress on such topics as Indian religious freedom. In

improvisational troupe: a group of performers who make up what they do as they go along, without a script or anything else to guide them.

litigation: the process of appearing in court to pursue a legal claim.

drafted: drew up.

Suzan Shown Harjo

addition, she kept track of whether the U.S. government was following internationally recognized principles of human rights and **self-determination.**

In 1981, a new president, Ronald Reagan, took office. His Republican **agenda** was far different than that of Jimmy Carter, a Democrat. So Harjo shifted her attention to other matters. She battled proposed budget cuts in Indian programs and attempts to turn over control of tribal and federal schools to the states. She also continued to support legal cases involving treaty rights, individual civil liberties, land claims, environmental protection, and restoring federal recognition to tribes that lost their official status as Indians as a result of government policies during the 1950s.

self-determination: freedom to choose one's own political future.

agenda: plan.

Heads National Congress of American Indians

In 1984, Harjo returned to the NCAI, this time as the organization's executive director. Over the next five years, she provided the leadership for the NCAI's national policy. Her particular focus was on legislative and litigation efforts and cultural concerns.

The year 1984 also marked the beginning of her current role at the Morning Star Institute. In addition, Harjo is the cofounder and vice president of Native Children's Survival. It is dedicated to "the healing of Mother Earth and her children." She is also developing new policy on Native Peoples' cultural property rights.

Harjo's connections with these and many other groups has made her a key player in a number of major Native American cultural activities. In 1989, for example, she was a leading force behind the law that established the National Museum of the American Indian. She was also one of the chief negotiators in an agreement with Smithsonian Museum officials regarding the return and reburial of Indian remains and sacred objects. (In 1990, this agreement led to a new law, the Native American Grave Protection and Repatriation Act.) In addition, she has worked with a national **coalition** *of Indian tribes and organizations as well as various environmental, human rights, and religious groups to win legal protection for sacred Indian sites and passage of the Native American Free Exercise of Religion Act of 1993.*

More recently, Harjo has taken up the fight against the use of Indian names and mascots for sports teams. She and many others who support her believe they are degrading and contribute to the problem of low self-esteem among young Native Americans. In 1994, Harjo was the lead **petitioner** *in a lawsuit filed with the U.S. Patent and Trademark Office that would force the Washington Redskins football team to drop its name, logo, and mascot.*

Harjo is also a strong **advocate** *of the arts. She herself is a published author of numerous essays, articles, and poems. To showcase the talents of other Native American artists and writers, she organizes exhibitions and poetry readings throughout the country. Through Native Chil-*

coalition: an alliance of different people or groups who come together to take action.

petitioner: a person who makes a formal written request.

advocate: promoter, supporter.

dren's Survival, she is involved in music, too, as the produc-
er of a series of videos featuring Indian performers who
combine traditional tribal and rock music.

Harjo is a frequent lecturer at events across the nation.
She talked about some of the issues that interest her most
in a speech she delivered on September 18, 1992. The
occasion was the opening session of the fourth annual
"Seeds of Change" Conference, held in Santa Fe, New Mex-
ico. The following excerpt was transcribed from an audio-
tape provided by Harjo.

Many of the people in the world think they know about
Native Peoples. And most of the things they know are wrong.
They know things about us and associate things with us that
have nothing to do with us. "Woo-woo-woo!" That's what
drunken white people do at closing time at bars. But that's
very much identified with Native People. "Boom-boom-
boom-boom-boom" is just an unimaginative musical director
for a Western film and his successors. Scalping. You know
who introduced commercial scalping in this hemisphere?
The French and British fur trappers. That's also where the
term "redskin" came from....

The French and British fur trappers used to drag in gunnysacks full of skulls of Native People for bounty. It was the way
they made a living. And they would bring in the wagons full
of Indian bodies. Well, that got to be right **cumbersome**,
'cause they were killing more and more Indians and had to
bring in greater gunnysacks and bigger wagons. So the people
who were paying the bounties agreed to pay bounty for the
scalps, rather than the skulls, and for the red skins, rather
than the whole bodies....

Now you don't even have to know that to know that there
is something wrong with identification of anyone from outside that group. That's name-calling....

Jack Kent Cooke [the owner of the Washington Redskins
football team] has said the name of the Redskins "is not
derogatory." Well, he said two things. He said, "There's not a
jot, whittle, chance in hell" that the name of the Redskins is

cumbersome: troublesome,
awkward.

derogatory: something that
expresses a low opinion,
insulting.

going to be changed "because it would cost too much money." Well, he's wrong. It would make him a fortune. The name-change contest, which myself and six other petitioners before the U.S. Patent and Trademark Board have offered to conduct for Jack Kent Cooke—I think it would be great fun.... I'm sure everyone can come up with wonderful names for this team that don't single out living human beings. Native People are the only living human beings singled out for abuse in the sports arena. Think about it....

Right now we're trying to reclaim our personal names, reclaim our Indian nations' names, because everyone's called something that we weren't called. Tsistsistas is the name of the Cheyenne People. The Lakota People had two words for us, Shyhela and Shyhanna—"the Red People" and "the People who talk so fast and funny you can't understand them." Or, if they're talking directly to us, "the People who speak and lead beautifully with their words." So, you be the judge....

Europeans had a lot of difficulty pronouncing names that are really quite simple. So they couldn't say "Shyhela," and they couldn't say "Shyhanna," and they couldn't say "Tsistsistas" for some reason, so they said "Cheyenne," and that stuck.

The Muscogees, that's our name for ourselves—that's my dad's People. And the British came in, and you may know the Muscogees by another name—Creek. And that's because the British were so imaginative that they said, "These people live around creeks. Let's call them...."

So, when we are identified as an era, as in cowboys and Indians, and when we are identified by the color of our skin or what any dictionary will tell you is the most derogatory or disparaging or demeaning word you can call a Native American—there is one dictionary definition our attorneys found out in legal research on the word "redskin" that simply says, "not the preferred word for Native Americans." The collective name for us—don't worry about Native Americans, Indians, Indigenous People (which is much too long), Native Peoples—everything is wrong and inadequate. So just mix it up, use every term interchangeably and try to find out what our real names are and refer to us as that. That's the best thing.

Tohono O'odham, for example—the People in Arizona who have a reservation that's larger than the state of Connecticut—went to the Bureau of Indian Affairs in the mid-'80s and said, "We want you to change your paper on us. You keep writing to us as Papago, and we don't like that term."

The woman at the BIA said, "Well, we have too much paper on you. We can't change this name."

They said, "Well, our name is the Tohono O'odham. It's not too difficult. Call us that, write to us."

And she said, "Well, why don't you like Papago?"

"Well, it means 'bean-eater.' It was just something that someone said, 'You're a bean-eater, we'll call you that,' and it was just a way of stripping us of our identity." And so on and so forth.

And she said, "Well, I wouldn't mind being called a bean-eater myself."

And they said, "Okay, every time we write to you, we'll write to you as Papago. And when you write to us, address us as Tohono O'odham."

It's very difficult—I mean, that took several years of negotiating with the Bureau of Indian Affairs. I don't mean to always **rag on** the BIA. It *is* one of the worst federal agencies, no doubt about it. And it will not improve as long as it's in the Interior Department, divorced from other people. And as long as it has to compete with the Bureau of Land Management and the Bureau of Reclamation and Fish and Wildlife Service and so forth. And is run by people who see as their jobs the management of Indian People.

The BIA pretty much is a losing battle on most Indian reservations because the families are pretty strong at home and they don't have much of a foothold. They don't do much good, but anymore they don't do much that's bad....

The Bureau of Indian Affairs is ... one of the oldest federal agencies, and it's the one that [General George Armstrong] Custer said to line up all the employees on his way out to Little Big Horn and said, "Now, don't do *nothin'* til you hear from me." Well, orders is orders!

rag on: criticize, nag, or scold.

I'm really pleased to have been able, with my Cheyenne brother, **Ben Nighthorse Campbell** [see entry] ... to not only get a memorial honoring our Indian heroes from that place and time, but to get rid of the name of Custer. And on this October 12, many of our People whose ancestors were there—of the Lakota and the Blue Clouds, the Arapahos, and the Cheyennes—will gather on the Greasy Grass at Little Big Horn, and that's when there will be dedicated the national battlefield that's just called simply Little Big Horn National Battlefield.

It didn't make any sense that it was called "Custer" anyway.... It was the only battlefield in the park system that was named after an individual. And you wouldn't think the United States would name it after a loser. It shows you how far people will go to find heroes. I agree that we all need our heroes, but it's important to look at the kind of people we're propping up and shaking the dust off [of].

Columbus, really?... I would, were I Italian, want as a hero someone who could at least have written to his mother in Italian. He couldn't do that. Not a very bright guy. Certainly lost, we all know that. What did he write, day one, in his journal? About "the Indios." Guess where he thought he was? He kept four separate journals, each **at variance with** the other, so we know that, at best, he told the truth one-quarter of the time.

He and his tiny men and their rats brought gifts of civilization here. Here, to this place that Columbus wrote about as "Paradise on earth." Well, they couldn't have that in Europe, could they? What was the system that was there?... It was a system ... of economic and religious slavery that meant no individual, no **inherent sovereignty**.... What was going on in Europe? There was top-down sovereignty. Divine right of kings. So, sovereignty flowed from God to kings to some of the people some of the time, and most of the people none of the time.

What happened? What kept it all together? The promise of Paradise.... Things might be lousy here, but don't worry about it. And they might get worse, but don't worry about it. Because, when you die, you will be glorified.

I have great respect for every person's religion. That was the missing ingredient from the other direction, by the

at variance with: not in agreement with.

inherent: inborn.

sovereignty: freedom from control by others.

way—respect. The only way to make the next five hundred years different from the past five hundred years is to begin with that single word—respect.

I do question the spiritual base of religions that would **dictate** that my children are going to a nightmare of a hell because they don't believe in the way of people who came from Europe. I don't know where they're going. I wish them well.

I don't understand a religion and its spiritual base that can … state in its basic document that "man shall have **dominion** over the beasts and the birds."

That is what's happened here. It began with Columbus and his men and his rats. And their diseases that were imported and that killed, by 1500, eight million people, in the Caribbean area, who had been alive in 1492. It was not simply a mowing down of people…. It was an **ecocide** of unimaginable proportions which is still going on, as so many of you know and are working to halt….

What we need to begin—a different course of action—is to forget about the kinds of heroes that we've been propping up. And to start celebrating those small and large acts of courage that exist within ourselves and our families and our neighbors, each one of us, and *celebrate* that, *applaud* it. How wonderful when someone acts in a courageous way! Give them encouragement so they *might* do it again. Learn from it.

But, if we constantly prop up false heroes—and heroes who are not going to be one-hundred-percent perfect, because nobody's one-hundred-percent—we're constantly going to be disappointed in those individuals or make mythic beings out of pitiful people. We need to begin with that respect within ourselves and look for the essence of your own culture.

One thing that Native Peoples still have is very powerful belief systems. One thing I like about the fairly recent movie *Thunderheart* was that it showed the practical, everyday nature of magic and power—that it's not the stuff that you should be misty-eyed about. It happens as a matter of course. You drink water in the day, you do a little magic during the day (or a lot, depending on the situation). You just have to train yourself for it. And the best way to train yourself for it is

dictate: order or command with the voice of authority.

dominion: supreme authority or control.

ecocide: destruction of the environment.

Suzan Shown Harjo

by exploring whatever routes you have, whatever clues you have to your own character and identity and culture. And then come to us as whole people so we can talk, so we can share, so we can enhance each other.

I'd like to commit some poetry, which I always try to do when I get outside of Washington, D.C. I live on a terrible reservation there—**abject** poverty, **rampant** alcoholism, checks bouncing everywhere, cutthroat politics. So I always feel like I'm getting away with something when I'm outside of Washington and can do something as **seditious** ... as commit poetry.... This one's called "Jumping Through the Hoops of History."

I wrote it—it's dedicated to Columbus and Custer (and we've talked about them), [Philip Henry] Sheridan, who was the other great military man in U.S. history who said, "The only good Indian's a dead one." And then his **protégé** was Colonel [John M.] Chivington, and they—both together with Custer—had a lot to do with the massacres of my relatives at Sand Creek [Colorado, in 1864] and the Washita....

This is also dedicated to John Wayne—well, you know why—and to all such heroes of yesteryear. I wrote it to get it off my chest, for one thing, and knowing that this would be a time of a lot of public stupidity, in addition to the funny hats and the parades and everything. And that some things had to be put in some sort of perspective. [Harjo is referring here to celebrations in 1992 marking the five hundredth anniversary of Christopher Columbus's arrival in the New World.]

The real push behind it was—the day I started to write this was the day I found out that, for the third decade in a row, our Indian teenagers took the prize. We're still the population in the country with the highest rate of teenage suicide. Most of that comes from low self-esteem. Most of that comes from the constant bombardment of negative imaging and having either ourselves written out of existence or written about wrongly.

Also, someone sent me a box of hollowed-out 45/70s [bullets].... It is a big bullet, folks. A little bitty bullet like this will drop a deer. This one ... had a special little treat, a little magnesium load.... It would explode on contact and just burn

abject: hopeless.

rampant: widespread.

seditious: something that inspires people to resist authority.

protégé: someone whose career is advanced by another person with influence.

holes in you. And it was known to cut people in half. This was made especially for the Cheyenne, the Lakota, and the Arapaho people *and* the buffalo—this 45/70. So all of that together made me think, "This is a heck of a day."

I had just finished a major battle, too, in Washington and around the country, just getting new law so we could get back our dead relatives from museums and educational institutions and federal agencies, and our religious items....

One thing that gave me that little extra push was finding out, in the Anthropological Archives in the Smithsonian's National Museum of Natural History, the **bills of lading** for the heads of my relatives from the Massacre at Sand Creek. So, not only were they mutilated and mowed down—people who are not abstract and not just numbers, but people who we have oral history about, who are family people. Some of whom were known by my grandparents. Several my mother remembered as a child. Not abstract and ancient history. This is *real, new* stuff to us. So, that kind of plays in here, too.

Anyway, I'm going to read this....

> 10 little, 9 little, 8 little Indians
> 7 little, sick little, live baby Indians
> poor little, me little, you little Indians
> the only good Indian's a dead 1

> *a lot of young Indians got dead in the '80s*
> > *just like the '70s and '60s*
> > *both 19 and 18 hundreds*
> > *and all the other 00s since 1492*
> *a sucker's #s game over the sale of*
> > *the centuries*
> > *with 99-year leases and 1¢-treaties*
> > *with disappearing ink on the bottom line*
> > *signed by gilt-eyed oddsmakers*
> > *whose smart $ bet on 0 redskins by half-time*

> *in the 4th quarter, when this century turned on us,*
> > *we were down to 250k in the u.s.*
> > *from the 50m who were here*
> > *but who just didn't hear about*
> *the lost italian, lurching his way from spain*
> > *with scurvy-covered sailors and yellow-fevered priests*

bills of lading: receipts listing goods that have been shipped.

Suzan Shown Harjo

at least 1,000 points of blight and plague
in 3 wooden boxes marked "india or bust"
and "in gold we trust"

columbus washed up on our shores, praising paradise
on earth
and kinder, gentler people
who fixed them dinner, but laughed so hard
at these metal-headed, tiny whitemen
that they fell to their knees
we please them, dear diary, columbus wrote home
they think we're gods
so the knights of the lost boats
spread syphilis and The word of the 1 true gods
and planted 00s of flags of the 1 true kings
and sang their sacred 3-g song

"a, b, c, d, g, g, g
glory, god and gold, gold, gold"

rub-a-dub-dub, a niña tub
rub-a-dub-dub, a pinta tub
rub-a-grub-grub, Native gold and lands
rub-a-chop-chop, Native ears and hands
rub-a-dub-dub, santa maria sub
rub-a-rub-rub, Indians out
8m by 1500, or thereabout

meanwhile, back in the land of wicked queens and fairy
tales
serfs were sewing and owing the churches
and paying dues to the papal store
all for the promise of the kingdom of heaven
starving and dying to make it to that pearly door
the inquisition kings reaped peasant blood$, but
wanted more
than those in robes could rob from the poor
so the captains of invention
designed the missions to go forth and mine
with tools of destruction to kill the time
so cristobal colon led the chorus in the same old song
kyrie, kyrie, kyrie eleison
a new world beat for average savages
who didn't change their tune

and were bound by chains of office
  and staked out to pave the yellow brick road
  at invasion's high noon
and wizards in satin read their rights in latin
  kyrie, kyrie, kyrie requiremento
  and a lot of Indians got dead
  as was, by god, their right
  to the sound of death songs in the night
    kyrie, kyrie, kyrie requiremento
and amerigo begat the beautiful
  and the bibles grew and the bullets flew
and the pilgrims gave thanks
  and carved up turkeys and other peoples' lands
and mrs. governor stuyvesant bowled with 10 bloody
                              skulls
  and begat up against the wall streets
  and shopping mauls on 00s of mounds
and the 7th cavalry prayed and passed the ammunition
  and loaded gatling guns 100k times
  and shot off extra special 45/70s
  for any Indians or buffalo
  between europe and manifest destiny
meanwhile, in most of Indian country
  no one heard about the ironhorse or the goldwhores
  or the maggots in the black hills
  with no-trespassing signs
  or what's yours is homestake mine's
  but that's what they called ballin' the jack
then it was 2 late, about a 25¢ to midnight
  and us without a second hand to tell the times were
                              a changin'
so, we jumped through the hoops of history
  on mile-high tightropes without a net
  with no time to look back or back out
  with no time to show off or cry out

    look, ma, no hands
          no hands
          no hands

and the calendar was kept by #s of sand creeks
  and washitas and wounded knees and acoma mesas
  and 00s of army blankets of wool and smallpox

and a lot of chiefs who made their marks
    no longer able to thumb their way home
    where x marked the spots on their babies
and pocahantas haunted england

    singing ring-a-ring-a-rosy
    ashes, ashes, all fall dead

and a lot of fences got built
    around a lot of hungry people
    who posed for a lot of catlins
    who shot their fronts
    and snapped their backs

    just say commodity cheese, please

and a lot of Indians got moved and removed
    relocated and dislocated
    from c to shining c
    from a 2 z
    from spacious skies to fort renos
    from purple mountains to oklahoma
    from vision quests to long walks
    from stronghold tables to forks in the road
    from rocks to hard places
    from high water to hell
    from frying pans to melting pots
    from clear, blue streams to coke

and we got beads
    and they got our scalps
and we got horses
    and they got our land
and we got treaties
    and they got to break them
and we got reservations
    and they got to cancel them
and we got christian burials
    and they got to dig us up
and they got america
    and america got us

    and they got a home where Indians don't roam
    (now follow the bouncing cannon ball)
    and they got a home where Indians don't roam

and a lot of young Indians got dead
and those were the glory daze
and we learned the arts of civilization
reciting the great white poets

    (oh, little sioux or japanee
    oh, don't you wish that you were me)

singing the great white songs

    (onward christian soldiers
    marching as to war
    to save a wretch like me
    amazin' race, amazin' race)

sailing down the mainstream

    (with land o' lakes butter maiden
    and kickapoo joy juice role models
    for good little Indian girls and boys)

and we got chopped meat
and we got buffaloed
and we got oil-well murders
and they got black-gold heirs
and they got museums
and we got in them
and they got us under glass
and we got to guide them
and they got the kansas city chiefs
and we got a 14,000-man b.i.a.
and we got pick-up trucks
and they got our names for campers
and they got rubber tomahawks
and we got to make them
and they got to take us to lunch
and we got to eat it
and they got richer
and we got poorer
and we got stuck in their cities
and they got to live in our countries
and they got our medicines
and we got to heal them
and we got sick
and they got, well, everything

and we got to say please and thank you
        and good morning, america
        you're welcome, y'all come
        and have a nice hemisphere

then, all of a sudden, a new day dawned
        and america yawned
        and the people mumbled
            something about equality and the quality of life
            some new big deal to seal the bargain
            and jack and jill went to the hill
            to fetch some bills to save us
            and the united snakes of america
            spoke in that english-only forked-tongue way
            about cash-on-the-barrelhead, hand-over-fist
            in exchange for Indian homes on the termination
                            list
            and bankers and lawyers and other great white
              sharks
            made buyers-market killings
            when more chiefs made their marks
            and lots of Indians packed their bags and
                            old-pawn
            for fun with dick and jane and busing with
                            blondes
            for a bleeched-out, white-washed american morn
            while we were just trying to live and get born

and a lot of young Indians got dead
        in america's 2 big wars
        and the little ones they tried to hide
            like the my-lais
            and other white lies
        and the millions on the grate-nation's main streets
            with holes in their pockets
            and tombstones for eyes
you see, america was busy lunching
        and punching clocks
        (and each other, don't tell)
        and pushing paper
        (and each other, do tell)
        and loving and leaving cabbage-patch/latch-key kids
        in the middle of the road and nowhere

(where everything got touched but their hearts
where $ bought the love they were worth)
and America's daddy and mommy looked
up from their desks
out from their ovens
over their shoulders
behind the times
down their noses
and right before their eyes
but just out of sight
behind flashlights in abandoned buildings
through crack in the walls
and in the halls of boarding schools
a lot of young Indians got dead, too
girls with bullets, booze and lysol for boyfriends
boys with nooses and razor blades for cold
comfort
and a few grandmas and grandpas
on their last legs anyway

and we who were left behind
sang songs for the dead and dying
for the babies to stop crying
for the burned-out and turned-out
for the checked-out and decked-out
ain't that just like 'em
we said over cold coffee and hot tears
for getting themselves dead
forgetting to tell us goodbye
for giving america no 2-week notice
forgiving america with their bodies
ain't that just their way
to gather us up and put us down
gee, kids really do the darndest things
like get themselves dead
like a lot of them did
just yesterday and today
and a lot of young Indians got dead
faster than they could say
tomorrow
oh, say, can't you see
they learned america's song and dance

from the rockets' red glare
to god shed his light on thee
they read america's history
where they weren't
or were only bad news
they laughed when president rip van reagan
told the russians the u.s.
shouldn't have humored us
they passed when senator slender reed said
this is the best deal for your land
find another country or play this hand
they learned the lessons about columbus
in child-proof, ocean-blue rhymes
along with other whiteboy-hero signs of the times
they saw the ships sailing, again
and a future as extras
in movies where Indians don't win
they knew they were about to be discovered, again
in someone else's lost and found mind
in an old-world/bush-quayle
new age/snake-oil
re-run as much fun
as the first scent of those sailors
fresh from the hold
exhaling disease, inhaling gold
and a lot of young Indians escaped just in time
to miss the good wishes and cheer
have a happy, have a merry
have a very nice columbus year

10 little, 9 little, 8 little Indians
7 little, sick little, live baby Indians
poor little, me little, you little Indians
the only good Indian's a dead 1

... I love you all. Thank you for listening. *Aho.*

Sources

Books

Notable Native Americans, Gale, 1995.

Periodicals

Dallas Morning News, "Columbus: Discoverer or Despoiler?" October 11, 1992.

Lear's, "An American Crusader: Suzan Shown Harjo of Washington, D.C.," July/August 1989, pp. 135–36.

Los Angeles Times, "Suzan Shown Harjo: Fighting to Preserve the Legacy—and Future—of Native Americans," November 27, 1994, p. M3.

Native Peoples Magazine, "Guest Essay," winter 1994, p. 5.

Newsweek, "I Won't Be Celebrating Columbus Day," fall-winter 1991 (special issue), p. 32.

New York Times, "Working Profiles: Suzan Harjo, Lobbying for a Native Cause," April 2, 1986.

Washington Post, "Bury My Heart at RFK," November 6, 1994.

Joseph

(In-mut-too-yah-lat-lat)
c. 1840–1904

Chief of the Nez Percé tribe

Among the saddest stories of Indian resistance against the westward migration of white settlers was that of Chief Joseph and his tribe, a small group known as the Nez Percés. (French explorers gave them that name, which means "pierced nose," after observing their custom of wearing nose rings.) Their ancestral home was a large area of land that stretched across what is now southeastern Washington, northeastern Oregon, and central Idaho. For the most part, they lived peacefully with neighboring tribes and the few white farmers and trappers they met while hunting and fishing. In 1848, however, control of the Pacific Northwest shifted from Great Britain to the United States. White American settlers then began heading into the territory in greater numbers. This led to tensions that eventually destroyed the Nez Percé way of life.

Joseph, who was born around 1840 in Oregon's Wallowa Valley, grew up during this troubled time. He was the son of a chief (also named Joseph) who repeatedly warned

"I HAVE ASKED SOME OF THE GREAT WHITE CHIEFS WHERE THEY GET THEIR AUTHORITY TO SAY TO THE INDIAN THAT HE SHALL STAY IN ONE PLACE, WHILE HE SEES WHITE MEN GOING WHERE THEY PLEASE. THEY CANNOT TELL ME."

his people to be careful in their dealings with whites. In 1855, however, some of the Nez Percés signed a treaty giving up most of their land. In return, U.S. government officials assured them that the Wallowa Valley could serve as their reservation. But eight years later, even this land was **ceded** to the whites in a treaty that not all the Nez Percés approved, including the band led by Joseph's father.

U.S. Army Orders Tribe to Reservation

Around 1871, Joseph assumed the title of chief from his father upon the older man's death. By this time, his band of Nez Percés were waging a war of **passive resistance** not only against further white expansion but also against attempts to move them to a reservation in Lapwai, Idaho. Before long, however, the discovery of gold in the Wallowa Valley increased pressure on U.S. authorities to make the Indians leave the area.

Finally, in the spring of 1877, U.S. Army General Oliver O. Howard issued an **ultimatum** to the Indians. He told them they had to agree to give up all of their land and move to the reservation within thirty days. If they did not, he would order his soldiers to force them out.

Chief Joseph was not a warrior, and he had no desire to fight with the whites. He saw himself mostly as a protector of the aged, the weak, and the helpless among his people. So he advised them to obey General Howard's order. His call for patience and peace did not sit well with everyone, however. While the Nez Percés were in the process of making their way to their new home in June 1877, several young male members of the tribe who bitterly resented the way they were being treated attacked and killed some white settlers. The incident touched off a series of skirmishes between the Nez Percés and the U.S Army. Chief Joseph showed unexpected military skill by defeating the better-equipped and more numerous government troops. Yet he knew that he could not continue to do so for very long, because more soldiers were already on the way from other nearby outposts. So the chief made a fateful decision—he and his people would try to escape to Canada.

ceded: granted or transferred (usually by treaty).

passive resistance: defying authority by refusing to cooperate.

ultimatum: a final demand, especially one that will result in immediate force or other direct action if it is rejected.

Chief Leads Tribe on Long Trek to Canada

Over the next eleven weeks, Chief Joseph led a band of several hundred Nez Percé men, women, and children on a retreat of well over a thousand miles through the rugged terrain of the Pacific Northwest. (Part of their route took them through what is now Yellowstone National Park.) On their trail were U.S. government forces as well as enemy Indians. At least a dozen times, they had all-out battles with the soldiers following them, and in most cases the Nez Percés defeated them or fought to a stalemate (tie). Throughout the chase, Chief Joseph impressed his opponents with his courage and his steady determination. They were also surprised that he never harmed the white settlers his band met along the way.

By late September 1877, the Nez Percés at last found themselves within about thirty miles of the Canadian border at a place in Montana known as Eagle Creek. But they had paid a high price to make it that far. In addition to those who had fallen in battle, there were many others who had died along the way from exhaustion, hunger, and disease. For the ones who had managed to survive, the coming winter promised severe weather and probable starvation.

Surrounded and vastly outnumbered by well-armed U.S. troops, Chief Joseph finally surrendered on October 5, 1877. His brief remarks to General Howard and General Nelson A. Miles are among the best-known and most heart-wrenching words ever spoken by a Native American. They are reprinted here from W. C. Vanderwerth's Indian Oratory: Famous Speeches by Noted Indian Chieftains, *University of Oklahoma Press, 1971.*

Tell General Howard I know his heart. What he told me before, I have in my heart. I am tired of fighting. Our chiefs are killed. Looking Glass is dead. Toohoolhoolzote is dead. The old men are all dead. It is the young men who say yes and no. He [Ollokot, Joseph's own brother] who led on the young men is dead. It is cold and we have no blankets. The little children are freezing to death. My people, some of

Joseph's now-famous words captured belated public sympathy: "I am tired; my heart is sick and sad. From where the sun now stands I will fight no more forever."

them, have run away to the hills and have no blankets, no food; no one knows where they are—perhaps freezing to death. I want to have time to look for my children and see how many I can find. Maybe I shall find them among the dead. Hear me, my chiefs. I am tired; my heart is sick and sad. From where the sun now stands I will fight no more forever.

99

While some of the Nez Percés did manage to slip away to Canada, Chief Joseph and his followers were sent to live in Indian Territory in what is now Oklahoma. There they still faced tremendous hardship. Many of them (including five of Chief Joseph's children) became sick and died. Chief Joseph did his best to bring their desperate condition to the attention of authorities. In 1879, he was allowed to go to Washington, D.C., to plead his case. On January 14, he testified before a special gathering of cabinet members, congressional representatives, and other government officials.

*"My friends," Chief Joseph began, "I have been asked to show you my heart. I am glad to have a chance to do so. I want the white people to understand my people. Some of you think an Indian is like a wild animal. This is a great mistake...." His statement to the officials was long and very detailed. First, he described his tribe's initial friendly contacts with white people and how they eventually came to be **at odds with** them over land. He then explained their confrontations with the U.S. Army and their attempt to escape to Canada. Finally, he spoke of his disappointment and sadness over how he and the rest of the Nez Percés had been treated and how they wanted to be treated instead. Joseph's concluding remarks from that meeting are reprinted here from W. C. Vanderwerth's* Indian Oratory: Famous Speeches by Noted Indian Chieftains, *University of Oklahoma Press, 1971.*

at odds with: in disagreement with.

"

I am glad we came [here to Washington]. I have shaken hands with a great many friends, but there are some things I want to know which no one seems able to explain. I cannot understand how the government sends a man out to fight us, as it did General [Nelson A.] Miles, and then breaks his word. Such a government has something wrong about it. I cannot understand why so many chiefs are allowed to talk so many different ways, and promise so many different things. I have seen the Great Father Chief [President Rutherford B. Hayes], the next Great Chief [Secretary of the Interior Carl Schurz], the Commissioner Chief [E.A. Hayt, head of Indian Affairs], the Law Chief [General Butler], and many other law chiefs [congressmen], and they all say they are my friends, and that I shall have justice, but while their mouths all talk right I do not understand why nothing is done for my people. I have heard talk and talk, but nothing is done.

Good words do not last long unless they amount to something. Words do not pay for my dead people. They do not pay for my country, now overrun by white men. They do not protect my father's grave. They do not pay for all my horses and cattle. Good words will not give me back my children. Good words will not make good the promise of your War Chief General Miles. Good words will not give my people good health and stop them from dying. Good words will not get my people a home where they can live in peace and take care of themselves. I am tired of talk that comes to nothing. It makes my heart sick when I remember all the good words and all the broken promises. There has been too much talking by men who had no right to talk. Too many **misrepresentations** have been made, too many misunderstandings have come up between the white men about the Indians.

If the white man wants to live in peace with the Indian he can live in peace. There need be no trouble. Treat all men alike. Give them the same law. Give them all an even chance to live and grow. All men were made by the same Great Spirit Chief. They are all brothers. The earth is the mother of all people, and all people should have equal rights upon it. You might as well expect the rivers to run backward as that any man who was born a free man should be contented when

misrepresentations: false statements made with the intent to deceive or be unfair.

Joseph   **111**

penned up and denied liberty to go where he pleases. If you tie a horse to a stake, do you expect he will grow fat? If you pen an Indian up on a small spot of earth, and **compel** him to stay there, he will not be contented, nor will he grow and prosper. I have asked some of the great white chiefs where they get their authority to say to the Indian that he shall stay in one place, while he sees white men going where they please. They cannot tell me.

I only ask of the government to be treated as all other men are treated. If I cannot go to my own home, let me have a home in some country where my people will not die so fast. I would like to go to Bitter Root Valley. There my people would be healthy; where they are now they are dying. Three have died since I left my camp to come to Washington.

When I think of our condition my heart is heavy. I see men of my race treated as outlaws and driven from country to country, or shot down like animals.

I know that my race must change. We can not hold our own with the white men as we are. We only ask an even chance to live as other men live. We ask to be recognized as men. We ask that the same law shall work alike on all men. If the Indian breaks the law, punish him by the law. If the white man breaks the law, punish him also.

Let me be a free man—free to travel, free to stop, free to work, free to trade where I choose, free to choose my own teachers, free to follow the religion of my fathers, free to think and talk and act for myself—and I will obey every law, or submit to the penalty.

Whenever the white man treats an Indian as they treat each other, then we will have no more wars. We shall all be alike—brothers of one father and one mother, with one sky above us and one country around us, and one government for all. Then the Great Spirit Chief who rules above will smile upon this land, and send rain to wash out the bloody spots made by brothers' hands from the face of the earth. For this time the Indian race are waiting and praying. I hope that no more groans of wounded men and women will ever go to the ear of the Great Spirit Chief above, and that all people may be one people. In-mut-too-yah-lat-lat has spoken for his people.

"

compel: force.

Chief Joseph and the Nez Percés were never allowed to return to their home in the Wallowa Valley. Instead, they were moved to the Colville Reservation in northern Washington during the mid-1880s. There Chief Joseph died in 1904 of "a broken heart," as the reservation doctor noted in his report.

Sources

Books

Aly, Bower, and Lucile Folse Aly, *American Short Speeches: An Anthology,* Macmillan, 1968.

Armstrong, Virginia Irving, compiler, *I Have Spoken: American History Through the Voices of the Indians,* Sage Books, 1971.

Beal, Merrill D., *"I Will Fight No More Forever": Chief Joseph and the Nez Percé War,* University of Washington Press, 1963.

Brown, Dee, *Bury My Heart at Wounded Knee: An Indian History of the American West,* Holt, 1970.

Haines, Francis, *The Nez Percés: Tribesmen of the Columbia Plateau,* University of Oklahoma Press, 1955.

Jones, Louis Thomas, *Aboriginal American Oratory: The Tradition of Eloquence Among the Indians of the United States,* Southwest Museum (Los Angeles), 1965.

Josephy, Alvin M., Jr., *The Nez Percé Indians and the Opening of the Northwest,* Yale University Press, 1965.

McLuhan, T. C., *Touch the Earth: A Self-Portrait of Indian Existence,* Outerbridge & Dienstfrey, 1971.

Nabokov, Peter, editor, *Native American Testimony: A Chronicle of Indian-White Relations from Prophecy to the Present, 1492–1992,* Penguin Books, 1991.

Notable Native Americans, Gale, 1995.

Rosenstiel, Annette, *Red and White: Indian Views of the White Man, 1492–1982,* Universe Books, 1983.

Sanders, Thomas E., and Walter W. Peek, *Literature of the American Indian,* Glencoe Press, 1973.

Vanderwerth, W. C., *Indian Oratory: Famous Speeches by Noted Indian Chieftains,* University of Oklahoma Press, 1971.

Witt, Shirley Hill, and Stan Steiner, editors, *The Way: An Anthology of American Indian Literature,* Knopf, 1972.

Susette LaFlesche

(Bright Eyes, Inshta Theamba)
1854–1903

Activist and writer of the Omaha tribe

> "IT CRUSHED OUR
> HEARTS WHEN WE SAW A
> LITTLE HANDFUL OF
> POOR, IGNORANT,
> HELPLESS, BUT PEACEFUL
> PEOPLE ... OPPRESSED BY
> A MIGHTY NATION."

During the late nineteenth and early twentieth centuries, several of the most prominent Native Americans in the country were members of a single family, the LaFlesches. Chief Joseph LaFlesche, also known as Iron Eye, headed the Omaha reservation in Nebraska. His son Francis, an expert on Omaha customs, was the first Native American to become a professional anthropologist. The chief's daughter Susan was the first Native American woman to graduate from a U.S. medical school. Perhaps the best known of Iron Eye's children, however, was his daughter Susette. Her efforts as a lecturer and a writer focused public attention on the often tragic consequences of the government's Indian resettlement policies.

Early Life

Susette LaFlesche was born on the Omaha reservation of mixed Native American and white heritage. Her father strongly encouraged his people to become Christians and adopt other traditions of white society. So obtaining an American-style education was of great importance in the LaFlesche household. Susette attended a Presbyterian mission school on the reservation until it closed when she was in her early teens. A couple of years later, she enrolled in the Elizabeth Institute for Young Ladies in Elizabeth, New Jersey. There she excelled as a student of both literature and writing, mastering the English language and gaining a thorough knowledge of American culture. After graduating in 1875, Susette returned to Nebraska. She eventually obtained a teaching position at the Omaha reservation school.

Around this same time, the Omahas watched with concern and fear as members of a neighboring tribe, the Poncas, were forcibly removed from their land in northern Nebraska and relocated to Indian Territory in present-day Oklahoma. (See box on page 118–119 for more information.) Many of the Omahas (including the LaFlesches) had family ties to the Poncas. Even more disturbing was the thought that the Omahas might be the next tribe ordered to move.

Rallies Support for Chief Standing Bear and the Poncas

Before long, the controversy had captured national attention. During the winter of 1878–79, Chief Standing Bear of the Poncas left Indian Territory without official permission to lead a group of his people back to their homeland in Nebraska. There he was arrested and brought to trial. One of those who testified on his behalf was Susette LaFlesche. Compelled by her own anger and sadness over Standing Bear's problems, she had begun challenging the government on behalf of the Poncas. Thanks in part to the information she assembled and presented in court, the chief received a favorable ruling, and the Poncas were eventually granted new reservation lands in Nebraska.

From then on, LaFlesche devoted herself to investigating and publicizing conditions among resettled Indians. She also **lobbied** for Indian rights in general.

In late 1879, for example, she and her half-brother, Francis, went on a lecture tour of the eastern United States.

lobbied: attempted to influence or persuade legislators to promote a program or policy.

*Accompanying them was Chief Standing Bear. Over the next six months, the three appeared before civic groups, literary clubs, and various organizations interested in Indian welfare. Using her Indian name, Bright Eyes, Susette LaFlesche served as Standing Bear's interpreter. She also spoke on her own as an **advocate** for him and his people. On November 25, she delivered the following speech to an audience in Boston, Massachusetts. It is reprinted here from Judith Anderson's* Outspoken Women: Speeches by American Women Reformers, 1635–1935, *Kendall/Hunt Publishing Company, 1984. LaFlesche's remarks were originally published in the* Boston Daily Advertiser *on November 26, 1879.*

,,

I have lived all my life, with the exception of two years, which I spent at school in New Jersey, among my own tribe, the Omahas, and I have had an opportunity, such as is **accorded** to but few, of hearing both sides of the "Indian question." I have at times felt bitterly toward the white race, yet were it not for some who have shown all kindness, generosity and sympathy toward one who had no claims on them but that of common humanity, I shudder to think what I would now have been. As it is, my faith in justice and God has sometimes almost failed me but, I thank God, only almost.

It crushed our hearts when we saw a little handful of poor, ignorant, helpless, but peaceful people, such as the Poncas were, **oppressed** by a mighty nation, a nation so powerful that it could well have afforded to show justice and humanity if it only would. It was so hard to feel how powerless we were to help those we loved so dearly when we saw our relatives forced from their homes and **compelled** to go to a strange country at the point of the bayonet.

The whole Ponca tribe were rapidly advancing in civilization; cultivated their farms, and their schoolhouses and churches were well filled, when suddenly they were informed that the government required their removal to Indian Territory. My uncle said it came so suddenly upon them that they could not realize it at first, and they felt stunned and help-

advocate: promoter, supporter.

accorded: granted, given.

oppressed: crushed or persecuted through the abuse of power or authority.

compelled: forced.

less. He also said if they had had any idea of what was coming, they might have successfully resisted; but as it was, it was carried rigidly beyond their control. Every objection they made was met by the word "soldier" and "bayonet."

The Poncas had always been a peaceful tribe, and were not armed, and even if they had been they would rather not have fought. It was such a cowardly thing for the government to do! They sold the land which belonged to the Poncas to the Sioux, without the knowledge of the owners, and, as the Poncas were perfectly helpless and the Sioux well armed, the government was not afraid to move the friendly tribe.

The tribe has been robbed of thousands of dollars' worth of property, and the government shows no **disposition** to return what belongs to them. That property was lawfully theirs; they had worked for it; the **annuities** which were to be paid to them belonged to them. It was money promised by the government for land they had sold to the government. I desire to say that all annuities paid to Indian tribes by the government are in payment for land sold by them to the government, and are not charity. The government never gave any **alms** to the Indians, and we all know that through the "kindness" of the "Indian ring" they do not get the half of what the government actually owes them. It seems to us sometimes that the government treats us with less consideration than it does even the dogs.

For the past hundred years the Indians have had none to tell the story of their wrongs. If a white man did an injury to an Indian he had to suffer in silence, or being **exasperated** into revenge, the act of revenge has been spread abroad through the newspapers of the land as a causeless act, **perpetrated** on the whites just because the Indian delighted in being savage.

It is because I know that a majority of the whites have not known of the cruelty practiced by the "Indian ring" on a handful of oppressed, helpless and conquered people, that I have the courage and confidence to appeal to the people of the United States. I have said "a conquered people." I do not know that I have the right to say that. We are helpless, it is true; but at heart we do not feel that we are a conquered people. We are human beings; God made us as well as you; and

disposition: inclination.

annuities: payments made on a regular schedule, usually once a year.

alms: charity.

exasperated: pushed to the point of extreme impatience or frustration.

perpetrated: carried out.

Chief Standing Bear and the Poncas

In 1879, national attention was focused on one of the most famous court cases in Native American history, the sad story of Chief Standing Bear and his people, a small, peaceful tribe known as the Poncas. At the heart of the case was the debate over the "personhood" of Indians. Many Americans believed at the time that an Indian was not really a person. Therefore, Indians were not entitled to enjoy the same individual civil rights guaranteed to whites under the terms of the Constitution—including the right to live where they wanted and to move around freely.

Chief Standing Bear's troubles dated back to 1858, when the Poncas reluctantly reached an agreement with the U.S. government that established their territory within a small reservation in northeastern Nebraska. Ten years later, however, the U.S. government negotiated a treaty with the Sioux Indians that basically overturned the earlier agreement with the Poncas. The new treaty gave Ponca lands to the Sioux without the knowledge or consent of the Poncas. In 1877, the Poncas endured yet another injustice when Congress ordered the U.S. Army to relocate the tribe to Indian Territory, hundreds of miles away in present-day Oklahoma. The journey was a heartbreaking one. Of the nearly six hundred Poncas who made the trip, about one-third died of disease or starvation within months after their arrival. Many others were left sick and disabled.

Among the dead were two of Standing Bear's children. Determined to return the bones of his son to the tribe's ancestral burial grounds in Nebraska, the chief left Indian Territory during the winter of 1878 to 1879. In doing so, he apparently ignored federal regulations that required him to ask the local Indian agent for permission first. Accompanied by thirty of his people—men, women, and children—he slowly made his way back to Nebraska. At the end of their three-month walk, the Poncas stayed for a while with the Omahas. It was on the Omaha reservation that Standing Bear was arrested by U.S. Army officers in April 1879.

The arrest sparked disbelief and outrage among the Omahas. The story attracted wider attention after Standing Bear vividly described his tribe's experiences to a newspaper reporter in the city of Omaha and then repeated it to members of a local church. "We told them [the government officials] that we would rather die than leave our lands," explained Standing Bear,

we are peculiarly his because of our ignorance and helplessness. I seem to understand why Christ came upon the earth and wandered over it, homeless and hated of all men. It brings him so much nearer to us to feel that he has suffered as we suffer, and can understand it all—suffered that we might feel that we belonged to him and were his own.

Susette LaFlesche

"but we could not help ourselves.... We were weak and sick and starved...."

Later that same year, Standing Bear went on a lecture tour of the eastern United States and shared his tragic story with others. He usually appeared on stage in traditional Ponca clothing while Susette LaFlesche interpreted for him. Afterwards, she often gave an eloquent speech of her own asking for justice for the Poncas.

Once the true reasons behind Standing Bear's decision to leave Indian Territory became more widely known, Congress was flooded with angry letters from people who were outraged by the treatment the chief had received. Federal authorities still would not reconsider their decision to take the case to court. They maintained that under the Constitution, Indians were not persons and therefore had no rights. They insisted that Standing Bear had to return to Indian Territory—even though he had reportedly broken up his tribe and said that he wanted to adopt white ways.

In the end, Federal Judge Elmer S. Dundy ruled in favor of Standing Bear. He declared that Indians were indeed persons under the laws of the United States. Therefore, he continued, no one had the power to hold Standing Bear in custody or force him to return to Indian Territory. This ruling made Judge

Standing Bear

Dundy the first government official to recognize the rights of individual Indians to personal freedom and legal protection.

Standing Bear was at last allowed to complete the sad task that had brought him back to Nebraska in the first place. At the urging of Susette LaFlesche and others, Congress launched an investigation into Ponca claims against the government. In 1880, federal authorities granted the tribe land for a reservation in Nebraska. There Standing Bear lived out his remaining years. He died in 1908 at the age of nearly eighty.

I will relate a single instance out of many, given me by my father, who knows the individuals concerned in it. I do not select it because it exceeds in horrors others told me by my Indian friends, but because it happens to be freshest in my memory. My father said there was in the Pawnee tribe a warrior holding a prominent position and respected by all the

Indians. A white man was given the position on the reservation of government farmer for the Pawnee tribe. The Pawnees expected, of course, that he would go around among them and teach them how to plough [plow] and plant. Instead of doing that, he had fenced in a large piece of land, and had that sown and planted with grain and produce of all kinds. The Indians planted it and thought they would receive a part, at least, of the harvest. They never got any of it.

The warrior mentioned above was one day in the field killing the blackbirds which had alighted in the field in large numbers. While engaged in doing this the powder gave out. He went to the government farmer's house to ask for more. He saw a jewelled **flask** hanging up in the outside of the door, and as the farmer came to the door he pointed to his gun to show that it was empty, and motioned to the flask to make known that he wanted some more powder. The government farmer shook his head and refused. The Indian, thinking he had misunderstood, raised his arm to take the flask to show him what he wanted. The government farmer, I suppose, thinking he, the Indian, intended to take the flask without his permission, raised a broadax lying on the ground, swung it in the air, and at one blow chopped the man's arm and cut into his side. The farmer then fled.

The Pawnee Indians gathered around the dying warrior, and were making preparations for war on the white people in revenge for the deed, but the dying man made them promise him that they would do nothing in return. He said, "I am dying, and when I am dead you cannot bring me back to life by killing others. The government will not listen to you, but will listen to the farmer and send its soldiers and kill many of you, and you will all suffer for my sake. Let me die in peace and know you will not have to suffer for me." They promised him, and none but the Indian people ever knew anything about it.

It is wrongs such as these which, **accumulating**, exasperate the Indians beyond endurance and prompt them to deeds of vengeance, which, to those who know only one side of the story, seem savage **barbarism**, and the Indians are looked upon with horror as beings whose thirst for blood is ever **unslaked**. I tell you we are human beings, who love and hate as you do. Our affections are as strong, if not stronger, than

flask: a narrow-necked container.

accumulating: adding up.

barbarism: backwardness, lacking a civilized nature.

unslaked: unsatisfied, unquenched.

yours; stronger in that we are powerless to help each other, and can only suffer with each other.

Before the tribal relations were voluntarily broken up by the Omahas, my father was a chief. He helped make some of the treaties with the government. He had been acquainted with the last eighteen agents who have **transacted** the business for one tribe on the part of the government, and out of those eighteen agents four only were good and honest men.

The following instance will show how these agents **squandered** the money of the tribe. About four years ago one of them, without **counselling** the tribe, had a large handsome house built ... at the expense of the Omaha tribe. The building was intended by the agent, he said, for an **infirmary**, but he could not get any Indian to go into it, and it has never been used for anything since. It is of no use to the tribe, but it was a good job for the contractors. The tribe is now **endeavoring** to have it altered, to use it as a boarding school for the Indian children.

I have been intimately acquainted with the affairs of the Poncas. The Poncas and Omahas speak the same language and have always been friends, and thus I have known all their sorrows and troubles. Being an Indian, I, of course, have a deep interest in them. So many seem to think that Indians fight because they delight in being savage and are bloodthirsty. Let me relate one or two instances which serve to show how powerless we are to help ourselves.

Some years ago an Omaha man was missed from one of our tribes. No one could tell what had become of him. Some of our people went to look for him. They found him in a pigpen, where he had been thrown to the hogs after having been killed by the white men.

Another time a man of our tribe went to a settlement about ten miles distant from our reserve to sell potatoes. While he stood sorting them out two young men came along. They were white men, and one of them had just arrived from the East; he said to his companion, "I should like to shoot that Indian, just to say that I had shot one." His companion **badgered** him to do it. He raised his revolver and shot him.

transacted: carried out.
squandered: wasted.
counselling: consulting.
infirmary: medical clinic.
endeavoring: trying.
badgered: urged to the point of harassment.

Four weeks ago, just as we were starting on this trip, a young Indian boy of sixteen was stabbed by a white boy of thirteen. The stabbing took place near my house. The white people in the settlements around wondered that the Indian allowed the white boy to stab him, when he was so much older and stronger. It was because the Indian knew, as young as he was, that if he struck a blow to defend himself, and injured the boy in defending himself, the whole tribe would be punished for his act; that troops might be sent for and war made on the tribe. I think there was heroism in that boy's act.

For wrongs like these we have no **redress** whatever. We have no protection from the law. The Indians all know that they are powerless. Their chiefs and leading men had been to Washington, and have returned to tell their people of the mighty nation which fills the land once theirs. They know if they fight that they will be beaten, and they only fight when they are driven to desperation or are at the last extremity; and when they do at last fight, they have none to tell their side of the story, and it is given as a reason that they fight because they are bloodthirsty.

I have come to you to appeal for your sympathy and help for my people. They are immortal beings, for whom Christ died. They asked me to appeal to the churches, because they had heard that they were composed of God's people, and to the judges because they righted all wrongs. The people who were once owners of this soil ask you for their liberty, and law is liberty.

99

LaFlesche's speeches during this well-publicized East Coast tour quickly established her as an Indian rights activist. Her words made a deep impression on her listeners. Among them were some of the most famous public figures of the day, including the poet Henry Wadsworth Longfellow. Many reform-minded people who had once been active in the fight against slavery turned their attention to the cause of Indian rights when they heard LaFlesche speak about the nation's unjust treatment of its native population.

redress: compensation, a way of righting a wrong done to someone.

LaFlesche spent most of the next few years on the road, lecturing extensively and even testifying on several occasions before Congress on conditions among the Omaha and Ponca tribes. In 1887, she took her message about the need for reform in Indian policy to overseas audiences during a ten-month speaking tour throughout England and Scotland.

Upon returning to America, LaFlesche settled once again in Nebraska. There she began a second career as a successful writer. She published numerous articles and stories (some for children) in a variety of midwestern newspapers and magazines, often under the name Bright Eyes.

Sources

Books

Anderson, Judith, *Outspoken Women: Speeches by American Women Reformers, 1635–1935,* Kendall/Hunt Publishing Company, 1984.

Armstrong, Virginia Irving, *I Have Spoken: American History Through the Voices of the Indians,* Sage Books, 1971.

Brown, Dee, *Bury My Heart at Wounded Knee: An Indian History of the American West,* Holt, 1970.

Brown, Marion M., *Susette LaFlesche: Advocate for Native American Rights,* Children's Press, 1992.

Clifton, James A., editor, *On Being and Becoming Indian: Biographical Studies of North American Frontiers,* Dorsey Press, 1989.

Nabokov, Peter, editor, *Native American Testimony: A Chronicle of Indian-White Relations from Prophecy to the Present, 1492–1992,* Penguin Books, 1991.

Notable Native Americans, Gale, 1995.

Wilson, Dorothy Clarke, *Bright Eyes: The Story of Susette LaFlesche,* McGraw-Hill, 1974.

Wilma Mankiller

1945–

Leader of the Cherokee tribe

"I THINK I CAN SAY WITHOUT THE TINIEST BIT OF FALSE PRIDE THAT WE ARE ONE OF THE MOST PROGRESSIVE TRIBES IN THE U.S. TODAY."

In 1987, Wilma Mankiller made history when she became the first woman elected chief of a major Native American tribe, the Cherokee Nation. Her victory was even more remarkable because it required her to overcome many obstacles, including poverty, racism, sexism, and several close brushes with death. As leader of the Cherokee Nation, Mankiller worked tirelessly to bring economic prosperity to her people while seeing to their many social and cultural needs as well. In the process, she became a near-legend in the Native American community for her dedication and compassion.

Early Life

Mankiller was born in Tahlequah, Oklahoma—the capital of the Cherokee Nation—to a Cherokee father named Charlie and a mother of Dutch and Irish background. (The family name comes from an old Indian military title meaning "one who safeguards the village.") One of eleven children in a close-knit and happy family, she spent the first ten years of her life not far from her birthplace. But every day was a struggle for the Mankillers. Barely able to get by on the few crops Charlie raised and sold, they finally accepted an offer from the federal government to move them to California. This was one of many thousands of such moves arranged by the Bureau of Indian Affairs during the 1950s to help "urbanize" Native Americans and make them blend in with mainstream white society.

In California, the Mankillers settled in a San Francisco ghetto. Life did not improve for them, however. The children were desperately homesick and had to put up with racist insults from their classmates at school. And Charlie Mankiller had trouble landing a steady job.

Eventually, however, the Mankillers adjusted to living in the city. Wilma finished high school and went on to college at San Francisco State during the 1960s with the goal of becoming a social worker. During this period she began associating with a group of young Native American activists. Through them, she gained a better understanding of her heritage that made her proud to be an Indian.

In 1969, some of these activists occupied Alcatraz Island in San Francisco Bay to protest the U.S. government's mistreatment of Indian people and to reclaim their treaty rights. Mankiller worked on the outside to round up support for the demonstrators. Her efforts drew her further into the growing American Indian Movement. By 1975, she had left California to return to Oklahoma and what she hoped would be an opportunity to work on behalf of the Cherokee people.

Survives a Near-Fatal Accident and Serious Illness

Mankiller spent the next few years developing and carrying out a number of economic and social self-help programs in the Cherokee community. She also resumed her education, this time at the University of Arkansas in Fayetteville. While driving back home after class one morning in late 1979, she was involved in a car accident. By coincidence, the driver of the other car was one of Mankiller's best friends. Mankiller was critically injured, and her friend was killed. Not long afterward, Mankiller was diagnosed with a serious muscle disease, myasthenia gravis. All of this was compounded by the kidney problems she had been suffering from since the early 1970s—problems that eventually became severe enough to require a kidney transplant.

Mankiller struggled for nearly a year to overcome the physical and emotional shock of everything that had happened to her. Once she was able to work again, she took up where she had left off. As director of the Cherokee Nation Community Development Department, she set up programs to help her people help themselves, mostly in the areas of health care and housing.

Mankiller's success soon attracted the attention of tribal leaders, including Principal Chief **Ross Swimmer** (see entry). In 1983, he asked her to be his running mate (for the post of deputy chief) in his reelection campaign. Despite facing opposition from some male members of the tribe who felt that a woman had no business being in the race, Swimmer and Mankiller managed to win by a narrow margin. Two years later, Swimmer resigned to head the Bureau of Indian Affairs during the administration of President Ronald Reagan. Mankiller then took over as principal chief, making her the first woman ever to hold the position.

Elected Principal Chief of the Cherokee Nation

In 1987, Mankiller decided to seek election as principal chief in her own right. Once again, she faced resistance. Some of the men, for example, were still not convinced that a woman should be chief. Also, Mankiller's continuing health problems were of concern. But with the encouragement and support of her husband, Charlie Soap, she was able to gather up enough strength and determination to defeat her opponent.

On August 14, 1987, in the Cherokee Nation capital of Tahlequah, Mankiller faced her people as their newly-elected principal chief and told them of her hopes and plans for the future. Her historic inaugural address is excerpted here from Native American Reader: Stories, Speeches and Poems, edited by Jerry D. Blanche, Denali Press, 1990.

❝

Good afternoon. I'd like to tell you how truly delighted I am to be here today. There's no greater honor I've ever had than to be chosen by my own people to lead them....

I heard someone say this week, "How are all these 'ordinary' people elected to the tribal council going to make the weighty decisions for the Cherokee Nation?" I can tell you quite frankly that "ordinary" people take very seriously the responsibility and trust that has been given them. I think you'll see a change in these people who have been elected to make decisions for you, merely from the weight of that responsibility. People say that crisis changes people and turns ordinary people into wiser or more responsible ones. As crises develop within the Cherokee Nation and we begin to resolve those crises, you will see many changes.

I'd like to talk just a little about the Cherokee Nation, where I see us today and where I see us going in the future. I think I can say without the tiniest bit of false pride that we are one of the most progressive tribes in the U.S. today. That progress we enjoy today, the Cherokee Nation that you see today—a very progressive, large, diverse organization—is not the result of the work of one person. It's the work of many, many people. There are a lot of people who laid the foundation for the work we're doing today....

We've grown very rapidly in the past fifteen years, just in the past ten years that I've been associated with the tribe. That growth has been phenomenal, and the **manifestation** of the growth over the past fifteen years is all around you. You can see the new Hastings Hospital, Cherokee Nation Industries, Cherokee Gardens, rural health clinics, the Head Start centers and many other examples of this growth. When I came to the Cherokee Nation ten years ago, there were two hundred or three hundred tribal employees. There are now well over seven hundred permanent employees, and several hundred more have seasonal employment.

That growth has not occurred without problems. Growth is a painful process. I'd like everybody to remember that we're still growing, we're still young. In the totality of Cherokee history, fifteen years isn't very long. And we've got many

manifestation: evidence; display.

more painful processes to work through before we reach a point where we will level off.

Our overall goal determined by the last tribal council and the last chief and deputy chief was a goal of self-sufficiency as total independence from federal aid. That's not at all what we mean. I personally think that the U.S. government owes us much in federal aid. We paid for much of what we receive today in lost lives and lost land. Our interpretation of self-sufficiency could simply be described as capability—the capability to do things for ourselves ... the capability to do things with some assistance from the BIA [Bureau of Indian Affairs], but basically running the tribe ourselves ... with some assistance from the IHS [Indian Health Service], but making the decisions ourselves. If you'll look where we are today, we're well on our way to self-sufficiency. Many people talk about self-sufficiency, self-reliance and **self-determination** in a **rhetorical** sense, but to translate that into reality is a very difficult task that I think the Cherokee Nation is doing fairly well.

We have an excellent group of elected officials, a very diverse group of people from various areas throughout the Cherokee Nation, from various backgrounds. We have some very serious challenges ahead of us. I will talk very briefly about one related to the constitution. Because the rest of the United States is talking about the U.S. Constitution, I'm going to talk about the Cherokee constitution.

In this election of 1987, the Cherokee voters overwhelmingly passed an amendment to our Constitution which would allow the council members to be elected by districts. One of the major tasks of this newly elected tribal council, the legislative body of the tribe, is to develop a plan for districting. That is a monumental undertaking. The voters have said "we want districting," but the details have to be worked out during the next four years.

I also think there's a need for a constitutional convention. In fact, our constitution requires us to have one within the next fifteen years. The reason we review our constitution is the same reason the U.S. government reviews its Constitution—it should reflect the collective values of the Cherokee people. As time changes our values and needs, the constitution needs a new look and some amendments. This amend-

self-determination: freedom to choose one's own political future.

rhetorical: questioning something for effect without expectation of an answer.

Wilma Mankiller

ment we just passed is the first to our constitution, but I certainly don't think it's the last. The Cherokee constitution ... basically provides a legal **infrastructure** for our government. That's our Bible, everything we do follows that so that's one of the very important challenges we have to undertake in the next four years....

Another important task we face is that of protecting tribal rights. By tribal rights, I mean the protection of those rights that are **afforded** us because we are tribal government. This is something that I, the deputy chief, and the tribal council are going to have to spend a great deal of time on. There are powerful anti-Indian lobbyists who are constantly trying to **diminish** tribal rights, and I think that what we have to do is constantly protect our tribal rights. Many of the services and programs we enjoy today are a direct result of the special government-to-government relationship with the U.S. government that has to be protected.

I also believe that we need to concentrate on the stimulation and development of the economy in this area. As I've told many of you before, we can't do economic development in a vacuum. We don't have the resources to do that by ourselves. We have to work in a team effort with the Oklahoma Chamber of Commerce, state government, local bankers, and the business community to develop the economy of this area. Oklahoma in general is suffering from a depressed economy. I believe the Cherokees are suffering even more. Our people are very hardworking. That's a well known fact. You can look at Cherokee Gardens, Cherokee Nation Industries, many of the industries in Arkansas that recruit and bus Cherokees across the border into Arkansas because they are good workers. We have hardworking people, but many of them don't have a place to work. One of our priorities is searching for ways to develop the economy of this area. That's critical.

We also must continue to move our health care system outward. When we proposed this eight or nine years ago, it seemed like a **radical** idea. At that time we didn't have rural health clinics and we were only developing a tribal-specific health plan and talking about moving services closer to the people. Today that's a reality. We have many clinics in outlying areas and are looking at developing more. We should

infrastructure: underlying foundation.

afforded: provided, granted.

diminish: decrease.

radical: revolutionary.

Mankiller with President Ronald Reagan, 1988

look very closely at our whole health care system and begin to place more emphasis on prevention and education.

With all of the progressive work we do in economic development, protection of tribal rights and in running a very complex organization, we must not forget who we are. We must pay attention to the protection and preservation of tribal culture. There are many definitions of tribal culture but we must sit down and define for ourselves those things we consider important to protect for future generations. In the past, promotion of tribal culture has been viewed as a function of the community and family, not of tribal government. But we've reached a point where we need to assume a leadership role. We need to explore what we as a government can do to promote and protect our culture.

Wilma Mankiller

I don't think that anybody, anywhere can talk about the future of their people or of an organization without talking about education. Whoever controls the education of our children controls our future, the future of the Cherokee people and of the Cherokee Nation. There are many new programs I'm going to propose and I'm sure the council will propose regarding education. We're doing a lot of innovative things in education but there's more we can do. We have always placed a great deal of importance on education and that has helped us as a people. We must continue to do that.

In our education programs, I would like to incorporate education about tribal government and tribal history. If we know where we've been as a people, our history, our culture and our ancestry we have a better sense of where we are today, and certainly, a better sense of where we're going.

I've talked about some of the battles we face in terms of education, economic development. It is easy to talk about these problems but it takes the teamwork of many people to address them.

Finally, while there are a lot of external threats to the Cherokee Nation, the really great threat is one that is internal.

As any young organization and as officials elected to tribal government, we must develop an environment where dissent and disagreement can be handled in a respectful way. Dissent is natural and good. Out of respectful dissent and disagreement comes change that is usually positive. As tribal officials we can set an example how to disagree in a respectful and good way. We all have many goals for our tribe that will require myself, the deputy chief, the tribal council, the tribal citizens and tribal employees working together to reach.

We certainly can't do it if we focus on our disagreements. If we begin to focus on the things that we agree, we can forge ahead. We come from different backgrounds and certainly we're going to disagree. We must figure a way to balance that and the things we can work. The darkest pages in Cherokee history, the greatest tragedies that occurred to us as a people came when we were divided internally.

People say I'm a positive person, that I focus on positive things. I do. We've done a lot. I'm very proud of the Cherokee Nation, I'm very proud of the many people in our communities, I'm very proud of our history, I'm proud to be Cherokee. But that doesn't mean I don't know there are a lot of serious problems in our organization, that there are a lot of serious problems we still face in the communities and that I don't realize how much work remains to be done. As we continue to work on these problems, we need to be aware that the things we do will have a profound effect on the future of the Cherokee Nation, its government and the Cherokee people.

We take our responsibility extremely seriously. We work very hard and we welcome your input. As I said, we didn't acquire instant wisdom by being elected but we do take our jobs seriously and I think you'll see that over the next four years.

This is a very exciting time for me, for all these people. I hope that in the next four years we return in a very real sense to the golden era of the Cherokee Nation....

With that, I ask for your continued support throughout the next four years. You have certainly been supportive during this time, during the election and during the eighteen months I served as principal chief prior to the election. I thank all of those who helped me....

So with that, again, I'd like to thank you for your attention, hope you'll stay very involved in the Cherokee Nation and continue to give us your ideas, your support and your prayers....

99

Once in office, Mankiller remained true to her promise to stress economic development and various social welfare programs, especially those having to do with education, housing, and health care. She also took steps to build up the self-esteem of her people and help them make the change from the old ways to the new while preserving what is best about their culture and value system. At the same time, Mankiller worked to overcome white society's stereotypes about Indians. These efforts brought her widespread recognition and honors, including being named to the National Women's Hall of Fame.

Mankiller with President Bill Clinton at a White House meeting between Indian leaders and the president, 1994

Mankiller has always downplayed her accomplishments. She preferred to share the glory with the people she felt were truly responsible for her success—namely, the employees, tribal council, and citizens of the Cherokee Nation. As she once declared, "It's up to all of us, every tribal member, to take part in making sure that we survive into the twenty-first century as a culturally distinct group of people. Every Cherokee, whether full-blood or mixed-blood, whether rich or poor, whether liberal or conservative, has a responsibility to honor our ancestors by helping to keep our government, our communities, and our people very strong."

To Mankiller, one of the most personally satisfying aspects of her success was that the opposition she once faced as a female chief gradually faded over time. "People *are used to me," she remarked at one point during her term in office. "I don't get treated differently than anybody else. If I do a good job, people are happy; if I do something they don't like, they let me know they are unhappy." In 1991, the Cherokee Nation's confidence in Mankiller's ability to govern was made clear when they re-elected her as their principal chief with over eighty percent of the vote.*

Retires after Serving Two Terms as Principal Chief

In April 1994, Mankiller announced that she would not seek reelection to a third term. She left office feeling certain that she had paved the way for other women to follow in her footsteps. And despite the many difficult problems still facing the Cherokee people, she thought that she had made some progress. "When I was younger, I was full of anger," she told an NEA Today *interviewer. "But you can't dwell on problems if you want to bring change, you must be motivated by hope, by the feeling you can make a difference."*

In her final "State of the Nation" address, delivered on September 3, 1994, Mankiller reflected on the accomplishments of her administration. She also thanked the many people who had stood by her through the years, "even if you didn't agree with me." Concluded the ever-modest Mankiller: "I have never overestimated my importance to the Cherokee Nation and Cherokee history. I don't think I leave any great legacy. I hope when I leave you will remember that I did what I said."

Sources

Books

Blanche, Jerry D., editor, *Native American Reader: Stories, Speeches and Poems,* Denali Press, 1990.

Mankiller, Wilma, and Michael Wallis, *Mankiller: A Chief and Her People,* St. Martin's, 1993.

Notable Native Americans, Gale, 1995.

Periodicals

Grand Rapids Press, "Outgoing Cherokee Chief Likes Nation's Direction," October 21, 1994, p. A9.

Ms., "Wilma Mankiller: Harnessing Traditional Cherokee Wisdom," August 1986, p. 32; January 1988, pp. 68–69.

NEA Today, "Wilma Mankiller: Destined to Lead," October 1994, p. 7.

News from Indian Country, "The Very Human Side of Cherokee Nation Chief Wilma Mankiller," January 31, 1994.

Parade, "She Leads a Nation," August 18, 1991, pp. 4–5.

People, "Activist Wilma Mankiller Is Set to Become the First Female Chief of the Cherokee Nation," December 1985, pp. 91–92.

Southern Living, "Chief of the Cherokee," November 1986, p. 190.

Time, "To Each Her Own: Combining Talent and Drive, Ten Tough-Minded Women Create Individual Rules for Success," fall 1990 (special issue); April 18, 1994, p. 27.

U.S. News and World Report, "'People Expect Me to Be More Warlike,'" February 17, 1986, p. 64.

Russell Means

1940–

Lakota activist

*One of the most vocal and visible Native American activists on the scene today is Russell Means. For more than twenty-five years, he has worked on behalf of indigenous peoples (people native to a certain region) throughout the world. Means first became a public figure during the early 1970s as one of the militant leaders of the American Indian Movement (AIM), a civil rights organization dedicated to improving the lives of Native Americans. (See entry on **Clyde Bellecourt** and **Vernon Bellecourt** for more information.) His forceful, often angry, power of speech as well as his striking physical presence and flair for drama quickly made him a symbol of AIM and its activities. During his involvement in the radical and sometimes violent Indian demonstrations of the 1970s, some Native Americans criticized Means as an arrogant man and a trouble-maker. But many of those who disagreed with some of his actions believed that Means brought much-needed hope to an oppressed people. Means left AIM during the late 1980s. Since then his tactics have changed greatly, but his goals,* *he says, remain the same. "My ultimate aim is the reinstitution of pride and self-dignity of the Indian in America."*

Early Life

An Oglala Sioux—or Lakota—Means was born in Porcupine, South Dakota, on the Pine Ridge Indian Reservation. He left there with his family at the age of six, however, and moved to California, where he grew up in and around the city of Oakland. Although trained as an accountant, he worked as a rodeo rider, Indian dancer, and ballroom dance instructor before returning to South Dakota in the late 1960s. There Means took a job in the tribal office on the Rosebud Reservation. In 1970, he left South Dakota for Cleveland, Ohio, where he headed the city's Indian Center.

Around this time, Means was introduced to the American Indian Movement, or AIM, when he attended an Indian conference in Minneapolis, Minnesota. AIM had been founded in 1968 by a group of Native American activists who believed that the federal government's supervision of Indian affairs would eventually lead to the total destruction of their people unless they took action to ensure their survival. This message greatly appealed to Means, who bitterly resented the fact that white society had forced him and his ancestors to give up their culture and their language.

Upon his return to Cleveland, Means established a local AIM chapter and immediately became involved in major AIM demonstrations across the country. On Thanksgiving Day of 1970, for example, he participated in the takeover of the Mayflower II, *a replica of the Pilgrims' ship, at Plymouth Rock in Massachusetts. And at South Dakota's Mount Rushmore, he was one of a number of Indians who set up a camp to dramatize Sioux claims to the Black Hills region.*

Returns to the Pine Ridge Reservation

Around 1972, having grown tired of living in the city, Means moved back to the Pine Ridge Reservation. There he gained personal fame as well as increased respect for AIM when he led a group of demonstrators across the state line into Nebraska to protest the brutal death of an Indian named Raymond Yellow Thunder. Two young white brothers had beaten up Yellow Thunder "just for fun." Then they paraded him around at a dance in the town of Gordon while inviting onlookers to kick him. Later, they stuffed him in a car trunk, where he died. AIM became involved in the case at the request of Yellow Thunder's family when it became obvious that local authorities did not plan to charge the brothers with any serious crime. Means successfully reached a settlement that resulted in the resignation of the police chief and a promise to deal with the racist attitudes that had led to Yellow Thunder's death.

Means went on to play key roles in many other AIM protests, among them the Trail of Broken Treaties march to Washington, D.C., in 1972. This was a march of about five hundred Native Americans protesting the government's policies toward Indians; after arriving in Washington to find an unreceptive government, Means led a takeover of the office of the Bureau of Indian Affairs that lasted for nearly a week. But he is no doubt best remembered for taking part in the 1973 occupation of the village of Wounded Knee on the Pine Ridge Reservation.

Achieves Fame as AIM Leader at Wounded Knee

The Wounded Knee incident began when several hundred AIM members and sympathizers rebelled against the reservation's head **administrator,** Dick Wilson. Most of Wilson's support came from Indians who believed that they should try to assimilate, or to set aside their native customs and become a part of white culture. Many of the tribal elders at Pine Ridge, however, wanted to maintain the old traditions. Some of them had also accused Wilson of corruption and **strong-arm tactics.** AIM activists agreed with the elders, and in a symbolic gesture of defiance, they took over the village of Wounded Knee. The choice of Wounded Knee was especially meaningful to them because in 1890 more than two hundred Sioux men, women, and children had been killed there by U.S. Army troops under orders to crush a spiritual movement known as the Ghost Dance.

When AIM took over at Wounded Knee, federal marshals and FBI agents were on the scene to reestablish control. This

administrator: a person appointed to manage and carry out the policies of others.

strong-arm tactics: methods of dealing with people that involve excess or undeserved force.

Madonna Gilbert, Lakota, Describes Wounded Knee Takeover

It was the traditional people who invited us down to Pine Ridge to help out in 1972 and 1973. At Calico, the elders said, What can we do to wake these Indians up? We have to take a stand somewhere! So we decided that the symbolic place would be Wounded Knee. What happened there was never expected; we figured we'd be there just two or three days, we were never told to bring food or anything, I just had my jacket and my purse! And my two kids! We didn't realize what was happening until we were surrounded. We never broke the law in any way or did one thing wrong; it was the feds who were breaking the law by being on the reservation without jurisdiction, without any real permission from the people. But the FBI made us out to be the criminals right away.... The first time me and Lorelei went out, we ran into a whole army of tribal police, sheriffs, U.S. marshals, FBI.... They handcuffed us, threw us in vans, called us "gooks" and a lot worse.... And that was America's elite with all their war toys—I mean, helicopters, APCs, the whole Vietnam number, blue jump suits, infrared lights, guns everywhere you looked; it was Wounded Knee and the Seventh Cavalry all over again.

From *In the Spirit of Crazy Horse*, 1991 edition, pp. 66–67.

touched off an armed standoff between the Indians and the U.S. government. Means served as one of the major spokespersons for the Native Americans during the seventy-one-day takeover and also helped negotiate with authorities. Afterwards, he and a number of other AIM leaders were arrested on various civil disobedience charges. Their eight-month trial ended when the judge threw the case out of court for misconduct on the part of government prosecutors.

By then, Means had become an international celebrity. With his solemn and intense looks—which were enhanced by his rough denim clothes, Indian jewelry, and long dark braids—he was indeed an impressive figure. He remained controversial both on and off the reservation, partly because some people felt he enjoyed being the center of attention a bit too much. In 1974, he lost a close election for tribal chairman to Dick Wilson. In his campaign, Means vowed to destroy the "white man's tribal government" and to reestablish "a type of government where all Indians would have a voice." Charges of corruption and illegal vote counting followed Means's narrow loss, increasing the hostile feelings between pro-AIM and anti-AIM forces.

Means became a target of some of those anti-AIM forces—over the next six years or so, he was shot at and wounded five separate times, arrested and charged with crimes four times, and sent to a South Dakota state prison. During the year he spent behind bars, he was stabbed by a fellow inmate. Most criminal charges against Means were connected with his participation in AIM activism. However, one of the charges against Means was for the 1975 murder of an Indian man in a bar in Scenic, South Dakota. Means was acquitted of those charges in 1976.

By the end of the 1970s there was internal division within the AIM organization. Although the group had organized under a national director—Dennis Banks—existing AIM factions from different geographical locations began to splinter off from the national coalition. Although he denied a "public split" with Dennis Banks, Means went off to lead the Dakota AIM. In 1981 this group and many traditional Lakota people established a camp on federal land in South Dakota, calling it Yellow Thunder Camp. This was a step in reclaiming the Black Hills land for Lakota use.

Champion of Native American Rights Worldwide

Despite many setbacks, Means continued his efforts to keep the concerns of Native American people in the forefront of the human rights movement throughout the 1970s and 1980s. Even though he left AIM in early 1988, he has remained much in demand around the world as a lecturer and spokesperson for various Indian causes. He has also testified before numerous governmental bodies, including a special U.S. Senate committee investigating the federal government's relationship with Native Americans.

The following speech on the state of Native American nations was delivered September 28, 1988, at a university in the western United States (perhaps Colorado). It is reprinted here from Native American Reader: Stories, Speeches and Poems, edited by Jerry D. Blanche, Denali Press, 1990. Means began his talk with an Oglala Lakota (Sioux) greeting, which he then translated for his audience.

66

What I said is, "Hello, my relatives. I am an ally, and I come from Yellow Thunder Camp in our very sacred holy land, the Black Hills."

Back in 1968–70, the state of the American Indian nations in the Americas of the Western Hemisphere was unchanged from 1492.... This is now 1988, and it still remains unchanged from 1492. In 1492 we were considered an "**expendable** people" by Columbus and the governments of Europe, including the Roman Catholic Church. It wasn't until 1897 ... that the Catholic Church declared us to be human beings....

We are an "expendable people." Go down to Brazil and you will see the government forcibly relocating and allowing miners and forestry employees to massively murder Indian people. Go to Paraguay where they still have bounties on the Aiche. Go to Chile, where [President Augusto] Pinochet is officially starving the Mapuche to get their remaining lands. Go to Costa Rica, where [the lumber and paper company] Weyerhauser is removing Indian people so they can get at their forests. Go to Nicaragua, where the entire government effort has not only relocated but mass murdered—and it continues to this day—the Indian people. Both the left or the right excuse it and would rather deal with dope dealers. Go to Mexico. Go to Alaska. Go to Canada. Come right here to the United States of America, where this government right here today, at this very moment, is relocating and starving to death and completely destroying an Indian nation, the Navajo, in Arizona....

Welcome to the Americas. Welcome to the Americas, my home, where the dust that you kick up as you walk is made up of the bones of my ancestors. Welcome. For what you have **appropriated** and for what we have given to you, I will tell you.

Sixty percent of the world's foodstuffs comes from us. Eighty percent of what the average American eats every day comes from us. Non-Indians are continually asking me, "What's some traditional Indian food?" What did you eat today? Did you go to a salad bar? That's all ours....

expendable: unimportant, not worth saving.

appropriated: grabbed, seized.

Sewage systems we gave to the Europeans. When Cortez and Pizarro and Coronado and all the rest of the conquistadors were over here destroying Indian people and our records, some of the people with them recognized that, hey, these Indians have sewage systems. Let's take it back to Europe and clean up Berlin and Rome and London and Madrid and Brussels, Paris. And voilà! In less than a generation the amount of disease and the plague that was **rampant** in Europe dramatically was reduced to less than one percent than what it had been before. Because of the introduction of sewage systems that we gave to the world.

I could go on and on and on....

Welcome to the Americas. But instead of the Europeans, the Asians, the Africans, the Middle Easterners, the Far Easterners ... saying "thank you," we are still an "expendable people." Does anyone talk about majority rule in Ecuador or Bolivia or Peru or Panama or the Northwest Territories of Canada or Guatemala? No. You don't hear about majority rule. Because those are Indians, *campesinos,* peasants. Do you see at the family of nations a red person sitting around the table with the family of nations? We are the only color of the human race not allowed to participate in the international community. That's an insult to your own humanity! Think about it! Look around! Your own humanity is being insulted! You live in this modern day and age when an entire people is not even considered to be a part of the international community....

[In] 1968 and 1969, 1970, Indians that protested back east were wearing Plains Indians outfits. American Indian people were attending conferences in ties, shined shoes and suits and bouffant hairdos, with pearl earrings on the women. They were afraid to wear beadwork, afraid to wear silver and turquoise. They were embarrassed to announce to the world that they are proud of who they are. I was fortunate to be in the vanguard of a cultural revolution that took place in the late 1960s and 1970s. That cultural revolution enabled our pride and self-dignity to once again become the criteria of what the American Indian nations are all about. It succeeded beyond our wildest plans and expectations, hopes or dreams.

When I sat in Minneapolis with **Clyde Bellecourt** [see entry] and Dennis Banks in 1969 and we took the American

rampant: widespread.

Indian Movement into a national and then international organization, I remember when we attended Indian conferences and they wouldn't allow us to speak because we looked "ridiculous" in headbands and beadwork and moccasins and we had a drum with us. Our own people.... That was the state of the American Indian nations.... The Indian people embarrassed about who they are.

It's changed that cultural revolution. We had to challenge the United States government militarily, and we won again! Again! Because we were right and we're still right.

But understand the state of the American Indian nations. Because we know. You see, at the advent of the opening up of half the world to the rest of the world, we allowed disease and overpopulation of Europe to dramatically decrease....

Means with Dennis Banks and other AIM members singing victory song after dismissal of charges in 1973 Wounded Knee takeover

But have you all learned? What's the disease today that's incurable? AIDS. The revolution comes around again, but this time there is no more Western Hemisphere, no more Indians.... There's no other place to go.

The message is the same: clean up. You want to cure AIDS? Clean it up. You want to cure all the other diseases, the cancers, every one that pops up every day? Clean up. As **Chief Seattle** [see entry] said, "Continue to contaminate your bed and one night you will suffocate in your own waste."

The state of the American Indian nations, that cultural revolution I was talking about of the 1970s. Here's the beauty of that experience: our traditional people gained respect. Our culture gained respect. And we're still struggling....

But let me tell you something about the state of the American Indian nations. There is Indian activism in virtually every Indian community. Wherever there's more than one Indian, there's activism.... And it's infected the world. Because of our cultural revolution the onslaught and attack on indigenous peoples worldwide is now **pervasive.**

They're getting our own people to call themselves "Native American." They're getting our own people to teach in universities like this about "we come from China." Understand that we do not come from China. That is a racist, a very racist concept that began with Thomas Jefferson, and he only wrote about it in passing, because of our physical characteristics. In fact, the reverse is true. **Geologists** know it's impossible for us to have migrated from the Western Hemisphere west. Because during the Ice Ages, the ice corridors that were formed along the northwest coasts of the Western Hemisphere made it impossible to migrate from here to the west, or, as the Europeans call it, the Far East....

Where are the **anthropologists** around here? Don't they ever visit with geologists? The archaeologists, the official grave robbers of intellectual institutions such as this? Any high school students that have aspirations towards robbing graves, I would suggest that it is one of the most disrespectful professions and dishonorable professions, if you want to call it that, in the world today. There are federal laws protecting grave robbers. What kind of ghouls are archaeologists?

pervasive: everywhere, widespread.

geologists: scientists who study rocks to learn about the history of the earth and life on it.

anthropologists: scientists who study the origins and physical, social, and cultural characteristics of human beings.

I live at Canyon de Chelly, on the Navajo [land] for **aeons**. Canyon de Chelly is part of a whole tourist route to go see where Indians used to live. Cliff-dwellers, they're called. The Anasazi people, they're called by "anthros" [anthropologists] and "archies" [archaeologists].... We never go there. We have respect for that. We have respect. But day in and day out tourists, non-Indian tourists are trampling all over those cliff dwellings. Every day of the year.... They want to know what happened. But you know that archaeologists and anthropologists will not consult with Indian people because that would prejudice their findings. So they have come to the conclusion by robbing some of our graves—and this is the most recent—that we were cannibals because these bones were all broken up and in mass graves in a mass area.

Of course, these graves are about six or seven thousand years old. They didn't take into account any earthquakes or a coyote or two hanging around digging up the earth or moles or worms, etc. They didn't even go over to the Hopi and say, "Hey, guys, how do you bury your people?" They came to the conclusion we're cannibals. I retorted that if I used the same criteria as anthropologists and archaeologists of these learned institutions, I will go to a Christian gravesite, dig up a grave, find a body in a coffin, and say, "Aha! Aha! The white man is saving his dead for future famines! They have found a way to preserve food." That's how ridiculous this grave-robbing has become in the **alleged** intellectual community. We have our own people believing this. In the same institutions not even protesting it!

I am sick and tired of the state of the American Indian. We had a beautiful cultural revolution, but you know what happens? The government and all institutions are making it even harder for us to know who we are. You see, in this country, the United States of America, the Indian people, we can be anything we want to be. Anything. We can even become archaeologists. But we can't be Indian. It's against the law in this country to be Indian. We can't pray. The last six decisions of the Supreme Court concerning our freedom of religion all denied it....

I'm going to give you a view of what American Indian people are doing to themselves, because we've become our own worst enemy.

aeons: a very long period of time—so long that it cannot be measured.

alleged: questionably true, so-called.

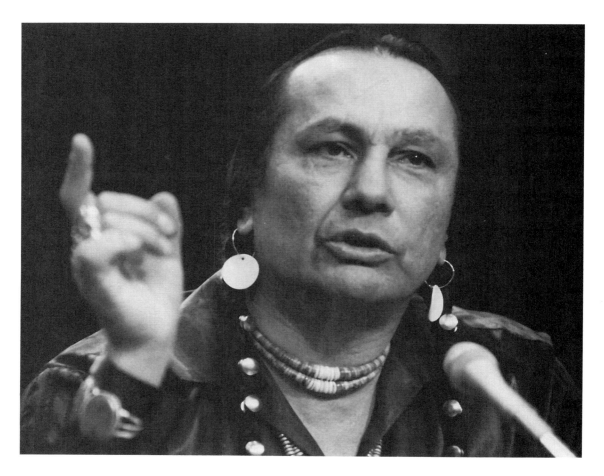

Means speaking in 1989: "The sanctity of life is too precious to allow this country to continue to be disrespectful."

Understand this about the U.S. government: they practice and perfect their colonialism on us, here, in the backyard of America, and then export it to the world.... We cannot, we do not have **self-determination**. It's called "self-administration," and that's my term. We get to **administer** someone else's policies.

Do you think Indian people are standing up? No. Do you know who they consider our leaders? The ones who suck off of Uncle Sam. Those are our alleged leaders, who are leaders by permission from the federal government. They're not my leader. Understand colonialism, where you're not allowed a choice of who your leaders are going to be. In fact, it insults your intelligence so much you refuse to participate in the society....

self-determination: freedom to choose one's own political future.

administer: carry out.

Russell Means

We still have a lot to give to the world. To be independent. We're not allowed to know who our heroes are. Our Indian children, every day, are bombarded with white and black heroes on TV and in school. And that's good, for the white children and the black children, and that didn't come without struggle. But our children—and you think our fancy, educated Indians are doing anything about making sure that their heroes are known to our own children? No. The only heroes they know, and that's because of us, AIM, are the ones from the last century.

What about our heroes from the first decade of this century? Or the second decades? Or the twenties? We had heroes, local and national heroes. And in the thirties, and the forties, and the fifties and the sixties and the seventies and the eighties. Our children don't know the names. In 1950 all the sports media in this country got together and they voted on who was the finest athlete in the first half century. You think they voted Jesse Owens? No! Jim Thorpe. They did it again in 1975....

I go around the Indian nation. I ask Indian teenagers and I ask Indian little kids. Just last week, I asked my daughter, who's in the third grade, "Who's Jim Thorpe?" "I don't know." And yet, one of the high schools on my reservation is called the Thorpes. Nobody on my reservation knows who Jim Thorpe is. None of the children.

I said, "Who's Billy Mills?" He won the 10,000 meters at [the Olympics in] Tokyo [Japan]. He's from my reservation. None of the kids know who Billy Mills is. That was just in 1964, for crying out loud....

I ask, "Who was the first Indian to become vice president of the United States of America?" Charles Curtis. [Curtis served with President Herbert Hoover from 1929 until 1933.] Everybody knows that, right? My own kids, other Indian kids don't know that.

I said, "Who's the first Indian ever to run for president of the United States?" I asked my daughter. She didn't know. I said, "It's your dad." [Means ran for president twice during the 1980s, once as the Libertarian candidate.]

But you see? I tell my own people: "Quit your complaining. You want to complain to somebody? Look in the mirror. And be a little bit independent."

But Indians and non-Indians: You're penalized today for being independent. If you're not part of the masses, you're penalized. Think about it. In every aspect of your life....

The state of the American Indian nations. I'm sick and tired of our own people. There's an entire people now in North Carolina who have Indian blood in their veins and want to be federally recognized. To me that's the **abomination** of what Indian people are. They actually believe that if you're federally recognized by the United States government, that somehow is a positive development. To me it is the most negative....

[Indian people] who refuse to be enrolled with their national ID number, refuse to recognize the United States of America, that is who our Indian leaders are. Not somebody funded by the federal government, funded by you all. You're the taxpayers. Funded by you. That's not my leader.

One thing about Indian people, and I just want to give you a small glimpse of who we are. Indian people are not tourists. We have homes that we never leave, and those that do are no longer Indian because they have no more connection.

Understand what that connection is. It's that dust I talked about earlier, that dust that comes from our Mother Earth. And only out of respect can you regain that. The Indian people are fooling themselves, not only in their culture, they've dropped their culture so they can call it a "powwow circuit," and they can dress any way they want to be, to the point where they fight their own people and are dependent on the federal government.

I come from the poorest county in the United States of America, the Pine Ridge Indian Reservation. The poorest county. I moved away from there last year to the home of my wife, a Navajo, Diné. Because that culturally is the way we do things. The man always moves to where the woman is from....

We have a way of life. We do not have a religion, we have a way of life. Our way of life is made up of one word: it's

abomination: something that provokes extreme disgust and hatred.

called "respect." But it means a lot more. Respect for our relatives' visions. When you understand that everything lives and that everything is sacred and the further you get away from what is natural the less important life becomes.

When you get yourselves locked into the asphalt jungles and there is no life, then even the human being's life is no longer important. My son, who is three years old, we live out on the Diné land in the desert, and I take him to the anthills and I show him and we sit there and we watch the ant people and I tell him about the ant people: "Have respect. Don't walk on their homes." He says, "Well, Reba does it." Reba's our horse. I say, "Reba's part of the earth. We know better."

If you have respect for the ant people then you'll have respect for people in Hiroshima. If you have respect for the ant people then you will have respect for people in Nicaragua or South Africa or anywhere else in the world.

The state of the Indian nation. Do you know the names of these mountains that are so beautiful right here, that you're so proud of you even put them on your license plates? When I moved down to Navajo, my wife didn't take me around. Just every time we traveled around she'd tell me the name of that mountain and that mountain and its history and whose land this is and what family has lived on that land and why.

This is the state of the Indian nations, but we're losing that because our educated Indians who have bought the white man's way will not allow our children to know our own heroes, our contemporary heroes, and what is beautiful and natural and respectful.

The state of the Indian nations. It's important that you know that you cannot break a branch when you're a child because you're breaking the arm of a living being. It's important to understand and be thankful for rain and not curse it because you have to walk in it. And to love the winter [snow], not because you can ski on it, but because it makes you strong as a person, as an individual.

If you know who you are I know who we are because I know the sacred colors. I know that pink stands for medicine. So I ask why? So my elders tell me. You go into the medicinal plants, all the plants that are good for you, inside the bud, not available to the naked eye. It's pink. Poisonous plants do not have that pink....

Have respect for colors. I know why orange is the color of water. And they say we primitives are not capable of abstract thought? I say, "Now wait a minute. How do you get orange the color of water? Why does that denote water?" Well, according to my nation, we live in the middle of a plains area. Orange is because when the moon comes up it's orange, and the moon controls water....

I know what orange means. To me it means the feminine power of birth. I know what it is to respect life because my grandfather told me my role in life, and I didn't know what he was talking about. I finally figured it out. Unfortunately, it took me thirty-seven years to figure it out. Because I had to go through sixteen years of white man education before I went back to school among my own people.

What I found out is that a long time ago, when the Lakota were sitting around the campfire, the men began to see the women grow with child. As they watched, they witnessed the miracle of life: birth. They watched a little longer and they saw that new life, that birth, being taken in the arms of woman and nurtured at her breast. They watched the child grow and become strong. Then they looked at one another. That was the end of my grandfather's story. I add this: The men looked at one another and said, "What are we doing here?"

So we look for the balance in life, the male-female balance of life which is in the universe, which is trapped in these trees, those grasses. All of life has a male-female balance, even you. If you understand the male-female balance then you don't have to worry about your rights, because every individual has a right.

In the 1970s, when I was younger and a militant and I wanted to change the world today, I went around to my people, **advocating** they pick up the gun. I said, "If we can't win let's get it over with. It's not worth watching the rape of our mother. It's not worth watching the massacre of her children. Let's get it over with."

But the old people would say, "Have patience, young man. Look around you. Understand who you are, where you come

advocating: promoting, supporting.

from, and why and where you are going. Understand that time is on your side and just because someone has invented a clock does not mean you have to hurry through life. Clocks are for those who are going to be trained to do the bidding of the master. Time is on your side. If you understand that you'll know how to utilize time. Therefore life is no longer a problem. Today is no longer a problem.... Nothing is a problem because you understand that there is no time."

The state of the American Indian nation. It's all good, and we don't have to pick up the gun because we understand about life. We understand that we don't need the gun because if that was true then all the grasshoppers in the world would get together and jump on you all. That doesn't happen. We understand immortality. The next world.

And immortality is today. You don't have to worry about tomorrow for peace of mind. That's why we're not tourists.

The old people will not travel for just any reason. I'll give you an example. Nineteen-eighty-two, the Bertrand Russell Tribunal, a very **formidable**, very **prestigious** international forum put together by **intellectuals** the world over, "anthros," and "archies," and all the alleged social scientists.... They decided to have a forum on the American Indians of the Western Hemisphere in Rotterdam [Netherlands] in 1982. So they invited us. And they came to us, the Indian people.

I was part of that.... We wanted our elders, our most revered elders, the traditional chiefs of our nation, to take our message over there.

So we arranged for our oldest chief, Fool's Crow, and his interpreter and another chief, Matthew King, a noble red man, to go over. We arranged a first class passage on an airplane. We got the St. Mark's Hotel in New York City to give them a three-bedroom suite free.

I was in our international affairs office at the UN arranging last-minute details. I got a call from my home in South Dakota.... They said, "Fool's Crow and Matthew King, they don't want to go."

So I call and I go around and I get the police to go after Matthew King and get him to a telephone and they get him on a telephone, and I said, "Look, your flight leaves early

formidable: something that inspires fear or awe.

prestigious: important, influential.

intellectuals: people who are prone to study, reflection, and speculation—the use of the intellect.

tomorrow morning. You get into New York City. We have first class. We have everybody ready. The airlines, the hostesses, everybody's going to treat you great. I've got you a suite in Rotterdam, and it's going to be first-class passage back."

He said, "Nephew, understand this. We're old people. That's a long way away. We might die over there. We don't want to go there. But you tell those Russell people that if they ever come to the United States and have a meeting, maybe we will attend."

Understand the beauty of that. Talk about individual **sovereignty**, independence. That was the ultimate statement. Here were all these educated Indians in the United States, Canada and the rest of the hemisphere, all the ones with their degrees, all the ones that like this kind of thing, we're hopping, including myself. I wasn't going, but I was all excited about it.

That really sat me down to look at what we are. All of that **materialism**, all of that ego-tripping, didn't mean a thing to these old people. All of these fancy titles after all of these fancy people that were putting on this tribunal....

"If those Russell people ever have a meeting over here, then maybe we'll come." I think that is the ultimate statement of sovereignty, individual sovereignty.

The state of the American Indian nations is an exciting state. I see that what goes around comes around. I understand that, because everything that is holy and sacred and good is round. Understand that also. That's part of the male-female balance. The sun is round, the moon is round. Walk up on a hill and you'll see that our sacred grandmother, the Mother Earth, is round. Everything sacred is round. So what goes around comes around.

Our people accomplished a socioeconomic phenomenon in the 1970s, in one decade, in less than fifteen years, not only in the United States of America but in Canada and the rest of the Western Hemisphere.

It's an exciting time to live, and we're fighting, but I'm sick and tired of the educated Indian, because to me they're not educated. They've educated their wisdom out. It's good. I have confidence in people who have education. I have one;

sovereignty: freedom from control by others.

materialism: excessive focus on things one can buy and own rather than on things of a spiritual or intellectual nature.

my children are getting theirs. I advocate Indians to go on to institutions of higher learning....

But understand that I know what **oppression** is. I know what sacrifice is. Understand that peoples who come from the barrio, the reservation, the ghetto, we know oppression. So we know how to struggle. We know what sacrifice is....

So it's an exciting time. And I see it's time now to go to my own people, slap them in the face and hear them say, "Thank you. I needed that."

Because we did it once before.... Understand that we're not through yet.

The **sanctity** of life is too precious to allow this society to continue to be disrespectful. I have grandchildren, nine grandchildren, and I fought so that my sons and my daughters would have a better way. And I'm not going to allow my sons and daughters to be satisfied so that their sons and daughters get back in the same old rut.

I'm not going to allow these **pseudo-Indians** who call themselves leaders, who the white man calls leaders. They're an insult to you and to me and to your government to allow these tribal governments to continue.

Understand that you are the next tribal peoples. You're going to be the new Indians of the twenty-first century. You're already feeling the squeeze. Understand. I know the beauty of the male-female balance. I know my creation story, and those that continue to suck off of Uncle Sam are my enemy and the enemy of everyone. It's not just limited to Indians. Maybe to all Native Americans, huh? The state of the Native American.

So I'll leave you with the words of Chief Seattle, and I quote part of his letter and speech to the then-president of the United States of America. He said, "Wave follows wave, and tribe follows tribe. It's the order of nature, and regret is useless. Your time of decay may be distant, but it will surely come. For even the white man's god who walked and talked with him as friend with friend could not escape our common destiny. We may be brothers after all. We shall see...."

oppression: unjust or cruel use of power and authority.

sanctity: the state of being safe from harm by others.

pseudo-Indians: false or fake Indians.

When Means left AIM in 1988, he said that he was eager to have more time to pursue other personal and professional interests. One of those interests turned out to be acting. He launched his new career with a well-received performance as Chingachgook in the 1992 film version of The Last of the Mohicans. In 1995, he was the voice of Chief Powhatan in Disney's animated feature Pocahontas and also served as a consultant on the project. In addition, he has appeared in the films Natural Born Killers, Wagons East, and Wind Runner. In 1996 he was working on a movie titled Wounded Knee, 1973. His future goals include producing and directing his own films to help educate the American people about Indians. In the same spirit, he has released a self-written and self-produced recording of rap music and protest songs called The Radical.

In 1995 Means published his autobiography, Where White Men Fear to Tread. The well-reviewed book tells the story of thirty years of angry protest. To most observers, Means has become more mellow since the book's release and the success of his movies. Several things brought about major changes in him, including his 1992 participation in an addiction clinic in Arizona, where he was treated for his anger.

Some Native Americans have been critical of Means's recent willingness to take part in the mainstream culture. In fact, his strongest critics accuse him of selling out for his own benefit. **Suzan Shown Harjo** (see entry), president of the Morning Star Institute, an Indian culture and arts organization, described Russell Means as a "sacrifice" in the Washington Post. "One of the great sadnesses for Russell is that he never enjoyed the trust of the people.... He wasn't in tribal government. Russell is a media-made figure. He was the available warrior poster boy for that time, when much of America needed that Indian who looked that way—to love and to hate, but mostly to fear." After many years of placing himself in the public eye, Means has taken a very practical view of the matter. "In America," he says, "you achieve visibility through entertainment or the arts."

Sources

Books

Blanche, Jerry D., editor, *Native American Reader: Stories, Speeches and Poems,* Denali Press, 1990.

Matthiessen, Peter, *In the Spirit of Crazy Horse,* Viking, 1983, new edition, 1991.

Means, Russell, and Marvin J. Wolf, *Where White Men Fear to Tread: The Autobiography of Russell Means,* St. Martin's, 1995.

Notable Native Americans, Gale, 1995.

Voices from Wounded Knee, 1973: In the Words of the Participants, Akwesasne Notes, 1974.

Periodicals

Chicago Tribune, "Dances with Disney: *Pocahontas* Is More Than a Movie to Russell Means," June 14, 1995.

Detroit News, "Russell Means' Acting Hasn't Cooled His Activism," October 12, 1992.

Grand Rapids Press, "A People's Man," March 21, 1993, p. A3.

Modern Maturity, "Russell Means: The Profound and Outspoken Activist Shares Some of His Most Ardent Convictions," September-October 1995, pp. 68–79.

"Russell Means Charts 'Cultural Chaos' of 'Growing Up Indian' in Biography," Knight-Ridder/Tribune News Service, December 6, 1995.

Washington Post, "Bury His Hate at Wounded Knee: Russell Means Says He's Found a Better Way to Help His People," December 7, 1995, p. D01.

Other

Incident at Oglala: The Leonard Peltier Story (documentary film), Carolco International, 1992.

Thunderheart (film), 1992.

Red Jacket

(Sa-Go-Ye-Wat-Ha)
c. 1756–1830

Chief of the Seneca tribe

One of the most famous members of the Iroquois confederation during the late 1700s and early 1800s was Red Jacket. (His colorful English-language name was inspired by the bright red British military coat he always wore.) The Iroquois confederation was a powerful alliance of six different Indian tribes—the Mohawk, Oneida, Onondaga, Cayuga, Seneca, and Tuscarora—whose original territory stretched over present-day New York State and much of southeastern Ontario, Canada. Red Jacket lived around the same time as several other major Iroquois leaders such as Cornplanter, who was a fellow Seneca, and **Joseph Brant** (see entry), a Mohawk. Unlike them, however, he considered himself first and foremost an orator rather than a warrior or a diplomat. In fact, Red Jacket's fame rests almost entirely on his legendary way with words.

Red Jacket was born near Lake Geneva, New York, around 1756. Nothing is known of his early life; he is not mentioned in historical records until the Revolutionary War

(1775–83). Although he was an ally of the British, he wanted the Iroquois to remain neutral in the struggle between Great Britain and her colonies. But more militant leaders such as Brant urged the member tribes to take part in the actual battles. Red Jacket himself did very little fighting on behalf of the British. This led some Indians to label him a coward.

A Spokesperson for the Senecas

After the war, Red Jacket became a principal spokesperson for the Senecas. He served as their representative at numerous councils and treaty sessions as well as at meetings with various officials of the new United States government. At first he favored establishing a closer relationship between Indians and whites. At a meeting in 1792 with President George Washington and other American officials, for example, Red Jacket even expressed a desire to see Indians learn the ways of white civilization. Later, he sold off vast amounts of Seneca land to white investors. Some historians now criticize that move as an attempt by Red Jacket to win the approval and friendship of whites.

Around 1800, however, Red Jacket gave up on the idea that Indians should try to become more like white people. He began urging his fellow Iroquois to reject European ways (including the Christian religion) and preserve their own beliefs and traditions before it was too late. He firmly believed that Indian ways worked best for Indian people, and he suggested that white people could probably gain by learning something from the Indians.

Clashes with White Missionary

Red Jacket's most famous statement on the subject of Christianity came in 1805. Sometime that summer, a Protestant missionary by the name of Cram left his home in Boston, Massachusetts, and set out for Buffalo, New York. Upon his arrival, he met with Seneca tribal leaders to ask for permission to preach among their people. Mr. Cram made his request as part of a **patronizing** speech in which he promised to teach his *"pagan"* audience about the one true way to worship.

patronizing: characterized by an attitude of superiority.

pagan: someone who either worships many gods or does not follow any religion.

At the end of the minister's remarks, Red Jacket stood up and angrily described what he and his people had already observed about the difference between Christian words and not-so-Christian actions. His response to the Reverend Mr. Cram is reprinted here from W. C. Vanderwerth's Indian Oratory: Famous Speeches by Noted Indian Chieftains, *University of Oklahoma Press, 1971.*

Friend and Brother! It was the will of the Great Spirit that we should meet together this day. He orders all things, and he has given us a fine day for our council. He has taken his garment from before the sun and has caused the bright **orb** to shine with brightness upon us. Our eyes are opened so that we see clearly. Our ears are unstopped so that we have been able to distinctly hear the words which you have spoken. For all these favors we thank the Great Spirit and him only.

Brother! This council fire was kindled by you. It was at your request that we came together at this time. We have listened with attention to what you have said. You have requested us to speak our minds freely. This gives us great joy, for we now consider that we stand upright before you, and can speak what we think. All have heard your voice and all speak to you as one man. Our minds are agreed.

Brother! You say that you want an answer to your talk before you leave this place. It is right that you should have one, as you are a great distance from home, and we do not wish to detain you. But we will first look back a little, and tell you what our fathers have told us, and what we have heard from the white people. Brother! Listen to what we say. There was a time when our forefathers owned this great island. [Red Jacket is referring here to the continent of North America, which many Indians believed was an island.] Their seats extended from the rising to the setting of the sun. The Great Spirit had made it for the use of Indians. He had created the buffalo, the deer, and other animals for food. He made the bear and the deer, and their skins served us for clothing. He had scattered them over the country, and had taught us how

orb: sphere; ball.

Redjacket eventually rejected Christianity along with European ways: "You have got our country, but you are not satisfied. You want to force your religion upon us."

to take them. He had caused the earth to produce corn for bread. All this he had done for his red children because he loved them. If we had any disputes about hunting grounds, they were generally settled without the shedding of much blood.

But an evil day came upon us. Your forefathers crossed the great waters and landed on this island. Their numbers were small. They found friends and not enemies. They told us they had fled from their own country for fear of wicked men, and had come here to enjoy their religion. They asked for a small seat. We took pity on them, granted their request and they sat down amongst us. We gave them corn and meat. They gave us poison [alcohol] in return. The white people had now found our country.

Tidings were carried back and more came amongst us. Yet we did not fear them. We took them to be friends. They called us brothers. We believed them and gave them a large seat. At length their numbers had greatly increased. They wanted more land. They wanted our country. Our eyes were opened, and our minds became uneasy. Wars took place. Indians were hired to fight against Indians, and many of our people were destroyed. They also brought strong liquors among us. It was strong and powerful and has **slain** thousands.

Brother! Our seats were once large, and yours were very small. You have now become a great people, and we have scarcely a place left to spread our blankets. You have got our country, but you are not satisfied. You want to force your religion upon us.

Brother! Continue to listen. You say that you are sent to instruct us how to worship the Great Spirit agreeably to his mind; and if we do not take hold of the religion which you white people teach we shall be unhappy hereafter. You say that you are right, and we are lost. How do you know this to be true? We understand that your religion is written in a book. If it was intended for us as well as for you, why has not the Great Spirit given it to us; and not only to us, but why did he not give to our forefathers the knowledge of that book, with the means of understanding it rightly? We only know what you tell us about it. How shall we know when to believe, being so often deceived by the white people?

Brother! You say there is but one way to worship and serve the Great Spirit. If there is but one religion, why do you white people differ so much about it? Why not all agree, as you can all read the book?

Brother! We do not understand these things. We are told that your religion was given to your forefathers and has been

tidings: news, reports.
slain: killed.

handed down, father to son. We also have a religion which was given to our forefathers, and has been handed down to us, their children. We worship that way. It teaches us to be thankful for all the favors we received, to love each other, and to be united. We never quarrel about religion.

Brother! The Great Spirit has made us all. But he has made a great difference between his white and red children. He has given us a different complexion and different customs. To you he has given the arts; to these he has not opened our eyes. We know these things to be true. Since he has made so great a difference between us in other things, why may not we conclude that he has given us a different religion, according to our understanding? The Great Spirit does right. He knows what is best for his children. We are satisfied.

Brother! We do not wish to destroy your religion, or to take it from you. We only want to enjoy our own.

Brother! You say you have not come to get our land or our money, but to **enlighten** our minds. I will now tell you that I have been at your meetings and saw you collecting money from the meeting. I cannot tell what this money was intended for, but suppose it was for your minister; and if we should conform to your way of thinking, perhaps you may want some from us.

Brother! We are told that you have been preaching to the white people in this place. These people are our neighbors. We are acquainted with them. We will wait a little while, and see what effect your preaching has upon them. If we find it does them good and makes them honest and less **disposed** to cheat Indians, we will then consider again what you have said.

Brother! You have now heard our answer to your talk, and this is all we have to say at present. As we are going to part, we will come and take you by the hand, and hope the Great Spirit will protect you on your journey, and return you safe to your friends.

99

enlighten: educate, provide insight (especially spiritual).

disposed: inclined; likely.

According to accounts of this exchange between the Reverend Mr. Cram and Red Jacket, the minister responded by refusing to shake hands with the Indians. He declared that there could be "no fellowship between the religion of God and the devil." The Indians reportedly just smiled and left the meeting.

*Red Jacket lived out the rest of his days trying to keep the Senecas away from the white man's religion and customs. He continued his efforts even after many members of the tribe—including some in his own family—became Christians. He remained friendly toward the United States government, however, and resisted attempts by other Indians such as the Shawnee chief **Tecumseh** (see entry) to draw the Senecas into an alliance that tried to block the westward expansion of white settlements.*

*In 1824, Red Jacket succeeded in having all missionaries temporarily expelled from tribal territory. But this only ended up creating tensions between those who had **converted to** Christianity and those who had not. The result was a bitter split in the Seneca nation. Red Jacket's own problems with alcohol and his excessive accusations of witchcraft against his followers made the situation even worse. In 1827, he was removed as a Seneca chief. He managed to win back his position shortly before he died and spent his last months sounding a final warning about the white man's greed and deception.*

Sources

Books

Armstrong, Virginia Irving, compiler, *I Have Spoken: American History Through the Voices of the Indians,* Sage Books, 1971.

Jones, Louis Thomas, *Aboriginal American Oratory: The Tradition of Eloquence Among the Indians of the United States,* Southwest Museum (Los Angeles), 1965.

McLuhan, T. C., *Touch the Earth: A Self-Portrait of Indian Existence,* Outerbridge & Dienstfrey, 1971.

Nabokov, Peter, editor, *Native American Testimony: A Chronicle of Indian-White Relations from Prophecy to the Present, 1492–1992,* Penguin Books, 1991.

converted to: become believers in.

Notable Native Americans, Gale, 1995.

Rosenstiel, Annette, *Red and White: Indian Views of the White Man, 1492–1982,* Universe Books, 1983.

Sanders, Thomas E., and Walter W. Peek, *Literature of the American Indian,* Glencoe Press, 1973.

Stone, William L., *The Life and Times of Sa-Go-Ye-Wat-Ha,* [New York], 1866.

Vanderwerth, W. C., *Indian Oratory: Famous Speeches by Noted Indian Chieftains,* University of Oklahoma Press, 1971.

Velie, Alan R., editor, *American Indian Literature: An Anthology,* University of Oklahoma Press, 1979.

Witt, Shirley Hill, and Stan Steiner, editors, *The Way: An Anthology of American Indian Literature,* Knopf, 1972.

Satanta

(White Bear)
c. 1830–1878
Chief of the Kiowa tribe

"I LOVE TO ROAM OVER THE PRAIRIES.... WHEN WE SETTLE DOWN WE GROW PALE AND DIE."

Known among the Americans he dealt with as the "Orator of the Plains" in recognition of his talents as a public speaker, Satanta was a warrior and chief of the Kiowa tribe. His territory stretched across the southern flatlands of the United States in present-day western Oklahoma, the panhandle of Texas, and part of New Mexico. Along with his fellow chiefs Satank and Kicking Bird, Satanta led the Kiowas' resistance against white settlements and white culture during the mid-nineteenth century. In both word and action, he made it clear that his people could neither understand nor accept the idea of abandoning their nomadic hunting existence to become farmers, as the whites wanted them to do.

Satanta was born around 1830, somewhere in the northern plains. Later, he moved south with the rest of his tribe. There he spent most of his life at war with white settlers and soldiers. New farms and ranches in Kiowa territory were destroying buffalo grazing land, and the angry Indi-

ans responded to this threat to their existence with count-less raids, particularly along the Santa Fe Trail. Satanta was an especially clever and colorful leader of one of the more militant bands of Kiowas. But besides his reputation as a brave and aggressive fighter, he was also famous as a speaker.

In October 1867, for example, Satanta spoke at the Medicine Lodge Council at Medicine Creek Lodge in south-ern Kansas. This ceremonial gathering was the largest of its kind ever held. In attendance were some five thousand Indians as well as a number of U.S. government officials. Many chiefs stood up to protest their treatment at the hands of whites. Among them was Satanta, whose words (originally delivered in Spanish) were widely quoted in magazines and newspapers of the day, including the New York Times. *Their simple **eloquence** caused the Americans who were present to refer to Satanta as the "Orator of the Plains." His speech is reprinted from W. C. Vanderwerth's* Indian Oratory: Famous Speeches by Noted Indian Chieftains, *University of Oklahoma Press, 1971.*

You, the commissioners, have come from afar to listen to our **grievances**. My heart is glad and I shall hide nothing from you. I understood that you were coming down to see us. I moved away from those **disposed for** war, and I also came along to see you. The Kiowas and Comanches have not been fighting. We were away down south when we heard you were coming to see us.

The Cheyennes are those who have been fighting with you. They did it in broad daylight so that all could see them. If I had been fighting I would have done it by day and not in the dark. Two years ago I made peace with Generals Harney, Sanborn and Colonel Leavenworth at the mouth of the Little Arkansas.

That peace I have never broken. When the grass was grow-ing in the spring, a large body of soldiers came along on the Santa Fe road. I had not done anything and therefore I was not afraid. All the chiefs of the Kiowas, Comanches, and Ara-

eloquence: forceful and persuasive power of speech.

grievances: complaints.

disposed for: inclined toward, leaning toward.

pahos are here today; they have come to listen to good words. We have been waiting here a long time to see you and are getting tired. All the land south of the Arkansas belongs to the Kiowas and Comanches, and I don't want to give away any of it. I love the land and the buffalo and will not part with it. I want you to understand well what I say. Write it on paper. Let the Great Father see it, and let me hear what he has to say. I want you to understand, also, that the Kiowas and Comanches don't want to fight, and have not been fighting since we made the treaty. I hear a great deal of good talk from the gentlemen whom the Great Father sends us, but they never do what they say. I don't want any of the medicine lodges [schools and churches] within the country. I want the children raised as I was. When I make peace, it is a long and lasting one—there is no end to it. We thank you for your presents.

All the headmen and braves are happy. They will do what you want them, for they know you are doing the best you can. I and they will do our best also. When I look upon you, I know you are all big chiefs. While you are in this country we go to sleep happy and are not afraid. I have heard that you intend to settle us on a reservation near the mountains. I don't want to settle. I love to roam over the prairies. There I feel free and happy, but when we settle down we grow pale and die.

I have laid aside my lance, bow, and shield, and yet I feel safe in your presence. I have told you the truth. I have no little lies hid about me, but I don't know how it is with the commissioners. Are they as clear as I am?

A long time ago this land belonged to our fathers; but when I go up to the river I see camps of soldiers on its banks. These soldiers cut down my timber; they kill my buffalo; and when I see that, my heart feels like bursting; I feel sorry. I have spoken.

Satanta

After several days of negotiations, Satanta and most of the other chiefs at the Medicine Lodge Council reluctantly signed a treaty handing over much of their territory to the U.S. government. In exchange, the government promised the Indians that they would receive food, clothing, and other supplies. Also under the terms of the treaty, the Kiowas were assigned to a reservation in present-day Oklahoma.

But the Kiowas soon grew restless and frustrated by attempts to turn them into farmers. Before long, an unhappy Satanta was once again leading raids across the prairie, killing white settlers and soldiers and stampeding livestock. The beginning of the end came in May 1871, when he and fellow chiefs Satank and Kicking Bird assembled a war party that ambushed an army wagon train traveling through Texas. The Indians killed eight of the twelve men driving the wagons and stole the freight and the mules.

Satanta was eventually arrested and convicted for his part in the raid. He was sentenced to hang, but humanitarian groups protested the harshness of the punishment. Thus, in 1873 Satanta was paroled on the condition that he never set foot outside the Kiowa reservation. The following year, when war broke out between the United States and the Comanches, he turned himself in to authorities hoping to show that he had not been involved. But because he had been away from the reservation on a hunting trip, Satanta was sent off to a state prison in Huntsville, Texas, to complete his life sentence.

Over the next few years, the Kiowa chief grew steadily weaker and more discouraged as he tried but failed to adjust to living behind bars. Finally, in September 1878, shortly after learning from a prison official that he would never be set free, Satanta reportedly committed suicide by jumping out of his window in the prison hospital.

Sources

Books

Armstrong, Virginia Irving, *I Have Spoken: American History Through the Voices of the Indians*, Sage Books, 1971.

Brown, Dee, *Bury My Heart at Wounded Knee: An Indian History of the American West,* Holt, 1970.

Jones, Louis Thomas, *Aboriginal American Oratory: The Tradition of Eloquence Among the Indians of the United States,* Southwest Museum (Los Angeles), 1965.

Notable Native Americans, Gale, 1995.

Vanderwerth, W. C., *Indian Oratory: Famous Speeches by Noted Indian Chieftains,* University of Oklahoma Press, 1971.

Seattle

(Seathl)
c. 1788–1866
Leader of the Duwamish and Suquamish tribes

"WHEN THE LAST RED
MAN SHALL HAVE
PERISHED FROM THE
EARTH AND HIS MEMORY
AMONG WHITE MEN
SHALL HAVE BECOME A
MYTH, THESE SHORES
SHALL SWARM WITH THE
INVISIBLE DEAD OF MY
TRIBE...."

Some of the most famous—and most disputed—words ever spoken by a Native American leader are those of Seattle, a chief of two Pacific Northwest tribes. Thanks to a speech of somewhat unclear origin, he is known today for his forceful and persuasive power of speech and his ability to foresee what lay ahead in the major environmental issues of the twentieth century. This has made him a powerful symbol of the ecology movement both in the United States and in Europe. Yet it is unknown whether Seattle ever really delivered the thought-provoking speech that so many people associate with him.

Early Life

Seattle was born and grew up among his people near the present-day city of Seattle, Washington, which was named after him. He was a young man when white settlers began arriving in large numbers throughout the Pacific Northwest. Like his father before him, he was friendly to the newcomers and encouraged his people to be helpful and cooperative as well. In fact, Seattle personally adopted some white traditions. During the 1830s, for example, French missionaries persuaded him to **convert to** Catholicism.

Tensions between Indians and whites increased, however, particularly after the discovery of gold in the area attracted hordes of miners who did not always respect the established boundaries and customs. Seattle continued to call for peace and patience, even refusing to take part in a war that broke out in the mid-1850s. So strong was his determination not to fight that in January 1855, he became the first Indian leader to sign the Fort Elliot Treaty. Under the terms of this document, he and his people gave away most of their land and agreed to move to a reservation along with several other Washington tribes.

Seattle's Words—or Not?

It was supposedly at the signing of the Fort Elliot Treaty that Chief Seattle turned to the territorial governor, Isaac Stevens, and spoke the words that have made him such a hero to environmentalists. This image of an angry Native American standing up to the forces that he felt were destroying his land and his way of life has been especially popular among Europeans for many years. (They have long considered Indians as very spiritual people who live in mystical harmony with nature.) It was not until the late 1960s and early 1970s, however—around the time the ecology movement began to gain more support—that a similar view of Native Americans emerged in the United States.

Rudolf Kaiser, a professor at the University of Hildesheim in Germany, has closely studied Seattle's environmental "speech." He has identified a number of different versions, including one that is described not as a speech but as a letter to President Franklin Pierce. None of these versions are anything like the two short speeches the chief was actually known to have given at the treaty ceremony. The texts of both of those speeches are stored in the government documents collection at the National Archives in Washington, D.C.

Professor Kaiser reported his findings in an essay entitled "Chief Seattle's Speech(es): American Origins and European

convert to: become a believer in.

Reception." It was published in the book Recovering the
Word: Essays on Native American Literature, *edited by
Brian Swann and Arnold Krupat (University of California
Press, 1987). In his essay, Professor Kaiser discusses his
efforts to track down and analyze four major versions of
Seattle's speech.*

According to the professor, the first version of Seattle's speech to appear in print was published in the Seattle Sunday Star *on October 29, 1887. A related article in the same newspaper explained that a doctor named Henry Smith had been present when the chief gave the speech in late 1853 or early 1854. As Smith recalled, the occasion was a reception for the new commissioner of Indian affairs for Washington Territory, Isaac Stevens. Impressed by Seattle's dignity and the seriousness of his message, Smith took detailed notes on the speech for his diary. He later used those notes to reconstruct the speech for the* Seattle Sunday Star. *(Unfortunately, Smith's diary has been lost, so there is no way to check his original notes.) Professor Kaiser thinks that Smith's account of what the chief said that day has served as the basis for everything that has appeared since then claiming to be the words of Seattle.*

Here is Smith's 1887 recollection of what Seattle had said back in the 1850s:

Yonder sky has wept tears of compassion on our fathers for centuries untold, and which, to us, looks eternal, may change. To-day it is fair, to-morrow it may be overcast with clouds. My words are like the stars that never set. What Seattle says the great chief, Washington ... can rely upon, with as much certainty as our pale-face brothers can rely upon the return of the seasons. [Smith noted here that "Washington" refers to George Washington, whom the Indians believed was still alive. He said that they recognized the name belonged to a president, and when they heard white people talk of the president at Washington, they misunderstood the name of the city to mean the name of the man then in office. Furthermore, according to Smith, the Indians also thought England's King George III was still alive. He had actually ruled during the time of the Revolutionary War (1775–83).] The son of the white chief says his father sends us greetings of friendship and good-will. This is kind, for we know he has little need of our friendship in return, because his people are many. They are like the grass that covers the vast prairies, while my people are few, and resemble the scattering trees of a wind-swept plain.

The great, and I presume also good, white chief sends us word that he wants to buy our lands but is willing to allow us to reserve enough to live on comfortably. This indeed appears generous, for the red man no longer has rights that he need respect, and the offer may be wise, also, for we are no longer in need of a great country. There was a time when our people covered the whole land as the waves of a wind-ruffled sea cover its shell-paved floor. But that time has long since passed away with the greatness of tribes almost forgotten. I will not mourn over our **untimely** decay, nor **reproach** my pale-face brothers with **hastening** it, for we, too, may have been somewhat to blame.

When our young men grow angry at some real or imaginary wrong and disfigure their faces with black paint, their hearts, also, are disfigured and turn black, and then their cruelty is relentless and knows no bounds, and our old men are not able to restrain them.

But let us hope that hostilities between the red man and his pale-face brothers may never return. We would have everything to lose and nothing to gain.

True it is that revenge, with our young braves, is considered gain, even at the cost of their own lives, but old men who stay at home in times of war, and old women who have sons to lose, know better.

Our great father Washington, for I presume he is now our father as well as yours, since [King] George has moved his boundaries to the north; our great and good father, I say, sends us word by his son, who, no doubt, is a great chief among his people, that if we do as he desires, he will protect us. His brave armies will be to us a bristling wall of strength, and his great ships of war will fill our harbors so that our ancient enemies far to the northward ... will no longer frighten our women and old men. Then he will be our father and we will be his children. But can this ever be? Your God loves your people and hates mine; he folds his strong arms lovingly around the white man and leads him as a father leads his infant son, but he has **forsaken** his red children; he makes your people **wax** strong every day, and soon they will fill the land; while our people are **ebbing** away like a fast-receding tide, that will never flow again. The white man's God cannot

untimely: occurring before the natural or proper time.

reproach: blame.

hastening: hurrying, speeding.

forsaken: abandoned.

wax: grow.

ebbing: dwindling.

love his red children or he would protect them. They seem to be orphans and can look nowhere for help. How then can we become brothers? How can your father become our father and bring us prosperity and awaken in us dreams of returning greatness?

Your God seems to be **partial.** He came to the white man. We never saw Him; never even heard His voice; He gave the white man laws but He had no word for His red children whose teeming millions filled this vast continent as the stars fill the **firmament.** No, we are two distinct races and must ever remain so. There is little in common between us. The ashes of our ancestors are sacred and their final resting place is hallowed ground, while you wander away from the tombs of your fathers seemingly without regret.

Your religion was written on tables of stone by the iron finger of an angry God, lest you might forget it. The red man could never remember nor **comprehend** it.

Our religion is the traditions of our ancestors, the dreams of our old men, given them by the great Spirit, and the visions of our **sachems,** and is written in the hearts of our people.

Your dead cease to love you and the homes of their **nativity** as soon as they pass the **portals** of the tomb. They wander off beyond the stars, are soon forgotten and never return. Our dead never forget the beautiful world that gave them being. They still love its winding rivers, its great mountains and its **sequestered vales,** and they ever **yearn** in tenderest affection over the lonely hearted living and often return to visit and comfort them.

Day and night cannot dwell together. The red man has ever fled the approach of the white man, as the changing mists on the mountain side flee before the blazing morning sun.

However, your proposition seems a just one, and I think my folks will accept it and will retire to the reservation you offer them, and we will dwell apart and in peace, for the words of the great white chief seem to be the voice of nature speaking to my people out of the thick darkness that is fast gathering around them like a dense fog floating inward from a midnight sea.

partial: biased, inclined to favor one group over another.

firmament: sky, heavens.

comprehend: understand.

sachems: chiefs.

nativity: birth.

portals: doors.

sequestered vales: secluded valleys.

yearn: have a strong desire for.

It matters but little where we pass the remainder of our days. They are not many. The Indian's night promises to be dark. No bright star hovers about the horizon. Sad-voiced winds moan in the distance. Some grim **Nemesis** of our race is on the red man's trail, and wherever he goes he will still hear the sure approaching footsteps of the **fell** destroyer and prepare to meet his doom, as does the wounded doe that hears the approaching footsteps of the hunter. A few more moons, a few more winters and not one of all the mighty **hosts** that once filled this broad land or that now roam in fragmentary bands through these vast solitudes will remain to weep over the tombs of a people once as powerful and as hopeful as your own.

But why should we **repine?** Why should I murmur at the fate of my people? Tribes are made up of individuals and are no better than they. Men come and go like the waves of the sea. A tear, a tamanamus, a **dirge**, and they are gone from our longing eyes forever. Even the white man, whose God walked and talked with him, as friend to friend, is not **exempt** from the common destiny. We may be brothers after all. We shall see.

We will **ponder** your proposition, and when we have decided we will tell you. But should we accept it, I here and now make this the first condition: That we will not be denied the privilege, without **molestation**, of visiting at will the graves of our ancestors and friends. Every part of this country is sacred to my people. Every hillside, every valley, every plain and grove has been **hallowed** by some fond memory or some sad experience of my tribe. Even the rocks that seem to lie **dumb** as they swelter in the sun along the silent seashore in solemn grandeur thrill with memories of past events connected with the late of my people, and the very dust under your feet responds more lovingly to our footsteps than to yours, because it is the ashes of our ancestors, and our bare feet are conscious of the sympathetic touch, for the soil is rich with the life of our **kindred**.

The sable braves, and fond mothers, and glad-hearted maidens, and the little children who lived and rejoiced here, and whose very names are now forgotten, still love these solitudes, and their deep **fastnesses** at **eventide** grow shadowy with the presence of dusky spirits. And when the last red

Nemesis: the Greek goddess of vengeful justice—therefore a symbol of anyone or anything that inflicts revenge.

fell: cruel, deadly.

hosts: crowds or multitudes (of people).

repine: feel sad or upset.

dirge: song or poem of grief that usually accompanies a funeral service.

exempt: excused, freed.

ponder: think about.

molestation: the act of disturbing or annoying someone.

hallowed: made holy.

dumb: silent.

kindred: people, relatives.

fastnesses: remote and secluded places.

eventide: evening.

man shall have perished from the earth and his memory among white men shall have become a myth, these shores shall swarm with the invisible dead of my tribe, and when your children's children shall think themselves alone in the field, the shop, upon the highway or in the silence of the woods they will not be alone. In all the earth there is no place dedicated to solitude. At night when the streets of your cities and villages shall be silent, and you think them deserted, they will throng with the returning hosts that once filled and still love this beautiful land. The white man will never be alone. Let him be just and deal kindly with my people, for the dead are not **altogether** powerless.

In 1969, American poet and writer William Arrowsmith published what he called a "translation" of Seattle's speech in the journal Arion. *(Six years later, it was reprinted in an issue of the* American Poetry Review.*) In his notes at the end of the speech, Arrowsmith explained that his "translation" was actually a modernization of Smith's original account—one that got rid of its nineteenth-century word choices and style. As a result, the two versions differ somewhat in vocabulary but not much in content.*

Without a doubt, however, the most famous version of Seattle's speech is the one many people throughout the world heard in a film called Home. *Around 1970, a man named Ted Perry was teaching at the University of Texas when he attended a rally on the environment. At the rally, he heard William Arrowsmith recite his "translation" of Seattle's speech. Some time later, Perry was approached by the Southern Baptist Radio and Television Commission about doing a film on the effects of pollution. Recalling Arrowsmith's appearance at the environmental rally, Perry contacted him and asked for permission to use the speech "translation" he had recited as the basis for his script. Arrowsmith agreed, and Perry went to work. Drawing his inspiration from Arrowsmith's words, he created an original work of fiction that shows Seattle as an angry, resentful Indian who condemns the white man for his carelessness toward the environment.*

altogether: completely.

Around 1972, Perry saw the completed film for the first time when it was broadcast on television. To his surprise, he noticed that he had not been given credit as the author of the script. Instead, viewers were left with the impression that what they had heard were the exact thoughts and words of Seattle. As a result, it is the following version of the chief's speech that has stirred the souls of ecology-minded people throughout America and Europe—even though it is very much the product of another man's imagination.

The Great Chief in Washington sends word that he wishes to buy our land.

The Great Chief also sends us words of friendship and goodwill. This is kind of him, since we know he has little need of our friendship in return. But we will consider your offer. For we know that if we do not sell, the white man may come with guns and take our land.

How can you buy or sell the sky, the warmth of the land? The idea is strange to us.

If we do not own the freshness of the air and the sparkle of the water, how can you buy them from us?

We will decide in our time.

What Chief Seattle says, the Great Chief in Washington can count on as truly as our white brothers can count on the return of the seasons. My words are like the stars. They do not set.

Every part of this earth is sacred to my people. Every shining pine needle, every sandy shore, every mist in the dark woods, every clearing, and humming insect is holy in the memory and experience of my people. The sap which courses through the trees carries the memories of the red man.

The white man's dead forget the country of their birth when they go to walk among the stars. Our dead never forget this beautiful earth, for it is the mother of the red man.

We are part of the earth and it is part of us. The perfumed flowers are our sisters; the deer, the horse, the great eagle, these are our brothers. The rocky crests, the juices in the meadows, the body heat of the pony, and man—all belong to the same family.

So, when the Great Chief in Washington sends word that he wishes to buy our land, he asks much of us.

The Great Chief sends word he will reserve us a place so that we can live comfortable to ourselves. He will be our father and we will be his children.

But can that ever be? God loves your people, but has abandoned his red children. He sends machines to help the white man with his work, and builds great villages for him. He makes your people stronger every day. Soon you will flood the land like the rivers which crash down the canyons after a sudden rain. But my people are an ebbing tide, we will never return.

No, we are separate races. Our children do not play together and our old men tell different stories. God favors you, and we are orphans.

So we will consider your offer to buy our land. But it will not be easy. For this land is sacred to us. We take our pleasure in these woods. I do not know. Our ways are different from your ways.

This shining water that moves in the streams and rivers is not just water but the blood of our ancestors. If we sell you land, you must remember that it is sacred, and that each ghostly reflection in the clear water of the lakes tells of events and memories in the life of my people. The water's murmur is the voice of my father's father.

The rivers are our brothers, they quench our thirst. The rivers carry our canoes, and feed our children. If we sell you our land, you must remember, and teach your children, that the rivers are our brothers, and yours, and you must henceforth give rivers the kindness you would give any brother.

The red man has always retreated before the advancing white man, as the mist of the mountain runs before the morning sun. But the ashes of our fathers are sacred. The graves are holy ground, and so these hills, these trees, this portion of the earth is **consecrated** to us. We know that the white man does not understand our ways. One portion of

consecrated: holy.

land is the same to him as the next, for he is a stranger who comes in the night and takes from the land whatever he needs. The earth is not his brother but his enemy, and when he has conquered it, he moves on. He leaves his father's graves behind, and he does not care. He kidnaps the earth from his children. He does not care. His father's graves and his children's birthright are forgotten. He treats his mother, the earth, and his brother, the sky, as things to be bought, **plundered**, sold like sheep or bright beads. His appetite will devour the earth and leave behind only a desert.

I do not know. Our ways are different from your ways. The sight of your cities pains the eyes of the red man. But perhaps it is because the red man is a savage and does not understand.

There is no quiet place in the white man's cities. No place to hear the unfurling of leaves in spring or the rustle of insect's wings. But perhaps it is because I am a savage and do not understand. The clatter only seems to insult the ears. And what is there to life if a man cannot hear the lonely cry of the whippoorwill or the arguments of the frogs around a pond at night? I am a red man and do not understand. The Indian prefers the soft sound of the wind darting over the face of a pond, and the smell of the wind itself, cleansed by a midday rain, or scented with the piñon pine.

The air is precious to the red man, for all things share the same breath—the beast, the tree, the man, they all share the same breath. The white man does not seem to notice the air he breathes. Like a man dying for many days, he is numb to the stench. But if we sell our land, you must remember that the air is precious to us, that the air shares its spirit with all the life it supports. The wind that gave our grandfather his first breath also receives his last sigh. And the wind must also give our children the spirit of life. And if we sell you our land, you must keep it apart and sacred, as a place where even the white man can go to taste the wind that is sweetened by the meadow's flowers.

So we will consider your offer to buy our land. If we decide to accept, I will make one condition: The white man must treat the beasts of this land as his brothers.

plundered: stolen or taken by force.

I am a savage and I do not understand any other way. I have seen a thousand rotting buffalos on the prairie, left by the white man who shot them from a passing train. I am a savage and I do not understand how the smoking iron horse can be more important than the buffalo that we kill only to stay alive.

What is man without the beasts? If all the beasts were gone, men would die from a great loneliness of spirit. For whatever happens to the beasts, soon happens to man. All things are connected.

Whatever befalls the earth, befalls the sons of the earth.

You must teach your children that the ground beneath their feet is the ashes of our grandfathers. So that they will respect the land, tell your children that the earth is rich with the lives of our **kin.** Teach your children what we have taught our children, that the earth is our mother. Whatever befalls the earth, befalls the sons of the earth. If men spit upon the ground, they spit upon themselves.

This we know. The earth does not belong to man; man belongs to the earth. This we know. All things are connected like the blood which unites one family. All things are connected.

Whatever befalls the earth befalls the sons of the earth. Man did not weave the web of life; he is merely a strand in it. Whatever he does to the web, he does to himself.

No, day and night cannot live together.

Our dead go to live in the earth's sweet rivers, they return with the silent footsteps of spring, and it is their spirit, running in the wind, that ripples the surface of the ponds.

We will consider why the white man wishes to buy the land. What is it that the white man wishes to buy, my people ask me. The idea is strange to us. How can you buy or sell the sky, the warmth of the land?—the swiftness of the antelope? How can we sell these things to you and how can you buy them? Is the earth yours to do with as you will, merely because the red man signs a piece of paper and gives it to the white man? If we do not own the freshness of the air and the sparkle of the water, how can you buy them from us?

kin: relatives, family.

Can you buy back the buffalo, once the last one has been killed? But we will consider your offer, for we know that if we do not sell, the white man may come with guns and take our land. But we are primitive, and in his passing moment of strength the white man thinks that he is a god who already owns the earth. How can a man own his mother?

But we will consider your offer to buy our land. Day and night cannot live together. We will consider your offer to go to the reservation you have for my people. We will live apart, and in peace. It matters little where we spend the rest of our days. Our children have seen their fathers humbled in defeat. Our warriors have felt shame, and after defeat they turn their days in idleness and contaminate their bodies with sweet foods and strong drink. It matters little where we pass the rest of our days. They are not many. A few more hours, a few more winters, and none of the children of the great tribes that once lived on this earth or that roam now in small bands in the woods will be left to mourn the graves of a people once as powerful and hopeful as yours.

But why should I mourn the passing of my people? Tribes are made of men, nothing more. Men come and go, like the waves of the sea.

Even the white man, whose God walks and talks with him as friend to friend, cannot be exempt from the common destiny. We may be brothers after all; we shall see. One thing we know, which the white man may one day discover—our God is the same God.

You may think now that you own Him as you wish to own our land; but you cannot. He is the God of man, and His compassion is equal for the red man and the white. This earth is precious to Him, and to harm the earth is to heap contempt on its Creator. The whites too shall pass; perhaps sooner than all other tribes. Continue to contaminate your bed, and you will one night suffocate in your own waste.

But in your perishing you will shine brightly, fired by the strength of the God who brought you to this land and for some special purpose gave you **dominion** over this land and over the red man. That destiny is a mystery to us, for we do not understand when the buffalo are all slaughtered, the wild horses are tamed, the secret corners of the forest heavy with

dominion: control, authority.

the scent of many men, and the view of the ripe hills blotted by talking wires. Where is the thicket? Gone. Where is the eagle? Gone. And what is it to say goodbye to the swift pony and the hunt? The end of living and the beginning of survival.

God gave you dominion over the beasts, the woods, and the red man, and for some special purpose, but that destiny is a mystery to the red man. We might understand if we knew what it was that the white man dreams—what hopes he describes to his children on long winter nights—what visions he burns onto their minds so that they will wish for tomorrow. But we are savages. The white man's dreams are hidden from us. And because they are hidden, we will go our own way. For above all else, we cherish the right of each man to live as he wishes, however different from his brothers. There is little in common between us.

So we will consider your offer to buy our land. If we agree, it will be to secure the reservation you have promised. There, perhaps, we may live out our brief days as we wish.

When the last red man has vanished from this earth, and his memory is only the shade of a cloud moving across the prairie, these shores and forests will still hold the spirits of my people. For they love this earth as the newborn loves its mother's heartbeat.

If we sell you our land, love it as we've loved it. Care for it as we've cared for it. Hold in your mind the memory of the land as it is when you take it. And with all your strength, with all your mind, with all your heart, preserve it for your children, and love it ... as God loves us all.

One thing we know. Our God is the same God. This earth is precious to Him. Even the white man cannot be exempt from the common destiny. We may be brothers after all. We shall see.

99

Another fairly well-known version of Seattle's speech was part of a display in the United States pavilion at the 1974 world exposition held in Spokane, Washington. Its author is unknown, but it is basically a shorter and somewhat more poetic version of what Ted Perry had written for his film script. As such, it probably enhanced the image of Seattle as a nineteenth-century **visionary** *with strong spiritual links to the ecology movement of the late twentieth century. Seattle's "speech" has even served as the basis of a popular children's book,* Brother Eagle, Sister Sky: A Message from Chief Seattle, *which was published in 1991.*

Chief Seattle and his people maintained friendly relations with the whites. They eventually settled on the Port Madison Reservation near what is now Bremerton, Washington.

Sources

Books

Armstrong, Virginia Irving, compiler, *I Have Spoken: American History Through the Voices of the Indians,* Sage Books, 1971.

Jones, Louis Thomas, *Aboriginal American Oratory: The Tradition of Eloquence Among the Indians of the United States,* Southwest Museum (Los Angeles), 1965.

McLuhan, T. C., *Touch the Earth: A Self-Portrait of Indian Existence,* Outerbridge & Dienstfrey, 1971.

Notable Native Americans, Gale, 1995.

Rosenstiel, Annette, *Red and White: Indian Views of the White Man, 1492–1982,* Universe Books, 1983.

Sanders, Thomas E., and Walter W. Peek, *Literature of the American Indian,* Glencoe Press, 1973.

Swann, Brian, and Arnold Krupat, editors, *Recovering the Word: Essays on Native American Literature,* University of California Press, 1987.

Vanderwerth, W. C., *Indian Oratory: Famous Speeches by Noted Indian Chieftains,* University of Oklahoma Press, 1971.

Witt, Shirley Hill, and Stan Steiner, editors, *The Way: An Anthology of American Indian Literature,* Knopf, 1972.

Periodicals

Newsweek, "Just Too Good to Be True," May 4, 1992, p. 68.

visionary: dreamer; someone who sees visions.

Sitting Bull

(Tatanka Yotanka)
c. 1831–1890

Chief of the Hunkpapa Sioux tribe

One of the best known and most colorful of the nine-teenth century's Indian leaders was Sitting Bull. He was a legendary figure even during his own lifetime. A skilled war-rior, statesman, and spiritual guide, he was a member of one of the many nomadic Sioux tribes whose lands stretched from central Canada to Mexico and from the Midwest to the Rocky Mountains. But much of his fame springs from the major role he played in the defeat of Gen-eral George Armstrong Custer at the Battle of the Little Bighorn. As a result of that stunning victory, Sitting Bull became a symbol of Native American resistance against the United States government.

Early Life

Sitting Bull was born near the Grand River in what is now South Dakota around 1831. His tribe was the Hunkpapa Sioux, a band that lived and hunted buffalo mostly in what is now Montana, Wyoming, and the Dako-

"I FEEL THAT MY COUNTRY HAS GOTTEN A BAD NAME, AND I WANT IT TO HAVE A GOOD NAME.... YOU ARE THE ONLY PEOPLE NOW WHO CAN GIVE IT A GOOD NAME, AND I WANT YOU TO TAKE GOOD CARE OF MY COUNTRY AND RESPECT IT."

tas. Sitting Bull was in his early twenties when he first made a name for himself among his people as a leader of a warrior society called the Strong Hearts. By the time he reached his mid-twenties he was a respected chief.

Sitting Bull reached adulthood about the same time white settlers began to head west in greater numbers. This invasion of farmers and ranchers threatened the very existence of the Sioux, who depended on being able to hunt freely over wide expanses of territory. Sitting Bull and his tribe managed to avoid the early conflicts that erupted between Indians and whites on the Plains. Things were especially quiet for them during the Civil War years (1861–65), when the flow of settlers slowed down and the U.S. Army was busy fighting back east.

After the war ended, however, the picture quickly changed. Homesteaders, ranchers, railroad workers, and others began to pour into the region in ever-increasing numbers. They pressured the federal government to send in troops to clear out the Indians, take over their land, and move them on to reservations to make it easier to control them.

"First Kill Me before You Take Possession of My Fatherland"

Sitting Bull had no intention of abandoning Sioux territory or traditions. He rejected the Fort Laramie Treaty of 1868 that negotiated a peace agreement between some Sioux tribes and the United States because it restricted his people's freedom to travel and hunt. The situation grew even more tense in 1874, when the discovery of gold in the Black Hills attracted hordes of would-be miners. (The Black Hills of South Dakota was a sacred area on Sioux land.) Some of them illegally entered Sioux lands while federal officials looked the other way. This touched off a series of battles between Sitting Bull's warriors and U.S. soldiers.

By this time, Sitting Bull was the leader of several bands of militant Sioux who felt as he did. The chief made clear at a council held around 1875 that he was not about to back down. "We cannot dwell side by side [with the white man]," he declared to his warriors. "Only seven years ago we made a treaty by which we were assured that the buffalo country should be left to us forever. Now they threaten to take that away from us. My brothers, shall we submit or shall we say to them: 'First kill me before you take possession of my Fatherland....'"

Finally, after months of growing conflict between the Sioux and U.S. troops, government officials ordered all Sioux hunting bands to report to their assigned reservations by January 1876. This was completely unacceptable to Sitting Bull and his people, who dreaded the thought of having to settle in one place as farmers. To them, that kind of life offered no spiritual fulfillment compared to riding and hunting across the plains.

Sitting Bull prepared for all-out war with the whites. He did not have to wait long. During the spring of 1876, three different U.S. military divisions moved into the Bighorn Valley area of eastern Montana. Their strategy was to attack the Sioux from several different directions. In this way, they figured they could eventually surround the Sioux and defeat them. What the soldiers did not know, however, was that they were about to encounter one of the largest groups of Native Americans ever to gather in a single place. Some twelve to fifteen thousand Plains Indians were camped at various spots along the Little Bighorn River.

Squares Off against General Custer

The first battle occurred on June 17, 1876, when Sitting Bull and his warriors clashed with U.S. soldiers in the Battle of the Rosebud. The Army was forced to retreat but immediately started making plans to strike again.

On June 24, a regiment that had been sent out to do some scouting in advance of the main body of troops spotted an Indian village. The officer in charge of the regiment was a cocky and flamboyant Civil War veteran by the name of General George Armstrong Custer. He completely underestimated the number of Sioux and Cheyenne warriors in the area. His fateful—and foolish—decision to attack the next morning led to his death as well as the deaths of 264 of his men in the famous Battle of the Little Bighorn. One of the masterminds behind this lopsided victory was Sitting Bull.

Sioux chiefs Sitting Bull, Swift
Bear, Spotted Tail, and Red
Cloud pose during negotiations,
c. 1880

But the Sioux and their allies did not have long to enjoy their moment of triumph over the forces of the United States. "Custer's Last Stand" also turned out to be the last major stand of Plains Indians against white expansion into their territory. The newspapers and magazines of the day came down especially hard on Sitting Bull for his role in the *battle. They portrayed him as a vicious savage who had cruelly massacred a courageous and heroic group of soldiers. With the U.S. Army on his trail, Sitting Bull fled to Canada with some of his followers. The loose alliance of Plains tribes that he had created soon fell apart without his leadership. And faced with the overwhelming power of the U.S. military, many of the smaller bands of Sioux surrendered.*

Rejects Terms of Surrender

Sitting Bull did not give up, however. Despite the hardships—including near starvation—that he and his people endured in Canada, they refused to return home and accept life on a reservation. At one point, a group of U.S. government officials visited him and urged him to surrender. Sitting Bull replied with a long summary of the white man's history of breaking promises and ignoring treaties. "We did not give you our country," he declared. "You took it from us.... You come here to tell us lies. We do not want to hear them.... You can go back. Say no more. Take your lies with you. I will stay...."

Finally, however, the hardships became too much to bear. On July 19, 1881, Sitting Bull and most of his followers crossed the border into the United States and surrendered to U.S. authorities. He spent much of the next two years as a prisoner. He was then allowed to settle on the Standing Rock Indian Reservation, which straddles the border between the present-day states of North and South Dakota. It was there that Sitting Bull testified before members of a special U.S. Senate committee in August 1883. The committee had been sent to the reservation to investigate conditions among Indians living in the former Sioux territory. Sitting Bull's plea on behalf of the welfare of his people is reprinted here from W. C. Vanderwerth's Indian Oratory: Famous Speeches by Noted Indian Chieftains, *University of Oklahoma Press, 1971.*

I came in with a glad heart to shake hands with you, my friends, for I feel that I have displeased you. And here I am to

Sitting Bull **189**

apologize to you for my bad conduct and to take back what I said.

I will take it back because I consider I have made your hearts bad. I heard that you were coming here from the Great Father's house some time before you came, and I have been sitting here like a prisoner waiting for someone to release me. I was looking for you everywhere, and I considered that when we talked with you it was the same as if we were talking with the Great Father. And I believe that what I pour out from the heart the Great Father will hear.

What I take back is what I said to cause the people to leave the council, and want to apologize for leaving myself. The people acted like children, and I am sorry for it. I was very sorry when I found out that your intentions were good and entirely different from what I supposed they were.

Now I will tell you my mind and I will tell everything straight. I know the Great Spirit is looking down upon me from above, and will hear what I say, therefore I will do my best to talk straight. And I am in hopes that someone will listen to my wishes and help me to carry them out.

I have always been a chief, and have been made chief of all the land. Thirty-two years ago I was present at the councils with the white man.... And since then a great many questions have been asked me about it, and I always said, wait. And then the Black Hills council was held, and they asked me to give up that land, and I said they must wait. I remember well all the promises that were made about that land because I have thought a great deal about them since that time.

Of course, I know that the Great Spirit provided me with animals for my food, but I did not stay out on the prairie because I did not wish to accept the offers of the Great Father, for I sent in a great many of my people and I told them that the Great Father was providing for them and keeping his agreements with them. And I was sending the Indians word all the time I was out that they must remember their agreements and fulfill them, and carry them out straight.

When the English [Canadian] authorities were looking for me I heard that the Great Father's people were looking for me, too. I was not lost. I knew where I was going all the time. Previous to that time, when a Catholic priest ... came to see me, I told him all these things plainly. He told me the wishes of the Great Father, and I made promises which I meant to fulfill, and did fulfill. And when I went over into the British possessions [Canada] he followed me, and I told him everything that was in my heart, and sent him back to tell the Great Father what I told him.

And General [Alfred] Terry sent me word afterwards to come in, because he had big promises to make me. And I sent him word that I would not throw my country away; that I considered it all mine still, and I wanted him to wait just four years for me; that I had gone over there to attend to some business of my own, and my people were doing just as any other people would do. If a man loses anything and goes back and looks carefully for it he will find it, and that is what the Indians are doing now when they ask you to give them the things that were promised them in the past. And I do not consider that they should be treated like beasts, and that is the reason I have grown up with the feelings I have.

Whatever you wanted of me I have obeyed, and I have come when you called me. The Great Father sent me word that whatever he had against me in the past had been forgiven and thrown aside, and he would have nothing against me in the future, and I accepted his promises and came in. And he told me not to step aside from the white man's path, and I told him I would not, and I am doing my best to travel in that path.

I feel that my country has gotten a bad name, and I want it to have a good name. It used to have a good name, and I sit sometimes and wonder who it is that has given it a bad name. You are the only people now who can give it a good name, and I want you to take good care of my country and respect it.

When we sold the Black Hills we got a very small price for it, and not what we ought to have received. I used to think that the size of the payments would remain the same all the time, but they are growing smaller all the time.

I want you to tell the Great Father everything I have said, and that we want some benefits from the promises he has made to us. And I don't think I should be tormented with anything about giving up any part of my land until those

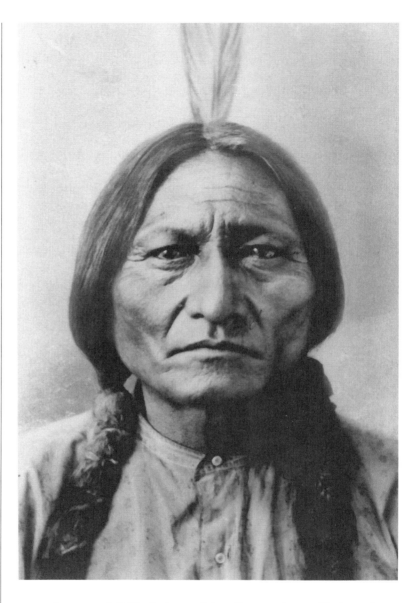

promises are fulfilled. I would rather wait until that time, when I will be ready to **transact** any business he may desire.

I consider that my country takes in the Black Hills, and runs from the Powder River to the Missouri, and that all of this land belongs to me. Our reservation is not as large as we want it to be, and I suppose the Great Father owes us money now for land he has taken from us in the past.

transact: carry out.

You white men advise us to follow your ways, and therefore I talk as I do. When you have a piece of land, and anything trespasses on it, you catch it and keep it until you get damages, and I am doing the same thing now. And I want you to tell this to the Great Father for me. I am looking into the future for the benefit of my children, and that is what I mean, when I say I want my country taken care of for me.

My children will grow up here, and I am looking ahead for their benefit, and for the benefit of my children's children, too; and even beyond that again. I sit here and look around me now, and I see my people starving, and I want the Great Father to make an increase in the amount of food that is allowed us now, so that they may be able to live. We want cattle to butcher.... That is the way you live, and we want to live the same way. This is what I want you to tell the Great Father when you go back home.

If we get the things we want, our children will be raised like the white children. When the Great Father told me to live like his people I told him to send me six teams of mules, because that is the way white people make a living, and I wanted my children to have these things to help them to make a living. I also told him to send me two spans of horses with wagons, and everything else my children would need. I also asked for a horse and buggy for my children. I was advised to follow the ways of the white man, and that is why I asked for those things.

I never ask for anything that is not needed. I also asked for a cow and a bull for each family, so that they can raise cattle of their own. I asked for four yokes of oxen and wagons with them. Also a yoke of oxen and a wagon for each of my children to haul wood with.

It is your own doing that I am here. You sent me here, and advised me to live as you do, and it is not right for me to live in poverty. I asked the Great Father for hogs, male and female, and for male and female sheep for my children to raise from. I did not leave out anything in the way of animals that the white men have; I asked for every one of them. I want you to tell the Great Father to send me some agricultural **implements**, so that I will not be obliged to work bare-handed.

Whatever he sends to this agency [reservation] our agent

will take care of for us, and we will be satisfied because we know he will keep everything right. Whatever is sent here for us he will be pleased to take care of for us. I want to tell you that our rations have been reduced to almost nothing, and many of the people have starved to death.

Now I beg of you to have the amount of rations increased so that our children will not starve, but will live better than they do now. I want clothing, too, and I will ask for that, too. We want all kinds of clothing for our people. Look at the men around here and see how poorly dressed they are. We want some clothing this month, and when it gets cold we want more to protect us from the weather.

That is all I have to say.

Except for a brief period during the mid-1880s when he toured with Buffalo Bill Cody's Wild West Show, Sitting Bull remained on the Standing Rock Reservation for the rest of his life. There he tried to keep as much of the Sioux culture alive as possible, even though he and his people were under intense pressure to adopt white ways. He also continued to speak out forcefully against the corrupt practices of many Indian commissioners. These government officials tried constantly to persuade the Sioux to give up even more of their land. On one occasion in 1889, Sitting Bull addressed a gathering of his fellow Indians and condemned the latest round of broken promises and worthless treaties. His speech to them is reprinted here from The Way: An Anthology of American Indian Literature, *edited by Shirley Hill Witt and Stan Steiner, Knopf, 1972.*

66

Friends and Relatives: Our minds are again disturbed by the Great Father's representatives, the Indian agent, the squaw-men, the mixed-bloods, the interpreters, and the favorite-ration-chiefs. What is it they want of us at this time? They want us to give up another chunk of our tribal land. This is not the first time nor the last time. They will try to gain pos-

implements: tools.

session of the last piece of ground we possess. They are again telling us what they intend to do if we agree to their wishes. Have we ever set a price on our land and received such a value? No, we never did. What we got under the former treaties were promises of all sorts. They promised how we are going to live peaceably on the land we still own and how they are going to show us the new ways of living, even told us how we can go to heaven when we die, but all that we realized out of the agreements with the Great Father was, we are dying off in expectation of getting things promised us.

One thing I wish to state at this time is, something tells me that the Great Father's representatives have again brought with them a well-worded paper, containing just what they want but ignoring our wishes in the matter. It is this that they are attempting to drive us to. Our people are blindly deceived. Some are in favor of the proposition, but we who realize that our children and grandchildren may live a little longer must necessarily look ahead and flatly reject the **proposition.** I, for one, am bitterly opposed to it. The Great Father has proven himself an *unktomi* [trickster] in our past dealings.

When the white people invaded our Black Hills country our treaty agreements were still in force but the Great Father ignored it—pretending to keep out the intruders through military force, and at last failing to keep them out they had to let them come in and take possession of our best part of our tribal possession. Yet the Great Father maintains a very large standing army that can stop anything.

Therefore, I do not wish to consider any proposition to **cede** any portion of our tribal holdings to the Great Father. If I agree to dispose of any part of our land to the white people I would feel guilty of taking food away from our children's mouths, and I do not wish to be that mean. There are things they tell us sound good to hear, but when they have accomplished their purpose they will go home and will not try to fulfill our agreements with them.

My friends and relatives, let us stand as one family as we did before the white people led us **astray.**

proposition: offer, deal.

cede: grant or transfer (usually by treaty).

astray: off the right path; away from what is proper.

Sitting Bull and his family at Fort Randall, Dakota Territory, after his 1882 surrender

Sitting Bull's words were spoken during a time of great **turmoil** and despair among the Plains Indians. Then came a ray of hope—the teachings of a Paiute Indian prophet named Wovoka. During the late 1880s, he began claiming that God had appeared to him in a vision. In this vision, God told him of a dance ceremony that would enable Indians to recover their lands, drive away the whites, reunite with their ancestors, and live in peace and prosperity. Known as the Ghost Dance, this ceremony found much support among the Plains tribes. By 1890, many of them were performing it nightly.

Such activities made U.S. authorities very nervous. They were afraid that the spiritual revival sparked by the Ghost Dance, along with Sitting Bull's appeals for unity among the

turmoil: restlessness, confusion.

Sioux, might cause a violent new Indian uprising. On December 15, 1890, two tribal police officers arrived at Sitting Bull's home during a Ghost Dance ceremony with orders to arrest him. At first, Sitting Bull was prepared to cooperate, but when his followers objected, he decided to resist. A riot then erupted around his cabin. In the confusion that followed, the police officers shot and killed Sitting Bull.

Just two weeks later, on December 29, about two to three hundred Sioux followers of Sitting Bull and the Ghost Dance were massacred by U.S. troops at Wounded Knee, South Dakota. Most of them were unarmed men, women, and children who had fled from the Standing Rock Reservation to seek safety elsewhere. Their deaths quickly led to the decline of the Ghost Dance movement and also ended Sioux efforts to defy white authorities. But the image of Sitting Bull as a powerful Indian leader who would not accept the loss of his lands or his traditions lives on today as a proud symbol of resistance.

Sources

Books

Adams, Alexander B., *Sitting Bull: An Epic of the Plains,* Putnam, 1974.

Brown, Dee, *Bury My Heart at Wounded Knee: An Indian History of the American West,* Holt, 1970.

Manzione, Joseph, *I Am Looking to the North for My Life: Sitting Bull, 1876–1881,* University of Utah Press, 1990.

McLuhan, T. C., *Touch the Earth: A Self-Portrait of Indian Existence,* Outerbridge & Dienstfrey, 1971.

Notable Native Americans, Gale, 1995.

Rosenstiel, Annette, *Red and White: Indian Views of the White Man, 1492–1982,* Universe Books, 1983.

Utley, Robert, *The Lance and the Shield: The Life and Times of Sitting Bull,* Holt, 1993.

Vanderwerth, W. C., *Indian Oratory: Famous Speeches by Noted Indian Chieftains,* University of Oklahoma Press, 1971.

Vestal, Stanley, *Sitting Bull, Champion of the Sioux,* University of Oklahoma Press, 1957.

Witt, Shirley Hill, and Stan Steiner, editors, *The Way: An Anthology of American Indian Literature,* Knopf, 1972.

Smohalla

c. 1815–1895

Spiritual leader of the Wanapam tribe

"ALL THE DEAD MEN WILL COME TO LIFE AGAIN. WE MUST WAIT HERE IN THE HOUSE OF OUR FATHERS AND BE READY TO MEET THEM IN THE BODY OF OUR MOTHER."

Smohalla was the founder of the so-called "Dreamer Religion," a philosophy that developed among the Indians of the Pacific Northwest during the late 1800s. No one is absolutely sure what tribe he belonged to, but it is known that he was born in eastern Washington State along the Columbia River, probably among the Wanapam people. Smohalla left there around 1850 after quarreling with a local chief. He then traveled for several years, making a name for himself as a warrior until he was wounded and left for dead during a skirmish with members of another tribe.

Gains Religious Following

Upon returning to his homeland—where his sudden reappearance was considered a miracle—Smohalla told of having visited the Spirit World. He claimed that religious truths and supernatural powers had been revealed to him in dreams or in a trancelike state. (This is how his movement eventually got its name.)

Smohalla's **creed** was a unique combination of several different elements. Through his contacts with Christian missionaries, Indian converts to Christianity, and fur traders, he had some knowledge of the Christian religion. He was especially drawn to the story of Christ's resurrection (rising from the dead), which became a theme of the Dreamer Religion. (Dreamers or prophets such as Smohalla supposedly received messages from the Great Spirit while in a deathlike state and then returned to life.) Although he did not approve of violence, he predicted that one day, with the help of the Great Spirit, all Indian people, living and dead, would rise up and drive the whites from their lands. He also embraced Native American ideas about nature and the environment, and he urged Indians to reject all aspects of white culture and return to their own traditions.

Smohalla's message found an eager audience among other Indians in the Northwest. Not only had they been steadily losing land to white settlers, they were also falling ill and dying from the strange new diseases the whites had brought with them. Their desperation and fear made Smohalla's promise of hope for a brighter future very appealing.

Reverence for Earth Mother

At the heart of Smohalla's message was his vision of a **benevolent** Earth Mother. As the following brief but impassioned statement attributed to him makes clear, he was very much opposed to any suggestion that he and his people should settle down and become farmers or ranchers like the whites. His much-quoted words are reprinted from Literature of the American Indian, *by Thomas E. Sanders and Walter W. Peek, Glencoe Press, 1973.*

My young men shall never work. Men who work cannot dream, and wisdom comes in dreams.

You ask me to plow the ground. Shall I take a knife and tear my mother's breast? Then when I die she will not take me to her bosom to rest.

creed: a set of guiding beliefs.
benevolent: kind and generous.

You ask me to dig for stone. Shall I dig under her skin for bones? Then when I die I cannot enter her body to be born again.

You ask me to cut grass and make hay and sell it, and be rich like the white men. But how dare I cut off my mother's hair?

It is a bad law, and my people cannot obey it. I want my people to stay with me here. All the dead men will come to life again. We must wait here in the house of our fathers and be ready to meet them in the body of our mother.

*Smohalla's words had a great impact on many tribes of the Pacific Northwest. One of his most famous followers was Chief **Joseph** (see entry) of the Nez Percés. However, many chiefs—both those who were open to white ideas and those who wanted to fight against the whites— did not get along with him very well. And even though he preached nonviolence, Smohalla often ran into trouble with U.S. authorities, who occasionally put him in prison.*

The Dreamers strongly resisted all attempts to turn them into farmers or ranchers, a decision that ultimately cost many of them their lives. As for Smohalla, he spent his final years on the Yakima Indian Reservation. Since his death, others have carried on his teachings to this day.

Sources

Books

McLuhan, T. C., *Touch the Earth: A Self-Portrait of Indian Existence,* Outerbridge & Dienstfrey, 1971.

Notable Native Americans, Gale, 1995.

Ruby, Robert H., and John A. Brown, *Dreamer-Prophets of the Columbia Plateau: Smohalla and Skolaskin,* University of Oklahoma Press, 1989.

Sanders, Thomas E., and Walter W. Peek, *Literature of the American Indian,* Glencoe Press, 1973.

Ross Swimmer

1943–

Leader of the Cherokee tribe

Ross Swimmer is an attorney and businessman who has served with distinction as principal chief of the Cherokee Nation and as head of the Bureau of Indian Affairs (BIA). The BIA, which is part of the Department of the Interior, is the agency that handles the relationship between the United States government and Native American tribes. With its large bureaucratic structure and a long history of political entanglements, corruption, and mismanagement, the BIA represents a major challenge to the Native American leaders who have tried to steer it to a more effective course. (See **Ada Deer** for more information.)

Early Life

Swimmer was born and raised in Oklahoma City, Oklahoma. He was the son of two lawyers—his father (who was half Cherokee) was in private practice, and his mother worked for the Federal Aviation Administration. Following in their footsteps, Swimmer earned a bachelor's degree in

"SHOULD WE CONTINUE TO EXPECT INDIANS TO BE ALCOHOLIC, UNEMPLOYED AND AT THE BOTTOM OF THE SOCIOECONOMIC SCALE? OR SHOULD WE EXPECT INDIAN PEOPLE TO HELP THEMSELVES?"

political science from the University of Oklahoma in 1965 and then studied for his law degree there, too. After graduation, he went to work with a local firm and was promoted to partner in 1970.

Two years later, however, Swimmer left Oklahoma City and began his long association with the Cherokee Nation. His first job was that of general counsel (attorney) at the Nation's headquarters in Tahlequah, Oklahoma. In 1975, his friend and mentor, W. W. Keeler, chose not to run for reelection as principal chief of the Cherokee Nation. So Swimmer decided to run for chief himself and won.

Serves as Principal Chief of the Cherokee Nation

The challenges Swimmer faced when he took office were considerable. It was a time of significant change in the relationship between federal and state governments and Native American tribes. Most notably, government officials were drastically cutting back on the amount of money budgeted for programs serving Indian communities. But during his three terms as chief, Swimmer successfully led the Cherokee Nation through these changes, calling for more **self-determination** *and self-sufficiency for his people to help them cope with decreasing federal and state financial support.*

To realize his goals, Swimmer developed management and marketing programs designed to help Cherokee businesses grow and prosper and thus boost employment rates. He also lobbied Congress for the right to sue companies that had long been mining Cherokee land, even though they had never asked for permission or offered to pay for what they had taken. In addition, Swimmer obtained funding for a new Indian Health Service hospital in Tahlequah and led efforts to update the Cherokee constitution.

In recognition of the work he had done to improve his tribe's economic standing, Swimmer was named cochair of President Ronald Reagan's Commission on Indian Reservation Economies in 1983. His continued devotion to the ideals of self-determination and self-sufficiency for Native Americans greatly impressed administration officials over

self-determination: freedom to choose one's own political future.

the next two years. In 1985, President Reagan again turned to Swimmer for help, this time to head the Bureau of Indian Affairs. Thanks to strong support from both Democrats and Republicans and enthusiastic recommendations from several prominent Native American leaders, his nomination sailed through the Senate.

Takes Charge of the Bureau of Indian Affairs

Once again, Swimmer faced an especially challenging situation. For many years, the BIA had been the target of harsh criticism both inside and outside the government for its wasteful and often corrupt practices. During his four years as head of Indian Affairs, Swimmer tried to apply the lessons he had learned as chief of the Cherokee Nation to Indian communities across the country. He promoted economic development and encouraged tribal governments to take a more active role in leading their people. He also made every effort to use his business expertise to help solve the problems facing federal Indian programs. His ultimate goal was to get rid of the BIA entirely and have reservations treated like state or local governments. Under his plan, each one would have had its own budget and the power to enforce the law over Indians and non-Indians who live there. Swimmer also called for tough measures to deal with corruption and mismanagement.

*Swimmer left the BIA in 1989 without having accomplished all that he had hoped. He returned to Oklahoma, where he signed on as an attorney with a Tulsa firm and specialized in Indian law. In 1992, **Wilma Mankiller** (see entry), his successor as Cherokee principal chief, named him president and CEO of Cherokee Nation Industries (CNI), an electronics company owned by the tribe.*

Founded in 1969 and based in the town of Stilwell, Oklahoma, CNI manufactures wiring harness and electrical cable assembly for the U.S. military. Although it is now the tribe's largest business enterprise, it struggled for a number of years before Swimmer helped make it a success while he was still chief of the Cherokee Nation. His goal for the 1990s is making sure CNI survives and grows in an era of cutbacks in defense spending. To that end, he has been actively seeking out nongovernment customers for the company's products.

As a well-known Native American leader with many achievements to his credit, Swimmer is often asked to share with others his thoughts on self-determination and self-reliance. On several occasions in the 1990s, he has given a variation of the following speech, which he has entitled "An Indian Crossroad." It is reprinted here from a copy provided by Swimmer himself.

We have reached the proverbial crossroad of Indian affairs. The question remains, however, where to go from here? Information **gleaned** from reports over the past twenty years ... leads to the conclusion that the federal government has helped Indians, literally, to death. Why?

Whether the policy was one of placing Indians on reservations to protect them from white society and vice versa; or the General Allotment Act of the 1880s, giving individual ownership of land to Indians so they could be competitive and self-reliant; or the reorganization days of the 1930s that would retribalize Indians to permit self-government; or the termination era of the 1950s that would encourage division of tribal resources and allow Indians to "become just like us"; or the self-determination days of the past twenty years, all of those policies were presented as a way of helping the Indians. Only one thing has been missing from each. That is Indian involvement in the development of the policy....

As principal chief of the Cherokees, I sometimes followed the blind lead of Washington **bureaucrats**. We built our share of ill-planned rural housing and industrial parks. We also operated numerous social programs that Washington bureaucrats told us would be good for the Cherokees. However, when we began listening to the rural Cherokee people about their problems and inviting them to participate in developing solutions, we also began to change the way the tribe did business.

Today, Indian people too often see their tribal governments as extensions of the Washington bureaucracy. People

gleaned: obtained.

bureaucrats: government officials, especially ones who follow a narrow and rigid set of rules.

The Trustee Relationship between the U.S. and Native Americans

There are two fundamental principles underlying many of the policies that have arisen between Native Americans and the U.S. government: the "plenary power" of Congress over Indian affairs and, with this power, the "trust responsibility" the federal government is required to maintain toward Indians.

The Constitution provides Congress with "plenary power"—the sole authority to regulate trade with Indian tribes. "Trade" has come to be interpreted to mean all aspects of federal-tribal relations. Originally, this simply meant that states could not challenge federal Indian policy. By the end of the nineteenth century, however, the Supreme Court argued that Indian tribes themselves could not challenge federal Indian policy, even when the policy involved modifying or ignoring their treaties. In the 1960s and 1970s, however, the Supreme Court ruled that Congress cannot, in its exercise of plenary power over Indian tribes, violate the Bill of Rights, and it cannot take away Indians' property without paying "just compensation." Thus, while Congress has the Constitutional power to modify or negate treaty rights, it must pay for any property that is lost by the tribe as a result of its actions. States have no authority to modify or ignore Indian treaty rights.

"Trust responsibility" means that Congress and the president, in exercising plenary power, must always consider the best interests of Native Americans. Legally, there are advantages to the trust relationship. In the 1930s, the Supreme Court determined that the government had not lived up to its end of the trust relationship in specific cases, and began ordering compensation to be paid to tribes for the mismanagement of their natural resources and financial investments. Today, because of this responsibility to tend to the best interests of Indians, the government's stated policy is to interpret Indian treaties in the way the Indians would have understood them at the time they were made.

The trust relationship has in the past been a justification for paternalism in dealing with Native Americans, meaning that, not unlike an overbearing father, the government felt it could best take care of Native Americans by controlling the social and political behavior of the different groups, regardless of their desires and traditions. For example, for many years federal policy maintained that it was in the best interest of Native Americans to be assimilated into—or blend in with—mainstream American society. Many Native Americans did not agree. The trust relationship also means that Native American groups do not own their land outright—their land may not be leased, mortgaged, or transferred without federal as well as tribal approval.

The policy of the U.S. government today is guided by a 1988 House Resolution, which confirms the "government-to-government" relationship between the U.S. and the tribes, as well as the so-called trust responsibility of the United States to provide the tribes with legal protection and economic assistance.

get good jobs at the tribes because that is where Washington puts the money first. The Bureau continues to act as trustee for the Indians' land, money and other resources, so it is not unusual for people to get confused about which **entity** is really in charge. In many cases, the Bureau is the only "bank" the people have ever known. The only distinction between the Bureau and the tribes is based on activities performed by the two groups. If the Bureau operated an employment assistance program in the 1960s, that program may now be operated by the tribe. If it was unsuccessfully operated by the Bureau then, it likely will be the same with tribes today.

Congress sees the tribes and Indian people in as many different ways as there are congressmen and senators. Senators on the Senate Select Committee for Indian Affairs state their **unequivocal** support for Indian **sovereignty**, yet are often the same ones who will not support tribal criminal **jurisdiction** over non-Indians, taxation by Indian tribes over non-Indians and their property, or exclusive rights to regulate, zone or otherwise manage all aspects of the reservations.

The administration sees Indian Affairs as an effort to **preside** over constant conflict. Often, the Bureau of Indian Affairs is pressured by a tribe and congressmen to make a loan or grant that has little chance of success. After the project fails, the BIA is blamed for making a bad decision. Within the Department of Interior, conflicts are the rule, rather than the exception.

So, what about this new crossroad? Do we keep helping Indians as we have or is it time for a change? The answer lies in Indian country, not Washington, D.C. Indian people have to answer that question. If they are satisfied with a maintenance program made up of ... federal aid, that can be continued easily enough. Should we continue to expect Indians to be alcoholic, unemployed and at the bottom of the socioeconomic scale? Or should we expect Indian people to help themselves, stop drinking, find employment, get educated and share in the economic benefits this country offers? I sincerely believe Indians will rise to the latter expectations, but only if they are free to decide how to use the resources available to get there.

Do Indians want tribal government as we know it today? Yes and no. What they do want is the freedom to have the

entity: person or group.

unequivocal: absolute, without any doubt whatsoever.

sovereignty: freedom from control by others.

jurisdiction: control and authority to interpret and apply the law.

preside: occupy a place of authority or control.

kind of tribal organization they desire and not be bound by rules for governing themselves set forth by the federal government. Some may desire to **leverage** their sovereignty and federal money to purchase needed governmental functions from other governments in their area and have money left over while supporting a much smaller tribal government.

Congress could solve unemployment on the reservations overnight—if the people want to go work. Simple **amendments** to the tax code or providing financial **incentives** to industry for creating jobs in Indian country could provide enough work to have full employment—if that is what people want. The cost would probably be no more than what we pay now to maintain people in a state of unemployment. There are now tribes with access to more jobs than tribal members, yet unemployment is high. Job creation alone won't reduce unemployment unless Indian people want to work, are able and capable, and sufficient incentives exist.

Congress could also address poverty in Indian country by authorizing the administration of social service programs through an incentive system for success instead of constantly rewarding failure. For instance, if money were provided to alcohol treatment centers, counseling programs, and others based on days, weeks, months, or years of **sobriety** achieved, instead of on total number of alcoholics counseled, treated or housed, we would see some dramatic successes. Particularly, if the money were then left on the table with the tribes to address other chronic social problems.

Teachers of Indian students at Bureau schools will soon be paid the highest salaries of any teachers in public or private education. Will test scores go up as a result? Likely not. Not until Indian parents agree to send their children to school, keep them there, and share in the responsibility for their education. Not until every teacher is held **accountable** for teaching students. Not until Bureau schools are used as places of learning and teaching instead of employment programs. Senators and congressmen can **mandate** and provide pay increases, but they cannot force parents to get involved in their children's education, make teachers teach or force school boards to hire competent people. Indian children can improve educationally if simply given the opportunity and a few incentives to make it all worthwhile.

leverage: provide with greater power and effectiveness.

amendments: additions.

incentives: motivations.

sobriety: the state of being sober.

accountable: responsible.

mandate: order.

I do not know if Indians will be allowed to answer the question about which road to take, but I suspect that if congressmen would visit Indian communities and talk to Indian people, the road taken would go in a far different direction than the one likely to be chosen for them.

99

Sources

Books

Maestas, John R., editor, *Contemporary Native American Address*, Brigham Young University, 1976.

Notable Native Americans, Gale, 1995.

Periodicals

Cherokee Advocate, "Ross Swimmer Named President, Chief Executive of CNI," April 30, 1992.

Economist, "In the Red," February 25, 1989, pp. 25–26.

Tecumseh

(Tecumtha)
c. 1768–1813

Leader of the Shawnee tribe

Tecumseh was a prominent spokesperson for midwestern Indians during a period when white settlers in significant numbers first moved westward along the valleys of the Ohio, Allegheny, and Monongahela rivers. (This encompasses territory in what is now western Pennsylvania, Kentucky, Ohio, and Indiana.) Tecumseh was among the most influential Indian leaders of his day, known to tribes from the upper Great Lakes to the Gulf of Mexico and from the Great Plains to the Northeast. His dream was to unite as many Indian groups as possible to resist the westward expansion of white settlers he was convinced would one day destroy the Indian way of life.

Turbulent Times for Native Americans

Tecumseh was born the son of a Shawnee chief near the present-day town of Springfield, Ohio. During the early 1700s the Shawnees had gotten along fairly well with the white hunters and traders who occasionally passed through

"LET US FORM ONE BODY, ONE HEART, AND DEFEND TO THE LAST WARRIOR OUR COUNTRY, OUR HOMES, OUR LIBERTY, AND THE GRAVES OF OUR FATHERS."

their territory. But as Tecumseh was growing up, an increasing number of permanent white settlements were established. This eventually led to trouble between the Indians and whites. Tecumseh's father, a respected chief, was killed in a battle with the incoming settlers, and Tecumseh's older brother is said to have promised the dying chief that he would never make peace with the white intruders. Tecumseh, who was trained as a warrior, first went into battle at the age of fourteen. He also fought with the British against the American colonists during the Revolutionary War (1775–83).

Opposes Treaty Process

After the war, Tecumseh educated himself about the historical and legal status of Native Americans. He soon became a fierce opponent of the treaties that had ceded Indian lands to white settlers. Tecumseh argued that the land belonged to all tribes, not just to one. Therefore, he insisted, any agreement that did not have the consent of all Indians was not valid.

Tecumseh spent much of the late 1780s and early 1790s battling in Shawnee war parties against white settlers throughout Ohio, Kentucky, and Tennessee. The new U.S. government responded with military action and, at first, they met with defeat. Then the United States assembled a stronger and better-equipped group of soldiers that crushed the Indians in 1794 at the Battle of Fallen Timbers near present-day Toledo, Ohio.

Tecumseh survived the battle and retreated with his followers, living first in western Ohio and then in Indiana. The next ten years or so were marked by occasional skirmishes with white settlers followed by periods of relative peace and quiet in the Ohio valley. Tecumseh—who by now had a reputation as a respected and charismatic leader—often served as a link between U.S. government officials and his people in negotiating sessions.

Drive to Unify Tribes

Around 1805, however, Tecumseh began traveling extensively, trying to convince other tribes of the need for *an alliance of Indians to stop the advance of white settlers. Joining him in this effort was his younger brother, Tenskwatawa, a mystical religious leader known as the Shawnee Prophet. Together they launched a resistance movement based on the idea that Indians could achieve spiritual rebirth by rejecting white ways and once again embracing their own culture. They especially condemned drinking alcohol, which they felt was responsible for many of the Indians' problems. Their ultimate goal, however, was to drive the whites back east over the Appalachian Mountains.*

This blend of religious and political goals found favor among a number of other Native Americans who also felt threatened by the westward march of white civilization. Within just a few years, Tecumseh and his brother had established a growing community of believers in a new village they called Prophetstown or Tippecanoe, located where

Tenskwatawa, the Shawnee Prophet (1778–1837)

Tippecanoe Creek meets the Wabash River in present-day Indiana. Keeping a close eye on all these developments was William Henry Harrison, then the governor of Indiana Territory (and later president of the United States). It did not take him long to realize that Tecumseh was an exceptional leader among the local Indians—someone who would make it very difficult to secure the area for white settlers.

Once Prophetstown was established, Tecumseh set out to win more support for his Indian alliance. In 1808, he headed to Canada, where he discussed his complaints about U.S. expansion with the British. During 1810 and 1811, he journeyed from the Great Lakes area across to the Plains and then down to the Gulf of Mexico, trying to persuade the chiefs of various tribes to recognize the dangers they were all facing from the whites.

In the area of present-day Mississippi, for example, Tecumseh took his case before a special council meeting of Choctaws and Chickasaws. His passionate plea for unity is reprinted here from W. C. Vanderwerth's Indian Oratory: Famous Speeches by Noted Indian Chieftains, *University of Oklahoma Press, 1971.*

❝

In view of questions of vast importance, have we met together in solemn council tonight. Nor should we here debate whether we have been wronged and injured, but by what measures we should avenge ourselves; for our merciless **oppressors**, having long since planned out their proceedings, are not about to make, but have and are still making attacks upon our race who have as yet come to no **resolution.** Nor are we ignorant by what steps, and by what gradual advances, the whites break in upon our neighbors. Imagining themselves to be still undiscovered, they show themselves the less **audacious** because you are **insensible.**

The whites are already nearly a match for us all united, and too strong for any one tribe alone to resist; so that unless we support one another with our collective and united forces; unless every tribe **unanimously** combines to **give check to** the ambition and **avarice** of the whites, they will soon conquer us apart and disunited, and we will be driven away from our native country and scattered as autumnal leaves before the wind.

But have we not courage enough remaining to defend our country and maintain our ancient independence? Will we calmly **suffer** the white intruders and **tyrants** to enslave us? Shall it be said of our race that we knew not how to **extricate** ourselves from the three most dreadful **calamities**— folly, inactivity and cowardice? But what need is there to speak of the past? It speaks for itself and asks, Where today is the Pequod? Where the Narragansetts, the Mohawks, Pocanokets, and many other once powerful tribes of our race? They have vanished before the avarice and oppression of the white men, as snow before a summer sun. In the **vain** hope of alone defending their ancient possessions, they have fallen in the wars with the white men.

Look abroad over their once beautiful country, and what see you now? **Naught** but the **ravages** of the paleface

oppressors: people who crush or persecute others through the abuse of power or authority.

resolution: settlement, decision.

audacious: bold.

insensible: unaware, unconcerned.

unanimously: with the agreement and consent of all.

give check to: stop.

avarice: greed.

suffer: tolerate, put up with.

tyrants: people who harshly use their authority or power.

extricate: free.

calamities: disasters.

vain: useless.

naught: nothing.

ravages: violent acts of destruction.

destroyers meet our eyes. So it will be with you, Choctaws and Chickasaws!

Soon your mighty forest trees, under the shade of whose wide spreading branches you have played in infancy, sported in boyhood, and now rest your wearied limbs after the fatigue of the chase, will be cut down to fence in the land which the white intruders dare to call their own. Soon their broad roads will pass over the grave of your fathers, and the place of their rest will be blotted out forever. The **annihilation** of our race is at hand unless we unite in one common cause against the common foe.

Think not, brave Choctaws and Chickasaws, that you can remain **passive** and **indifferent** to the common danger, and thus escape the common fate. Your people, too, will soon be as falling leaves and scattering clouds before their **blighting** breath. You, too, will be driven away from your native land and ancient **domains** as leaves are driven before the wintry storms.

Sleep not longer, O Choctaws and Chickasaws, in false security and **delusive** hopes. Our broad domains are fast escaping from our grasp. Every year our white intruders become more greedy, **exacting**, oppressive and **overbearing**. Every year **contentions** spring up between them and our people and when blood is shed we have to **make atonement** whether right or wrong, at the cost of the lives of our greatest chiefs, and the **yielding** up of large tracts of our lands.

Before the palefaces came among us, we enjoyed the happiness of unbounded freedom, and were acquainted with neither riches, **wants** nor oppression. How is it now? Wants and oppression are our **lot;** for are we not controlled in everything, and dare we move without asking, by your **leave?** Are we not being stripped day by day of the little that remains of our ancient liberty? Do they not even kick and strike us as they do their blackfaces? How long will it be before they will tie us to a post and whip us, and make us work for them in their cornfields as they do them? Shall we wait for that moment or shall we die fighting before submitting to such **ignominy?**

Have we not for years had before our eyes a sample of their **designs**, and are they not sufficient **harbingers** of their

annihilation: total destruction.

passive: inactive.

indifferent: uninterested, unconcerned.

blighting: destructive, deadly.

domains: territories that are absolutely owned or ruled by an individual or group.

delusive: misleading, deceptive.

exacting: harshly demanding.

overbearing: bossy.

contentions: arguments.

make atonement: pay for an injury or loss.

yielding: giving.

wants: needs.

lot: fate.

leave: permission.

ignominy: disgrace.

designs: plans.

harbingers: signs, clues.

future determinations? Will we not soon be driven from our respective countries and the graves of our ancestors? Will not the bones of our dead be plowed up, and their graves be turned into fields? Shall we calmly wait until they become so numerous that we will no longer be able to resist oppression? Will we wait to be destroyed in our turn, without making an effort worthy of our race? Shall we give up our homes, our country, **bequeathed** to us by the Great Spirit, the graves of our dead, and everything that is dear and sacred to us, without a struggle?

I know you will cry with me: Never! Never! Then let us by unity of action destroy them all, which we now can do, or drive them back whence they came. War or extermination is now our only choice. Which do you choose? I know your answer. Therefore, I now call on you, brave Choctaws and Chickasaws, to assist in the just cause of liberating our race from the grasp of our faithless invaders and heartless oppressors. The white **usurpation** in our common country must be stopped, or we, its rightful owners, be forever destroyed and wiped out as a race of people.

I am now at the head of many warriors backed by the strong arm of English soldiers. Choctaws and Chickasaws, you have too long borne with **grievous** usurpation inflicted by the arrogant Americans. Be no longer their **dupes.** If there be one here tonight who believes that his rights will not sooner or later be taken from him by the avaricious American palefaces, his ignorance ought to **excite** pity, for he knows little of the character of our common foe.

And if there be one among you mad enough to undervalue the growing power of the white race among us, let him tremble in considering the fearful **woes** he will bring down upon our entire race, if by his criminal **indifference** he assists the designs of our common enemy against our common country. Then listen to the voice of duty, of honor, of nature and of your endangered country. Let us form one body, one heart, and defend to the last warrior our country, our homes, our liberty, and the graves of our fathers.

Choctaws and Chickasaws, you are among the few of our race who sit **indolently** at ease. You have indeed enjoyed the reputation of being brave, but will you be indebted for it

bequeathed: handed down; given.

usurpation: takeover or seizure by force and without the right to do so.

grievous: causing pain or suffering.

dupes: fools.

excite: arouse, cause.

woes: suffering, grief.

indifference: lack of interest or concern.

indolently: lazily.

Tecumseh and General William Henry Harrison

more from report than fact? Will you let the whites **encroach upon** your domains even to your very door before you will assert your rights in resistance?

Let no one in this council imagine that I speak more from **malice** against the paleface Americans than just grounds of complaint. Complaint is just toward friends who have failed in their duty; accusation is against enemies guilty of injustice. And surely, if any people ever had, we have good and just reasons to believe we have ample grounds to accuse the Americans of injustice; especially when such great acts of injustice have been committed by them upon our race, of which they seem to have no manner of regard, or even to reflect. They are a people fond of innovations, quick to **contrive** and quick to put their schemes into effectual execution

encroach upon: trespass on, invade.

malice: hatred.

contrive: invent, plot.

no matter how great the wrong and injury to us; while we are content to preserve what we already have. Their designs are to enlarge their possessions by taking yours in turn; and will you, can you longer **dally**, O Choctaws and Chickasaws?

Do you imagine that that people will not continue longest in the enjoyment of peace who timely prepare to **vindicate** themselves, and **manifest** a determined resolution to do themselves right whenever they are wronged? Far otherwise. Then **haste** to the relief of our common cause, as by **consanguinity** of blood you are bound; lest the day be not far distant when you will be left single-handed and alone to the cruel mercy of our most **inveterate** foe.

99

Despite this eloquent plea, Tecumseh was no match for the Choctaw chief Pushmataha. He spoke before the same council and argued against Tecumseh's proposal. Pushmataha insisted that the Americans were their friends and that the Great Spirit would punish the Indians for breaking their treaties with the white man.

This reaction was fairly typical among the older chiefs Tecumseh met during his travels. Not only did they feel threatened by his militant brand of leadership, they also could not quite bring themselves to form alliances with other Indians, especially ones who had been their enemies for many generations. As a result, Tecumseh won most of his support among younger, more militant Indians who were not content to let whites overrun their lands.

In any event, Tecumseh's prediction about what would happen to the Choctaws and Chickasaws eventually came true. During the early 1830s, they were forced off their land and sent west along the Trail of Tears to Indian Territory. (See box for more information.)

When Tecumseh returned home to Prophetstown in late 1811 after his long journey, he found that the community had been destroyed by Governor William Henry Harrison and U.S. Army troops. (During his presidential campaign some thirty years later, Harrison played up this great "vic-

dally: dawdle, delay.

vindicate: protect oneself from attack; to avenge.

manifest: show.

haste: hurry.

consanguinity: relationship, kinship.

inveterate: firmly established; habitual.

The Trail of Tears

In 1830, the U.S. Congress passed the Indian Removal Act with the enthusiastic support of President Andrew Jackson. This new law served as the foundation of the country's Indian policy for about the next thirty years. During the 1830s and 1840s in particular, Indian tribes still living east of the Mississippi River were ordered to leave their homes, abandon their possessions, and set out on foot for what is now Oklahoma. There they were expected to settle on poor-quality reservation land. In the Southeast, army troops helped herd thousands of reluctant Cherokees, Creeks, Seminoles, and Choctaws along a route the Cherokees named the Trail of Tears. Many died from hunger, disease, and exposure before reaching their destination.

tory" at the so-called Battle of Tippecanoe.) Soon after, the British and Americans fought each other in what became known as the War of 1812. With his dreams of an Indian **confederation** *in ruins, Tecumseh headed for Canada and joined the British forces so that he could fight against the Americans. He then distinguished himself as a warrior and was put in charge of all Indian forces during the battle for Detroit (which the Americans lost) in August 1812.*

Within just a short time, however, the tide began to turn against the British. In September 1813, a major naval battle took place on Lake Erie between American and British forces. Led by Commodore Oliver Hazard Perry, the Americans defeated the British fleet and effectively ended their domination of the Great Lakes. Tecumseh tried but could not persuade his British allies to stay and fight on land. Instead, they fled to Canada, where they finally agreed to stand up to the advancing American troops. Less than a month later, while fighting alongside British forces near Chatham, Ontario, Tecumseh was shot and killed in the Battle of the Thames. At the head of the victorious American army was his longtime enemy, William Henry Harrison.

Sources

Books

Armstrong, Virginia Irving, compiler, *I Have Spoken: American History Through the Voices of the Indians,* Sage Books, 1971.

confederation: alliance, association, or league.

Eckert, Allan W., *A Sorrow in Our Heart: The Life of Tecumseh,* Bantam Books, 1992.

Edmunds, R. David, *Tecumseh and the Quest for Indian Leadership,* Harper, 1987.

Jones, Louis Thomas, *Aboriginal American Oratory: The Tradition of Eloquence Among the Indians of the United States,* Southwest Museum (Los Angeles), 1965.

McLuhan, T. C., *Touch the Earth: A Self-Portrait of Indian Existence,* Outerbridge & Dienstfrey, 1971.

Nabokov, Peter, editor, *Native American Testimony: A Chronicle of Indian-White Relations from Prophecy to the Present, 1492–1992,* Penguin Books, 1991.

Notable Native Americans, Gale, 1995.

Rosenstiel, Annette, *Red and White: Indian Views of the White Man, 1492–1982,* Universe Books, 1983.

Sanders, Thomas E., and Walter W. Peek, *Literature of the American Indian,* Glencoe Press, 1973.

Sugden, John, *Tecumseh's Last Stand,* University of Oklahoma Press, 1990.

Vanderwerth, W. C., *Indian Oratory: Famous Speeches by Noted Indian Chieftains,* University of Oklahoma Press, 1971.

Velie, Alan R., editor, *American Indian Literature: An Anthology,* University of Oklahoma Press, 1979.

John Trudell

1947–

Activist, actor, and musician of the Sioux tribe

During the 1970s, John Trudell was a major spokesperson of the American Indian Movement (AIM). More recently, however, he has blended his activism with various forms of entertainment and creative expression. Through his acting, his poetry, and his music, he hopes to communicate the struggle for Native American rights in new and different ways.

Early activism

Trudell was born and raised on the Santee Sioux Reservation, located on the border of South Dakota and northeastern Nebraska. He left there to serve in the U.S. Navy for four years during the Vietnam War. His military experience made him acutely aware of the racism directed at blacks, Asians, and other minorities such as himself.

After his tour of duty ended in the late 1960s, Trudell began associating with other young Native Americans who felt it was time to challenge the status quo (existing state of

"OUR ENEMY IS NOT THE UNITED STATES, OUR ENEMY IS NOT THE INDIVIDUAL WHITE MAN. OUR ENEMY IS THE COLLECTIVE WHITE MAN."

affairs). They struck their first major blow on November 20, 1969, when about ninety Indians from a number of different tribes occupied Alcatraz Island, the site of a former federal prison in San Francisco Bay. Ten days later, Trudell joined his fellow activists on Alcatraz, and there they remained for most of the next nineteen months. The goal of this group—known as the Indians of All Tribes (IAT)—was to dramatize the government's seizure of Indian land and its restrictions on Native American hunting and fishing rights. IAT issued a land claim for Alcatraz based on the terms of the Fort Laramie Treaty of 1868, which stated that unused federal land could be taken over by Indian people.

At the peak of the takeover in mid-1970, as many as a thousand people had gathered on the island to protest the mistreatment of Native Americans and to demand that the site be turned into an Indian educational and cultural center. Throughout the occupation, Trudell served as the voice of "Radio Free Alcatraz." This daily radio program broadcast the concerns of the Indian occupiers from stations in the California cities of Berkeley and Los Angeles as well as from New York City.

Defeat at Alcatraz

During this same period, Trudell also traveled and lectured extensively, winning support wherever he could for the IAT and its land claims to Alcatraz. But the occupation ended on June 11, 1971, when U.S. marshals removed the last of the demonstrators from the island. Although Alcatraz ultimately became a national park, it remains a powerful symbol of courage and **solidarity** *to many Native Americans.*

Trudell officially joined the American Indian Movement (AIM) during the spring of 1970 and soon became the group's national spokesperson. (See entries on **Clyde and Vernon Bellecourt** *and* **Russell Means** *for more information on AIM.) He participated in several more occupations of federal land and government buildings early in the decade, including one at an abandoned missile range in California in 1971 and another at the Bureau of Indian Affairs (BIA) office in Washington, D.C., in 1972. The BIA incident*

solidarity: unity, cooperation.

occurred in connection with the Trail of Broken Treaties, a march that brought together thousands of Indians from across the country. Once in Washington, the demonstrators unsuccessfully tried to present the U.S. government with a formal list of their demands. When officials refused to hear them out or to provide them shelter, in anger and frustration some of them took over the BIA offices. For five days, they squared off against riot police and federal authorities. The vandalism and other damage that resulted from the takeover gained publicity—mainly unfavorable—for AIM.

Involvement with AIM and the Pine Ridge Incident

In 1973, Trudell was elected cochair of AIM. That year, he took part in the much-publicized siege near the village of Wounded Knee on South Dakota's Pine Ridge Indian Reservation. The confrontation began in February when several hundred AIM members and **sympathizers** gathered at Pine Ridge to take a stand against the mistreatment of Indians. Their anger was focused in particular on a man named Dick Wilson, the reservation's head **administrator**.

Most of Wilson's support came from Indians who believed that they should try to leave behind their native customs and become a part of white culture. Many of the tribal elders, however, wanted to maintain the old traditions. Some of them had also accused Wilson of corruption and **strong-arm tactics**. AIM activists agreed with the elders, and in a symbolic gesture of defiance, they took over the village of Wounded Knee. (Wounded Knee already held a somber place in history as the site of an 1890 massacre of more than two hundred Sioux men, women, and children by U.S. Army troops.) Federal marshals and FBI agents immediately moved in to reestablish government control. The resulting armed standoff lasted seventy-one days, ending only when federal negotiators promised to set up a meeting between Sioux elders and several White House representatives.

Within a year or so after the siege ended, Trudell delivered the following talk to a Native American audience in which he stressed the need for unity, **sobriety**, and commit-

sympathizers: supporters, promoters.

administrator: a person appointed to manage and carry out the policies of others.

strong-arm tactics: methods of dealing with people that involve threats, bullying, and violence.

sobriety: the practice of remaining sober (refusing to drink alcoholic beverages).

ment to the goals of AIM. (The exact date and occasion of his remarks are unknown.) Those who have heard him speak have described him as **charismatic,** *tense, and sharp-witted. In the words of singer and fellow activist Buffy Sainte-Marie, for example, Trudell "was the orator who could make sense of a complicated situation and really move the individual listener on an intimate level.... [He was] a person in control of a powerful* **righteousness.** *He stood up for our native people...." His speech is reprinted here from* Contemporary Native American Address, *edited by John R. Maestas, Brigham Young University, 1976.*

I want to talk about commitment for our organization. I think commitment is the number one thing we should be thinking about. We've got to have commitment so strong that when we get mad at each other we can overlook it. We have got to have commitment so strong that we will never accept "no" for an answer. We have to have commitment so strong that we will not accept their excuses or lies as an answer. We have to have commitment so strong that we will live and we will die for our people.

We have got to start thinking in terms of love. You know we get caught up in hating the white man for what he's done to us and that hate shows. It shows in our own organization. We start playing the white man's games, and we start fighting each other. We're out for the good of Indian people but if we don't like something someone does, then we start backstabbing and calling names, and we criticize. We need to be open and talk to these individuals that the individuals are displeased with and confront them with how we feel.... The white man manipulates and we react. It's ridiculous....

I wonder about respect. We speak of respect. We study respect, and we use the word many times. But then we go and pour alcohol into our bodies. We do not respect our bodies when we do this. We rip off from each other. We do not respect our brothers when we do this. We do not respect our brothers when we talk about them behind their backs. These are things that we have to start thinking about.

charismatic: especially charming or appealing.

righteousness: a sense of being morally right or justified in doing something.

John Trudell

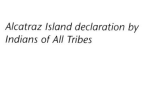

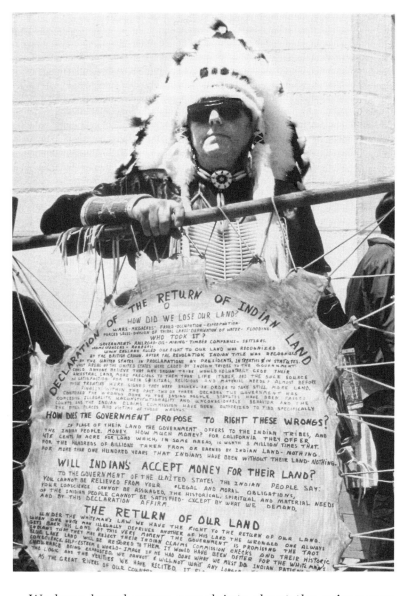

We have heard many complaints about the **grievances** against the white man and against the Bureau of Indian Affairs and against the state. We have got to understand such things as **colonialism**. We've got to understand the methods the white man uses to put us under his thumb. *Colonialism*.

That means the white man comes to our country and takes our lands away from our people and puts us into reservations

grievances: complaints.

colonialism: control by one power over a dependent area or people.

and he continues to control three-fourths of the reservation and our lives. That is colonialism. When we have white landlords and white officials that sit there looking good and we go hungry and sit there without our rights—that is colonialism. Those in the Interior Department sit back and get rich and get fat, and they keep us from gaining the working knowledge and experience we need to control our lives again. That is colonialism. Colonialism is when the white man controls our land and he does our thinking for us, and then he continues to keep us disoriented and keep us at each other's throats. This is colonialism.

Our enemy is not the United States, our enemy is not the individual white man. Our enemy is the collective white man. If the collective white man sits back and he allows this to happen—then he is our enemy. The white man is the one who has to accept this before there can be peace, love and understanding between the races. They have got to understand that he is in the wrong....

It was white people that created jails, and it was white people that robbed our land. It was white people that sat back in the corner and allowed their government to do it. They come to us and talk to us of love and brotherhood. It was the white people that sold us guns, guns that got us killed.... They sell us guns and make some money off of us. They use us. They've got it set up so that they can play off of our fears, emotionalism....

They still think they can teach us a lesson with their clubs and their guns and their Bible. But you look at the overall strategy that they've got, and we can see they are using **intimidation** because they want to isolate us like the SLA and the Black Panthers. [The SLA, or Symbionese Liberation Army, was a radical group made up of black militants and their white supporters. In 1974, they kidnapped newspaper heiress Patty Hearst and demanded a ransom of over $200 million to feed the poor of California. The Black Panthers were also militant revolutionaries. They operated mostly in the ghettos of the country's bigger cities during the late 1960s and early 1970s.] They abuse us by calling us names, and they intimidate us by coming in with their clubs and beating us. They come in with their tear gas, and they shoot, and they make the communities afraid of us because they

intimidation: actions intended to frighten or threaten.

John Trudell

want to isolate us. They do not want us talking of freedom. They do not want the black man to think about freedom. They do not even want their own people to think about freedom.

They try to intimidate us and tell us that they have power, but the truth is that they have no power. They have guns, bombs, airplanes, laws and other methods of destruction, but that is not power. Power comes from the people. Power comes from love for the people. Power comes from not fighting each other. Power comes from standing together. Power comes from the right to live—that is power. We've got the power, and all we have to do is put it together. But we do not have to take this crap from the white people. We will have to continue to put up with it until we pull ourselves together. The biggest contradiction that I have seen within the American Indian Movement is that we don't respect each other. We say we do, but we don't act it....

I've heard a lot of talk about legal aid, about laws, and I don't see much hope of depending on the white man's laws. I don't see much hope in depending on the white man's understanding. Something that I firmly, honestly believe is that things aren't going to change. The technology has changed, but the civilization hasn't. The white man's civilization has always been one of creating a government and making that government stand. Always. The violence is the same. The corruption is the same. The manipulation of people's lives and his mind is the same. Their civilization is the same. Their technology is all that has changed, and this is something that we have got to expect.

At any time, they come out and tell us these things take time, and I've heard that fifty thousand times in the last year. These things take time—1876 was when the American government was celebrating its first illegal anniversary. They had problems with the blacks. They had problems in the [Ulysses S.] Grant [presidential] administration.... What has changed from 1876 to 1974? Now you can see it on TV, now we come to a microphone and talk about it. The technology has changed but the system hasn't. We must not be fooled by them. We must put ourselves in their position, and we must condition our minds and condition them to say "no," becoming a collecting voice of "no" from the people. That is the only way that we are going to be able to correct them. We must have the courage to tell them NO, NO, NO!

We must stop becoming drunk. You don't know how many times we have tried to reason with you. Drunk, drunk—the biggest damn problem we have is being drunk. How much money do we make and spend on alcohol? Alcohol is the number-one weapon against the Indian people. One hundred years ago they started pumping the alcohol through us and have used it against us since the first white man put his foot on this land. They have taken our religion, they have taken our children. They are taking our land and giving us alcohol, and alcohol is fast becoming the new God of the Indian people. Alcohol is becoming the new way of life.

We hold our gatherings, and many people come. But first they go out and drink, and then they have to ask us for gas money to get home. You know the American Indian Movement has a hard time getting money—it's real hard. All the money we are getting now, they are taking it and wrapping it up in the courts. They are making us give the money back to them. Because we have to fight these legal hassles in the courts, we have to take the money right back into the court system.

No matter what the record happens to be, the actions are always different. It is only us that can change it. We **oppress** ourselves because we listen to them. Maybe we listen to their lies because we don't want to deal with the truth, but if we are going to talk about revolution, if we are going to talk about freedom, if we are going to talk about humanities and people's rights, we are going to have to deal with the truth. We are going to have to recognize it. We're going to have to understand it. We're going to have to learn to work with it. And when that truth hurts us, then we are going to have to sit down and evaluate ourselves too. We needn't worry about the truth or being criticized. We are not perfect, but too many times within our own organization, that is the biggest problem that we come up with. We are too good to be criticized and too good to be humble. We are too good to express love. We want to show that we are free by fighting each other, and that is getting us nowhere.

We need to start thinking. We need to start being ourselves. We need to stop being manipulated by the white man

oppress: crush or persecute through the abuse of power or authority.

John Trudell

Trudell, both artist and activist, explains: "I'm not really trying to entertain or deliver a message. I'm trying to communicate."

in his media and political systems, courtrooms, poolrooms, and by his alcohol industry. We've got to start taking action of our own....

We had better start preparing ourselves and pulling ourselves together. Let's start being a family. You know the American Indian Movement is the only family I've got. When I come into my family, I don't like to see name-calling and accusations. I don't like to see people shooting each other because when we do that we only please the white man.

You know, I don't buy this crap that Indians have always fought and can't get along. Too many times we listen to them.... Too many times we get sucked into believing it. All we've got to relate to is that we are the Indian people, and when the white persons came over here, we showed them how to live, we showed them how to survive, and they were peaceful toward us, and they were nice because they did not know how to live here. Once they found out how to live here, they then started killing us and stealing our land. Then they brought the black man in, and then started their history of oppression of the people of this land. They told us we were going to live in a free democracy. They told us we had human rights, and they got us to believe it.... They never say that we are losing our freedom....

We can't decide what our education will be. We cannot decide what our religion will be and can't get it recognized because we aren't free. Free? There is no freedom in this country unless you are extremely rich or unless you have liberated your own self. Which is our main concern—ourselves. What are we going to do with ourselves? Are we going to be able to accept criticism? Are we going to be able to recognize that the whole Indian community is a priority? Everybody has to start thinking about not spending all of our money on good ole booze and a fun time. We are going to have to start thinking about not stabbing others in the back because we don't agree with what they say. We've got to have open minds because we do not like the way things are being done. When our opinions are expressed and put down, we should not be mad and want to jump on each other's backs. We should accept the fact that we are all together and we all believe in the same thing, and this has got to be the number one priority.

99

Trudell remained cochair of the American Indian Movement through the end of the 1970s. He served as coordinator of the group's defense efforts on behalf of Leonard Pelti-

er, an Indian convicted of the shooting deaths of two FBI agents on the Pine Ridge Indian Reservation in June 1975. (See entry on Clyde and Vernon Bellecourt for more information on the Peltier case.) But Trudell may have paid a steep price for supporting that cause. In February 1979, his wife, mother-in-law, and three children died in a mysterious house fire at their home on the Duck Valley Reservation in Nevada. The blaze broke out only a few hours after Trudell was arrested for burning an American flag on the steps of the FBI building in Washington, D.C., during a pro-Peltier demonstration. Investigators later determined that the house fire had been deliberately set. Trudell believes to this day that government agents had something to do with the crime.

In the aftermath of that tragedy, Trudell turned to writing poetry to help deal with his loss. He also continued to make appearances at various benefits for Indian and environmental causes. Many times, he recited his poems (which have a distinct social and political flavor) and delivered fiery speeches. Eventually, these attracted the attention of musicians Jackson Browne and Bonnie Raitt. With their encouragement, Trudell began to set some of his thoughts to music. He experimented first with traditional Native American sounds and then with modern electric rock.

Since then, he has released two CDs, AKA Graffiti Man (1992) and Johnny Damas and Me (1994). Both try to make a personal as well as a political statement through a blend of tribal voices and instruments and contemporary music. As Trudell explained to a Billboard reporter, "I'm trying to achieve a genuine **fusion**.... I'm not really trying to entertain or deliver a message. I'm trying to communicate. Politics will always be a part of me, but that's all it is—a part. I'm a whole person just trying to express my feelings, and hopefully others can relate to them."

Trudell has also become involved in various film projects. In 1992, for example, he served as a consultant to the makers of Incident at Oglala, a documentary on the Leonard Peltier case. (He appeared on-camera, too, in several interview clips.) That same year, he acted in the thriller Thunderheart, which is based on some of the events that

fusion: union, blend.

took place on the Pine Ridge Indian Reservation during the 1970s. Trudell played a character modeled after Peltier.

Sources

Books

Maestas, John R., editor, *Contemporary Native American Address,* Brigham Young University, 1976.

Matthiessen, Peter, *In the Spirit of Crazy Horse,* Viking, 1983, new edition, 1991.

Notable Native Americans, Gale, 1995.

Voices from Wounded Knee, 1973: In the Words of the Participants, Akwesasne Notes, 1974.

Periodicals

Billboard, "Native American Song, Then and Now," May 9, 1992, p. 5; "Trudell Inspires Unusual Ryko Promo," January 29, 1994, pp. 13–14.

Interview, "Rocking a Difference and Rolling a Change," April 1992, pp. 98–103.

Other

Incident at Oglala: The Leonard Peltier Story (documentary film), Carolco International, 1992.

Thunderheart (film), 1992.

Index

Index

Plenary power 205

Plymouth Rock (Massachusetts) 137

Pocahontas 154

Poetry 91, 97, 219, 229

Police harassment 3, 139

Politics 54, 56, 63, 67

Ponca 115-123

Pontiac 47

Poverty 1, 3, 37, 40

Prison 2-3, 78-79

The Problem of Indian Administration 35

Prophetstown 211, 216

Protection and preservation of tribal culture 4-5, 9-10, 57, 63, 69, 89, 130, 132, 142, 162, 167, 186, 194, 199, 211, 221

Protest 1, 20, 125

Pushmataha 216

R

Racism 1, 3, 12, 19-20, 23, 57, 70, 79, 91-92, 110, 119, 125, 132, 138, 142, 189, 219

"Radio Free Alcatraz" 220

Raitt, Bonnie 229

Reagan, Ronald 90, 126, 130 (ill.), 202

Red Cloud 188 (ill.)

Red Jacket 156-163, 156 (ill.), 159 (ill.)

"Red Power" movement 2

Reform movement 31, 33, 119, 123

Religion 6, 9, 15, 47, 89, 95, 115, 138, 145, 157, 171, 174, 196, 198, 211

Relocation 3, 7, 23, 26, 78, 108, 116, 118, 125, 141, 167-168, 171, 174, 186, 204, 217

Republican party 58

Resettlement policies 3, 7, 23, 26, 78, 108, 114, 116, 118, 125, 141, 167-168, 171, 174, 186, 204, 217

Revolutionary War (1775–83) 47-48, 72, 156, 210

Rocky Mountains 185

Roosevelt, Franklin D. 43

Roosevelt, Theodore 86

S

Sainte-Marie, Buffy 222

Sand Creek Massacre (1864) 97

Santa Fe Trail 165

Satank 164

Satanta 164-169, 166 (ill.)

Sauk (Sac) 25-30

Seattle 144, 153, 170-184, 172 (ill.)

Seattle, Washington 170

"Seeing Red" 89

Self-determination 10, 69, 146, 202, 204

Seminole 217

Senate Indian Affairs Committee 38

Seneca 71, 156-162

Sexism 126, 133

Shawnee 209

Shawnee Prophet. *See Tenskwatawa*

Sheridan, Philip Henry 97

Shyhanna 93

Shyhela 93

Sioux 31, 118, 185, 219

Sitting Bull 31, 185-197, 185 (ill.), 188 (ill.), 192 (ill.), 196 (ill.)

Six Nations of the Haudenosaunee. *See Iroquois Confederacy*

Six Nations Reserve 48

Smohalla 198-200

Social service programs 3, 8, 19, 66, 126, 132, 207

Society of American Indians (SAI) 33

Sovereignty 10, 12, 52, 206

Spain 77

Spiderwoman Theatre Company 89

Sports 55

Sports team names 23, 57, 91

Spotted Tail 188 (ill.)

Standing Bear 118, 119 (ill.)

Standing Rock Indian Reservation 189

Stevens, Isaac 171

Stillwater State Prison 2

Stilwell, Oklahoma 203

Strong Hearts 186

Success 58

Suicide 97

Suquamish 170

Swift Bear 188 (ill.)

Swimmer, Ross 126, 201-208, 201 (ill.)

T

Tahlequah, Oklahoma 124, 202

Tecumseh 25, 162, 209-218, 209 (ill.), 215 (ill.)

Tenskwatawa 211 (ill.)

Termination Resolution (1953) 66-67, 204

Texas 85, 164

Theater 89

Thorpe, Jim 147

Thunderheart 96, 229

Tippecanoe 211

Tohono O'odham 94

Toledo, Ohio 210

Trail of Broken Treaties (1972) 4, 138, 221

Trail of Tears 216-217

Treaty rights 4, 10, 26, 49, 108, 111, 118, 125, 171, 186, 190, 195, 210, 220

Tribal recognition 67

Tribal rights 129

Trudell, John 219-230, 219 (ill.), 227 (ill.)

Trustee relationship 205

Tsistsistas 93